The Copyeditor's Guide to

Substance

&Style

Learn how to find and fix basic errors in text and graphics, in print and online

3rd Edition

Completely Revised

THE EDITORS OF EEI PRESS

The Copyeditor's Guide to Substance & Style, 3rd edition: Learn how to find and fix basic errors in text and graphics, in print and online. ©2006. Complete revision of the 1996 edition, *Substance & Style: Instruction and Practice in Copyediting.*

EEI Press offers other books on editorial topics and publishes *The Editorial Eye*, a subscription newsletter. See www.eeicommunications.com/press for more information, tables of contents, excerpts, and a sampler of articles.

EEI Press offers discounts for quantity orders from bookstores, nonprofits, associations, and educational organizations. Review copies are available to instructors evaluating textbooks for course adoption. For more information, call or write to

EEI PRESS®
A Division of EEI Communications

66 Canal Center Plaza, Suite 200
Alexandria, VA 22314-5507
tel 703-683-0683 • fax 703-683-4915
e-mail press@eeicommunications.com
www.eeicommunications.com/press

Library of Congress Cataloging-in-Publication Data: Available on request.

ISBN 0-935012-26-5

Cover design by Scott Baur

Table of Contents

Sidebars and Illustrations

Acknowledgments

Many people at EEI have had a hand in this book over the years. Foremost is the author of the original edition, Mary Stoughton, whose professional influence on hundreds of copyediting students—and her appreciative former colleagues—still reverberates years after her retirement from EEI.

A major goal for the third revision of Stoughton's text was to add an overview of basic online editing tools and techniques. To that end, EEI Press was fortunate to work with Rob Kunkle, a senior manager at the American Psychiatric Association and an experienced editor-writer who has worked for Johns Hopkins University, Washingtonpost.com, and EEI Communications. Kunkle wrote the online editing chapter.

Lee Mickle, a longtime EEI editor and project manager, edited the online chapter and worked with Ed Gloninger, EEI's production manager, to clarify and verify technical points. Judy Cleary copyedited the chapter and reviewed it as a non-tech user.

Editor Mickle selectively updated the book to better reflect contemporary publishing practices and workplace realities that have changed the role of editors: tight budgets (which make choosing the right level of edit an economic necessity) and the outsourcing of editorial, writing, and production work (which make electronic workflow the standard).

This new edition also contains updated advice on editing tables, written by Patricia Caudill when she was EEI's quality control manager. Learning to systematically parse graphic material for clarity, accuracy, and accessibility is merely another of the difficult but essential skills that a copyeditor acquires with time and painstaking practice.

Robin Cormier, EEI's vice president and director of publishing; Jane Rea, EEI's editorial services manager; and Linda Jorgensen, EEI Press manager, were the book's quality control reviewers. Courtney Cornelius gave the manuscript a magnificently thorough thumping as its out-the-door reviewer. And these proofreaders ably plowed through more checking and correction rounds than we care to count: Heather McDonald, Stephanie Franks, and Norman Klinetop. With a steady hand, Heather McDonald also did the demanding manual markup for the answer keys and the Copyediting Marks chapter.

Scott Baur, design services manager, redesigned the book to be a more convenient size, with more readable type and a simpler format. Rebecca Hunter, desktop publishing specialist, executed the layout with extraordinary care and skill. Sharon Martin and Rae Benedetto provided patient production assistance, and Ed Gloninger oversaw the production process.

Finally, we must acknowledge the EEI Training students, *Editorial Eye* subscribers, and EEI Publications clients over the years who have inspired much of the advice in this guide.

If you have a copyediting question that's not answered in these pages, send it to press@eeicommunications.com and we'll help you come up with an answer. It's what we do here....

Foreword

All editors try to ensure that a written message says what its author meant to say in the clearest way possible. Removing obstacles is the name of the game. But love of the English language and a sharp eye for detail do not necessarily make for a good copyeditor (although they help).

This book is meant for all would-be and working editors:

- Those who think they would like to be editors, and find themselves having to edit, but lack the training to do so.

- Those who work on publications of any sort (newsletters, newspapers, journals, fact sheets, catalogues, brochures—the list is endless) and would like to do a better job of it.

- Those who need to polish documents of any kind (letters, proposals, reports, research papers, and so on) and would like to learn a more systematic way of doing so, even if they are not "real" editors.

- Those who, discovering that written communications raise a whole set of issues that knowledge of subject matter alone doesn't solve, would like to master the basics of copyediting to improve their own work.

- Those who have professional editing experience but want to refresh themselves on the basics and work more efficiently online.

The Copyeditor's Guide to Substance & Style, the third and completely revised edition of *Substance & Style: Instruction and Practice in Copyediting,* is designed to work for self-instruction and for the classroom. After each topic is discussed, you can do exercises to help you sharpen your skills. A glossary of common grammatical and editorial terms will help when you encounter professional jargon. Illustrations and examples will help you see how to apply rules and concepts.

You will learn *how* to make copyeditor's marks and *what* to mark. You will learn the rule of grammar or style that governs each decision. Just as important, you will see examples of when it's best to leave something alone. (We recall with dismay a new copyeditor, flexing her muscles, explaining, "If I don't know what something means, I just delete it.")

The Copyeditor's Guide to **Substance**&*Style*

This revised edition has three new chapters:

- Citations and References: The Supporting Documentation

- Tables and Graphics: Making Data Easier to Grasp

- Electronic Editing Basics: Improving Workflow, Efficiency, and Quality.

We've added 22 new sidebars and illustrations, and the table of contents includes all sub-section titles for easier reference. Those familiar with previous editions will find updated versions of the editor's checklist to assign the correct level of effort and the matrix showing how different styles affect your editing. Those new to editing will appreciate the much-expanded discussion of the core tasks to master in the Copyediting: Working with Text chapter.

If you persevere, you'll absorb the basic skills and habits of mind needed for copy-editing, which you can then apply on the job. As you do that, you'll want to adapt the editing guidelines in this book to fit your own situation. For example, if you work exclusively online, you won't need to spend much time on editorial marks for hard copy. If you always work on short articles with immediate deadlines, you probably won't have time to make the three "passes" (or readings) we recommend—but you'll still want to use a checklist of tasks to focus your efforts.

The fundamental judgments that professional copyeditors must make and the principles they consistently apply are covered in *The Copyeditor's Guide to Substance & Style*. The techniques recommended have worked for hundreds of client publications and hundreds of students in the copyediting classes offered by EEI Communications (formerly Editorial Experts, Inc.). Colleges, universities, in-house training programs, and book and periodicals publishers use *The Copyeditor's Guide to Substance & Style*. It has proved its mettle in the workplace and in the classroom, and this is an extensively improved edition.

But this is just one resource. Editors are increasingly expected to be knowledgeable about editing and design software, print and Web readability issues, project management, and even public speaking (for training their peers). We encourage you to take a look at the dozens of editorial and software classes available from EEI Training. A catalog can be downloaded from www.eeicommunications.com.

You may also wish to augment the material in this book with other EEI Press books for publishing professionals, such as *The Great Grammar Challenge*, and a subscription to *The Editorial Eye*, EEI's flagship newsletter on publications standards, practices, and trends. You'll find an annotated list of other printed and online resources that EEI Press editors have selected for their colleagues at www.eeicommunications.com/press.

As T.S. Eliot famously said, "Most editors are failed writers—but so are most writers." Copyeditors join writers in the ongoing challenge of serving busy, distracted, reluctant readers when they give the working parts of good writing—word usage, punctuation, sentence structure, grammatical relationships—a tune-up. They also rise to emergencies: They fix the flat tires and broken windshields of prose.

Those of us at EEI Press who worked on this updated edition of *Substance & Style* salute those with a serious commitment to fostering well-written English. The trained copyeditor—that's you, now or in the near future—is potentially the writer's true ally and the best friend a reader could ask for. Don't be daunted by how much more there is to learn. It's worth it.

—Linda B. Jorgensen
Manager, EEI Press

INTRODUCTION TO COPYEDITING:
What It Is and What It Isn't

Editor: One who revises, corrects, or arranges the contents and style of the literary, artistic, or musical work of others for publication or presentation; one who alters or revises another's work to make it conform to some standard or serve a particular purpose. (Webster's Third International Dictionary)

Good editing should be invisible; editors, however, are not. Ask an author about editors as a breed and the response may range from profound gratitude to contempt. All too often the relationship between authors and editors is adversarial, but it needn't be so. Ideally, authors and editors complement each other, both striving to convey ideas seamlessly to the reader.

The negative stereotype of the editor/author relationship was captured by a *New Yorker* cartoon that showed two men with muttonchop whiskers sitting across a desk. One, holding a manuscript, is saying to the other, "Come, come, Mr. Dickens, it was either the best of times or the worst of times. It could not have been both." An author produces the perfect sentence and the editor quibbles over trifles; editors are "comma people," authors are "content people." Like most stereotypes, this one contains a grain of truth. Authors in general are more concerned with content and editors with its expression. As a division of labor, this one is as valid as any other.

This book addresses a particular kind of editing called copyediting. Copyeditors examine a manuscript sentence by sentence. By the time a copyeditor gets the manuscript, larger decisions, such as additions, deletions, or reorganizations, have already been made by other editors or reviewers.

Copyediting is different from substantive editing, which is concerned with those larger decisions. A copyeditor examines a manuscript for spelling, grammar, punctuation, consistency, and conformity to style. As one longtime editor put it, "The ultimate goal is to produce a sentence that sounds as if it could have been written no other way....You, the editor, are a bridge between two people, the person who has written and the person who will or may read."

Copyeditors take a manuscript and polish the language; they strive to make the author's meaning as clear as possible, to save readers from editorial inconsistencies that at best distract them from the content and at worst cloud the author's meaning. Copyeditors make sure that a manuscript will stand up to the scrutiny of both the author's peers and the general public. The copyeditor is often the last line of defense against absurdities that creep into print and embarrass the most diligent authors.

Editing in general and copyediting in particular are skills you learn by doing. However, most editors share common traits—a love of the written word, an appreciation of language in all its richness, a desire to see order emerge from chaos in the form of a manuscript that sings or speaks from the heart. The intellectual challenge is always there, but more than anything else, editing is fun—so much fun that it's easy to get carried away.

The following example shows "before-and-after" examples of substantive editing, copyediting, and proofreading.

This is the original.

The giraffe's circulatory system is specially adopted for it's long neck. A giraffe's hear weighs more that 24 pounds and pumps approximately 16 gallons of blood a minute. They have a special valve in the blood vessels of their neck. This special value allows them to been down to get a drink of water without passing out from the rush of blood to the brain.

The idea that giraffes are moot is a myth. Though normally silent, giraffes may sneeze, blear, snore, cough, and even make a very-low mooing sound. When upset, they snort and growl. Another myth about giraffes are that they don't lie down to sleep, in fact they do but only for a few minutes. They usually rest standing up, flicking their ears and keeping one eye open, always alert of what is going on. Giraffes only sleep deeply for a few minutes at a time. Another myth about giraffes is that its front legs are longer than their hind ones. In fact the length of both front and hind is about the same (the foreleg is only 1/10th longer than the hind.) It is the high shoulders which give the false impression of a difference in limb length too.

Definitions

These definitions are in chronological order. A manuscript usually goes through the following steps on its journey from idea to publication.

Writing to specification (as opposed to creative writing) means starting from an idea, with no manuscript or with notes alone; it includes research, interviews, consultations, draft preparation, and revisions.

Substantive editing includes reorganizing, rewriting, writing transitions and summaries, helping plan schedules, attending meetings, and consulting with authors and publishers.

Copyediting means reviewing a "finished" manuscript (copy) for spelling, grammar, consistency, and format. Copyeditors also check the completeness, accuracy, and format of tables, bibliographies, references, and footnotes. Copyediting doesn't usually include rewriting or reorganization, but it does include reducing wordiness and reviewing the content for logic.

This version shows online proofreading, the first level of editorial service. The proofreader has corrected basic spelling and format errors, as well as egregious grammar and usage errors that would be picked up in a "light copyedit" or "editorial proofread." (Proofreading on paper uses a very different system of marking from copyediting.)

The giraffe's circulatory system is specially ~~adopted~~ <u>adapted</u> for it's long neck. A giraffe's hear<u>t</u> weighs more ~~that~~ <u>than</u> 24 pounds and pumps approximately 16 gallons of blood a minute. They have a special valve in the blood vessels of their neck. This special ~~value~~ <u>valve</u> allows them to ~~been~~ <u>bend</u> down to get a drink of water without passing out from the rush of blood to the brain.

The idea that giraffes are ~~moot~~ <u>mute</u> is a myth. Though normally silent, giraffes may sneeze, blea<u>t</u>, snore, cough, and even make a very-low mooing sound. When upset, they snort and growl. Another myth about giraffes ~~are~~ <u>is</u> that they don't lie down to sleep~~;~~ in fact they do but only for a few minutes. They usually rest standing up, flicking their ears and keeping one eye open, always alert of what is going on. Giraffes only sleep deeply for a few minutes at a time. Another myth about giraffes is that its front legs are longer than their hind ones. In fact the length of both front and hind is about the same (the foreleg is only 1/10th longer than the hind.) It is the high shoulders which give the false impression of a difference in limb length too.

Proofreading means checking the final typeset version (proof) against the manuscript version to find typographical errors and deviations from typesetting or word processing instructions. Proofreaders query (question), but normally don't change, editorial errors and inconsistencies.

As with any other task, it's important to know how copyediting fits into the larger picture. This understanding makes instructions more relevant and can even determine the level of effort you expend. Copyeditors aren't expected to redo the work of the author and substantive editor, but rather to polish and complete it. Everyone works together to produce a harmonious whole.

Because copyeditors need to be very familiar with the rules of the language, this book incorporates a review of grammar and punctuation and includes examples and alternate

This version shows a standard online copyedit, the second level of editorial service. The editor has corrected spelling and other basic errors and changed wording to improve clarity and flow. See Chapter 3 for the standard copyediting marks used on hard copy.

The giraffe's circulatory system is specially ~~adopted~~ <u>adapted</u> for it~~'~~s long neck. A giraffe's heart weighs more ~~that~~ <u>than</u> 24 pounds and pumps ~~approximately~~ <u>about</u> 16 gallons of blood a minute. ~~They~~ <u>Giraffes</u> have a special valve in the blood vessels of their neck~~. This special value~~ <u>that</u> allows them to ~~been~~ <u>bend</u> down ~~to get a drink of~~<u>for</u> water without passing out from ~~the~~ <u>a</u> rush of blood to the brain.

The idea that giraffes are ~~meet~~ <u>mute</u> is a myth. Though normally silent, giraffes ~~may~~ <u>can</u> sneeze, bleat, snore, cough, and even make a very-low mooing sound. When upset, they snort and growl. Another myth about giraffes ~~are~~ <u>is</u> that they don't lie down to sleep~~:~~<u>;</u> in fact they do <u>lie down</u> but only for a few minutes <u>at a time</u>. They usually rest standing up, flicking their ears and keeping one eye open, always alert ~~of~~<u>to</u> what is going on. Giraffes ~~only~~ sleep deeply for <u>only</u> a few minutes at a time. Another myth about giraffes is that ~~its~~ <u>their</u> front legs are longer than their hind ones. In fact<u>,</u> ~~the length of both~~<u>the</u> front and hind <u>legs are</u>~~is~~ about the same <u>length</u>~~(—the foreleg~~<u>front</u> legs ~~is~~<u>are</u> only ~~1/10th~~ <u>10 percent</u> longer than the ~~hind~~<u>back legs~~)~~. It is the <u>giraffe's</u> high shoulders ~~which~~<u>that</u> gives the ~~false~~ impression of a difference in limb length~~ too~~.

solutions. Exercises will teach concepts and test skills. Often there's no right or wrong answer; some solutions are simply better than others.

The basic tools of the copyeditor's trade are a dictionary and a style manual. Editing often means ensuring conformity to a style, and this book compares some commonly used styles on such points as punctuation, abbreviation, and numbers. It also discusses what a style decision is and how it differs from a rule of grammar. Copyeditors who work for a publisher will need to become familiar with that publisher's preferred style. Freelance copyeditors may need to switch among several styles for different clients—a more demanding task. Chapter 11, Editorial Style: Manuals and Word Lists, compares several widely used style manuals.

Bear in mind that a copyeditor is not an English teacher. An English teacher is justified in pointing out problems in a composition and expecting the student to correct them. The copyeditor's job is to eliminate those problems.

This version shows a substantive edit, the third level of editorial service. The editor has reorganized and rewritten much of the text to make it more logical, accessible, and useful.

Giraffes have some unusual characteristics. The giraffe's circulatory system is specially adapted for its long neck. An adult giraffe's heart, which weighs more than 24 pounds, pumps about 16 gallons of blood a minute. A special valve in the blood vessels of the neck allows the animal to bend down to drink without passing out from a rush of blood to the brain. A number of myths about giraffes need to be refuted:

That they are mute. Although normally silent, giraffes can sneeze, bleat, snore, and cough. When upset, they snort and growl.

That they don't lie down to sleep. In fact, they do, but only for a few minutes at a time. They usually rest standing up, flicking their ears and keeping one eye open, alert to what is going on.

That their forelegs are much longer than their hind ones. In fact, the forelegs are only about 10 percent longer than the hind ones; the giraffe's high shoulders are responsible for the illusion that the legs are very different in length.

The Publications Team

Nutritionists have a food pyramid; publications people have a work team pyramid. Here's one typical way it is stacked: Overseeing the publishing process is the project manager. The editorial assistant works with the project manager, while the researcher is more likely to work with the writer. The writer's draft goes through the hands of the substantive editor and the copyeditor. Following the writer's review of the edits and responses to queries, the manuscript enters the production process. A designer develops specs for the finished product. The desktop publisher and Web specialist make the designer's concept a reality. The proofreader and quality control specialist ensure that no mistakes have crept in along the way. The printing specialist (or production manager) selects an appropriate printer for the job and monitors its progress. Voilà—an error-free, professional-looking publication makes it to the goalpost!

Exercise 1:
Spelling Test

Instructions: Cross through every misspelled word and write out the entire word with the correct spelling in the blank provided.

_____ The occurrence of a misspelled word in print is totaly

_____ impermissible. The affect is disastrous, an embarrass-

_____ ment to the printer, a distraction to the reader, and a

_____ slurr on the writer's competence. Misspelling is a sign

_____ that the role of the proofreader has been slighted or

_____ misunderstood. Although the proofreader is principly

_____ committed to seeing that the proof follows the copy

_____ accurately, there is a further committment to preventing

_____ the author, editor, or printer from looking rediculous.

_____ A practitioner of proofreading is never presumtuous in

_____ correcting (or—better—querying) an incorrect spelling.

_____ Let no conscientious proofreader wholey acquiesce to

_____ the rule of "follow copy" in regard to spelling.

Exercise 1 Answers

The occurrence of a misspelled word in print is ~~totaly~~   **totally**

impermissible. The ~~affect~~ is disastrous, an embarrass-   **effect**

ment to the printer, a distraction to the reader, and a   _____

~~slurr~~ on the writer's competence. Misspelling is a sign   **slur**

that the role of the proofreader has been slighted or   _____

misunderstood. Although the proofreader is ~~principly~~   **principally**

committed to seeing that the proof follows the copy   _____

accurately, there is a further ~~committment~~ to preventing   **commitment**

the author, editor, or printer from looking ~~rediculous.~~   **ridiculous**

A practitioner of proofreading is never ~~presumtuous~~ in   **presumptuous**

correcting (or—better—querying) an incorrect spelling.   _____

Let no conscientious proofreader ~~wholey~~ acquiesce to   **wholly**

the rule of "follow copy" in regard to spelling.   _____

Exercise 1, continued

Instructions: Choose one of the two letters in parentheses to complete the word.

1. comput_r   (e;o)
2. deduct_ble   (a;i)
3. defend_nt   (a;e)
4. depend_nt   (a;e)
5. dissen_ion   (s;t)
6. super_ede   (c;s)

7. inadvert_nt   (e;a)
8. indispens_ble (a;i)
9. m_mento   (e;o)
10. resist_nt   (a;e)
11. sep_rate   (a;e)
12. tox_n   (e;i)

Exercise 1 Answers

1. comput<u>e</u>r   (e)
2. deduct<u>i</u>ble   (i)
3. defend<u>a</u>nt   (a)
4. depend<u>e</u>nt   (e)
5. dissen<u>s</u>ion   (s)
6. super<u>s</u>ede   (s)

7. inadvert<u>e</u>nt   (e)
8. indispens<u>a</u>ble (a)
9. m<u>e</u>mento   (e)
10. resist<u>a</u>nt   (a)
11. sep<u>a</u>rate   (a)
12. tox<u>i</u>n   (i)

For words such as *dependent*, *dissension*, and *memento*, your dictionary may list more than one spelling. Always use the first spelling, which is the one more commonly preferred. Because dictionaries vary, be sure to use the one your client or employer prefers. Also, assume nothing. Don't automatically change the word *materiel* to *material* or *tranches* to *branches*: Check the context and look it up.

GRAMMAR:
You Have to Know It to Correct It

2

Unlike spelling, which lends itself to correction by spell-checkers (although they are far from infallible), grammar is less susceptible to automatic correction. A sentence that's grammatically unclear or downright incorrect undermines the reader's faith in the author.

Copyeditors are more than grammarians. A sentence fragment, for example, is grammatically incorrect, yet it can be an effective rhetorical device. A good copyeditor will consider whether its effectiveness outweighs its "incorrectness." Good editors share a love for and an appreciation of language. You have to like words to edit well, but you also have to know how the language works—why certain constructions are allowed and others aren't. Further, it's important to remember that the written word is more formal than the spoken word. Although the gap between the two is narrower than it used to be, some strictures remain. Should this distinction strike you as artificial, remember that in some languages (French, for example), entire tenses are no longer spoken, just written.

You need to hone your skills to be able to find and fix grammatical problems that weaken prose. You also need to know the names of faulty constructions so that you can explain your editorial changes to an author. As a copyeditor, you should generally notice most misplaced modifiers, unclear antecedents, and agreement problems upon even a cursory reading. Exercise 2 is a pretest to give you an idea of the grammatical problems you may encounter. It includes sentences with subject-verb disagreements, misplaced modifiers, and unclear (or missing) antecedents for pronouns. Rewrite or reorder the words to fix the problems you find, remembering always that you must preserve the author's meaning.

Answers and explanations appear in the answer key, which follows the pretest. The errors in Exercise 2 are discussed in detail in the following chapters. This book does not cover every point of English grammar. A list of useful printed and online references can be found at www.eeicommunications.com/press.

Exercise 2: Sentence Correction

Instructions: After each sentence, write the name of the grammatical and other problems you find. Then reorder words or rewrite sentences as needed to correct that problem.

1. Unhappy and depressed, the movie made me feel worse.

2. They only ate what they wanted to eat.

3. Without his wife, his life became onerous.

4. When the artist finished the painting of the boat, he immediately covered it with varnish.

5. My mother has a friend who is very tall.

6. The president said he expected everyone to support the offensive at the press conference last night.

7. Of all the quilts submitted, Laura's design was the most unique.

Exercise 2, continued

8. Hopefully, I have completed my income tax form correctly.

9. He thinks that he'll take a shower, and after that go to bed.

10. Lord Byron was young, well born, and had nice manners.

11. He hated politics and all elected officials were considered dishonest by him.

12. My favorite foods are: pizza, popcorn, and watermelon.

13. The congregation is not rich, but they certainly are generous.

14. If he was as clever as he is bold, he would be very successful.

15. Neither the coach nor the players is going.

16. Would Scarlett O'Hara have been happier if she would have married Ashley Wilkes?

17. Shakespeare's sonnets are about lovers who agonize over it.

The Copyeditor's Guide to **Substance**&*Style*

Exercise 2 Answers

It's important to have corrected these sentences, but it's essential to know why they need correction and also how to defend the changes you've made. Following are the edited sentences, showing the correct marks and explanations of the problems needing correction.

1. *Because I was*
~~U~~nhappy and depressed, the movie made me feel worse.

   Misplaced modifier (a word or phrase not logically or grammatically describing what it was meant to): As the sentence was originally written, the movie was unhappy and depressed.

2. They ~~only~~ ate what they wanted to eat.

   Misplaced modifier: Here the word *only* modifies *what they wanted*, not *ate*.

3. Without his wife, *he found* his life ~~became~~ onerous.

   Misplaced modifier: *His life* wasn't *without a wife*; *he* was. Such constructions are common in conversation but unacceptable in print.

4. When the artist finished the painting of the boat, he immediately covered it with varnish.

   Unclear antecedent (a substantive word, phrase, or clause referred to by a pronoun): What does the word *it* refer to—the painting or the boat? Actually, it could be either. If the answer isn't clear from the context, you as an editor would have to query the author.

5. My mother has a friend ~~who is~~ very tall.

   Wordiness: Some words could be cut out of this sentence with no loss of meaning.

6. The president said he expected everyone to support the offensive at the press conference last night.

   Misplaced modifier: You're permitted to doubt that the offensive took place at the press conference.

7. Of all the quilts submitted, Laura's design was ~~the most~~ unique.

   Modification of absolutes: Some words, such as *unique*, denote an absolute quality that can't carry a qualifying adjective such as *more* or *most*. Either something is unique or it's not. *Critical* is a similar sort of word, one that's modified regularly and incorrectly. A situation is critical or it's not: *Very critical* and *extremely critical* are redundant.

8. ~~Hopefully,~~ *I hope,* I have completed my income tax form correctly.

   Incorrect modifier: *Hopefully* used as an independent comment has crept into contemporary speech. Like *obviously* and similar terms, it's meant to modify the entire sentence. Some grammarians, however, consider this usage incorrect and prefer that *hopefully* be changed to *I hope* in this example.

9. He thinks that he'll take a shower and ~~after that~~ go to bed.

   Wordiness and incorrect punctuation: *Take* and *go* are two equal parts of the predicate forming a compound verb. A comma shouldn't separate the parts of a compound verb.

10. Lord Byron was young, well born, and ~~had nice~~ *well* manner~~s~~ *ed*.

    Faulty parallelism: Similar constructions must be treated similarly. The words following the verb weren't all predicate adjectives.

Exercise 2 Answers, continued

11. He hated politics and ~~all elected officials were considered dishonest by him.~~

    Faulty parallelism: The two independent clauses weren't parallel in structure.

12. My favorite foods are /pizza, popcorn, and watermelon.

    Incorrect punctuation: The colon is incorrect; use it only after a complete sentence.

13. ~~T~~he congregation is not rich, ~~but they~~ certainly ~~are~~ generous.
    (Although ... is)

    Incorrect antecedent: Although the sentence is perfectly comprehensible to readers, *they* has no antecedent. *Congregation*, the intended antecedent, is singular; *they* is plural.

14. If he ~~was~~ *were* as clever as he is bold, he would be very successful.

    Incorrect mood (the manner in which the action of the verb is conceived by the writer): This sentence should contain a subjunctive verb (condition contrary to fact), one of the few remnants of this form in the language. He's obviously *not* as clever as he is bold.

15. Neither the coach nor the players ~~is~~ *are* going.

    Subject-verb disagreement (*neither...nor* or *either...or*): When these forms are used, the verb agrees with the subject nearest to it—in this case, *players*. The verb must be plural.

Exercise 2 Answers, continued

16. Would Scarlett O'Hara have been happier if she ~~would have~~ *had* married

    Ashley Wilkes?

    Too many conditionals (*would haves*): One will suffice. Only the *if* clause
    needs a subjunctive verb. Scarlett didn't marry Ashley; thus, the situation is
    contrary to fact.

17. Shakespeare's sonnets are about ~~lovers~~ *people* who agonize ~~over it.~~ *about being in love*

    Implied antecedent (a usage common in everyday speech but not acceptable
    in writing): *It* refers to an imbedded idea, which must be spelled out.

    ———————————————

    The errors in these sentences are typical of the problems you'll find while editing
    You'll also be faced with style questions (one or 1, exercise 10 or Exercise 10),
    as well as tables, charts, and references. The following chapters are designed to
    prepare you for anything and to help you become that bridge between author
    and reader.

COPYEDITING MARKS 3

Editorial marks are a sort of shorthand that has evolved over time. These marks are not universal, but they're nearly so. Today, more and more publishers are editing manuscripts electronically, or online, a subject covered in detail in Chapter 15. But that practice is still not universal. If you're editing on paper (hard copy), editorial marks save you hours of writing detailed instructions. Used clearly and correctly, the marks can avoid needless revisions, costs, and annoyance.

The marks that follow are standard for editors. Some organizations use slightly different ones for particular purposes. If your office uses variants, by all means conform, but keep in mind that someone else (an "outside" author or keyboarder, for instance) may need a key to your notation.

Editors and proofreaders use the same marks, but place them differently. Editors mark in the text line, because the keyboarders need to read every line as they work. In addition, most manuscripts are double-spaced, so the editor has room to mark above the text. Proofreaders, working at a later stage in the editorial process, mark in the margin of the typeset material, so the keyboarder making corrections need only run an eye down the margin to see what to do.

Delete

Delete one character, several letters, or a whole word with a looped cancel mark (𝓎). If you want to delete an entire passage, box it in and draw an X through it.

Delete this letter.   Delete this letter.

Delete this word word.   Delete this word.

Close Up

To close up space entirely, use this mark (⟳), often called close-up hooks.

tooth‿paste   toothpaste

tooth‿brush   toothbrush

Using only the top half of the mark means to decrease the space, or to leave a word space, or to take out any extra space, depending on the context.

Now ⌒ is the time.   Now is the time.

Delete and Close Up

When you combine the delete symbol with the close-up hooks, you get a mark that looks like this: ⟆ . Use it when you want to delete a letter in the middle of a word or at the end of a word, just before a punctuation mark.

Noₒw is the tiₘme.   Now is the time.

Now is the timeₑ.   Now is the time.

Insert

When you want to insert a letter or a phrase, use a caret (∧). Always place your insertions above the line, and always place the caret precisely where you want the insertion to be.

all good

Now is the time for ∧ men   Now is the time for all good men

A brace (‿) under the insertion helps direct the eye to the proper place.

is the

Now ∧ time for all good men   Now is the time for all good men

If you're inserting a letter at the beginning or end of a word, you must use close-up hooks as well. To some people this practice seems superfluous, but without the hooks it's often impossible to tell where such insertions belong in heavily edited copy. For example, what did the editor intend here, *fields* or *snow*?

s

field ∧ now

The use of close-up hooks would have told you.

field now	field snow
field now	fields now

If you want to add space rather than a word, use a caret and a space mark (#). Some editors draw a line to separate the two words rather than using the symbol.

Insertspace	Insert space
Insertspace	Insert space

Lowercase

A slash through a capital letter means that the letter should be lowercase. If you wish to lowercase several letters in a row, you can use a slash with a "hat" on it.

Lowercase	lowercase
LOWERCASE	lowercase

Capitals

To make a lowercase letter or word uppercase, put three lines under the letters to be changed.

capital	Capital
all caps	ALL CAPS

Small Caps

Small caps are capital letters that are only as big as lowercase letters; they're often used for acronyms, such as VISTA, or combined with regular capitals for names in signature lines. To mark for small caps, use two lines under the words or letters.

Robert E. Brown	ROBERT E. BROWN
Robert E. Brown	ROBERT E. BROWN

Some people choose two lines to indicate regular caps, but such usage isn't standard.

Italics

The underline symbol (___) is used to signify both italics and underscore. To differentiate between the two forms, write the instruction (*ital* or *score*) in a circle in the margin. Keyboarders know not to enter or "set" anything circled in the margin. Circle all instructions, specifications, or queries, so that no one will put them into the text by mistake.

 <u>The Sound and the Fury</u>   *The Sound and the Fury*

 <u>The Sound and the Fury</u>   <u>The Sound and the Fury</u>

To remove italics, put a series of hatch marks through the line, or put a delete mark at the end. The latter, however, is very easy to miss in heavily edited copy.

<u>remove italics</u>

<u>remove italics</u>

Boldface

To indicate boldface, use a wavy line (∿∿∿) and to remove it, write and circle , which means *lightface*.

boldface
∿∿∿∿∿   **boldface**

 remove boldface
∿∿∿∿∿∿∿∿   remove boldface

Transpose

The transposition mark looks like this: ⟨. You can use it to transpose both letters and words.

transpose   transpose

words transpose   transpose words

You can also transpose around something that you've left untouched, although it's often better to rewrite the words. Be sure to keep transpositions easy to read and don't make transpositions within transpositions.

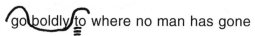

To boldly go where no man has gone

Replace

To mark for replacement, slash through the incorrect letter and put its replacement above the line. To replace an entire word, cross it out and write the correction above it to avoid any possibility of misunderstanding.

slash

splash

Spell Out/Use the Other Form

If you want to use the complete word instead of an abbreviation, circle the abbreviation. Circling also indicates that you want the other form.

seven

Company

General Motors

Note that the circle works both ways:

7

Co.

GM

If the circled text results in an ambiguous instruction, write out what you want. For instance, does *Calif.* become *CA* or *California*? Is *GM General Motors* or *General Mills*? Is *VA Virginia* or the *Veterans Administration*? Don't ask the person who must follow through on your markup to guess.

Paragraph

A symbol called the pilcrow (¶) is used to denote the beginning of a paragraph. This sign, which dates back to Middle English, is universally understood. Some editors use a sign that looks like an *L* (L) to mark a paragraph break, but this mark is too often lost in heavily edited copy and therefore is used less often.

¶ Need a new paragraph   L Need a new paragraph

Run On

Conversely, if you don't want a paragraph where one already exists, then you mark to run on (↶). You can use the same symbol to mark the end of a considerable deletion as well.

We were told to
speak to John Brown.
He is Assistant
Manager

John Brown, Manager of

Assistant Manager of

the Bethesda branch

Transfer

To move material to an adjacent line, brace or circle the passage and use an arrow to show where you want it to go.

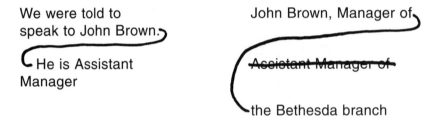

Be sure your marks and instructions are clear and accurate when you are

moving material to an adjacent line Brace or circle material to be moved

Box material to be moved to a different position on the same page and run an arrow to the new position.

Move this line down.

Copy marked this way is easy for keyboarders to read.

If you want to move material to another page, say from page 3 to page 4, follow this procedure: On page 3, circle the material to be moved, label it *Insert A*, and draw an arrow pointing toward the right-hand margin. In a circle, write *Move to page 4*. On page 4, draw an arrow from the left margin to the place of insertion and write in a circle, *Insert A from page 3*. See below for an example of this markup.

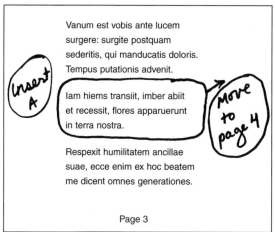

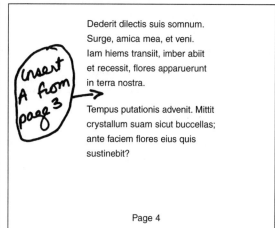

Superior/Inferior Characters

A character that goes above the line (superscript), as in a formula or footnote reference, is marked this way: $\vee$.

footnote$\underset{\vee}{|}$ footnote[1]

A character that should go below the line (subscript) is marked this way: $\wedge$.

H$\overset{\wedge}{\cancel{2}}$O H_2O

Punctuation Marks

A **comma** is marked this way: $\mathcal{S}$. The caret makes the mark stand out on the page and indicates that it goes below the line.

The **period** looks like a bull's-eye: $\odot$. Without the circle, the period can be mistaken for a random dot on the page.

The **semicolon** and the **colon** can also have carets, $\overset{\wedge}{;}$/ $\overset{\wedge}{:}$, although some editors use the marks alone, $;$/ $:$, or circle them, $⦷$/$⦶$.

Apostrophes and **quotation marks** are placed in upside-down carets to indicate their placement above the line: $\vee\!\!'$ and $\vee\!\!"$.

Question marks and **exclamation points** use the traditional handwritten symbols ❓ and ❗.

The **hyphen** looks like an equal sign: ⸗ . This is the traditional mark, although a single line is used as well.

Dashes are of two sorts and are marked this way: ⅟M and ⅟N . **Em-dashes** are the traditional kind: two hyphens if a software code isn't used or a long typeset line (—). Unless we specifically say en-dash, we mean em-dash. En-dashes will be discussed in Chapter 10.

If a manuscript has words hyphenated at the ends of lines, you'll need to decide whether the hyphen is part of the word or not and mark the hyphen accordingly.

If a hyphen appears only because a line is too short for the whole word, you must mark this "soft" hyphen for deletion. Failure to delete the hyphen produces such oddities as "We lack a quo-rum." If the word always has a hyphen (anti-inflation), then you must mark it to stay (a "hard" hyphen), so that it will be carried over into later iterations.

In the first case, you mark to delete and close (⟲); in the second, you add a line (⸗) to make the existing hyphen into the editor's mark. Regardless of which kind of hyphen appears at the end of a line, you must mark it, and it's generally advisable to mark all hyphens that might cause misunderstanding. Marking hyphens is discussed further in Chapter 10.

> He opened the tooth⟋paste tube.

> You should install child⸗proof locks on these doors.

Here is an example of each of these punctuation symbols correctly marked by an editor.

comma	Yes⸲
period	he said⊙
semicolon	I was late⟋therefore I lost.
colon	We will discuss the following⟋

hyphen	tamper‑proof seal
apostrophe	Mind your P's and Q's.
quotation marks	"Go," he said.
question mark	Did you say that?
exclamation point	Down!
em-dash	The brothers—Manny and Moe—
en-dash	1939–1945

Stet

Finally, if you edit in ink and later discover that you've made a mistake, use the stet symbol (stet), which means to ignore the correction and let the original stand. (*Stet* comes from Latin and means *let it stand*.) To stet text, put a series of dots under it and use the stet symbol right next to it.

Little Bo Peep has lost her sheep. (stet)

Placement Notations

Sometimes an editor must indicate where material should appear on the page or in a table. If you want a line to begin at the left margin (*flush left*), use this mark: ⌐ . If you want the line to be moved to the right margin (*flush right*), use this mark: ⌐ . If a head, for example, should be centered, put the two marks together like this: ⊐⊏ . Another way to ask that material be centered is to use this symbol: ctr .

Copyediting ⌐

⌐Date

⊐Chapter 1⊏

To align, or make margins or columns even, use two parallel lines. But be sure to say in a marginal notation how you want the column or the passage aligned if it isn't obvious. (For example, write "align on the decimal" and circle the instruction.)

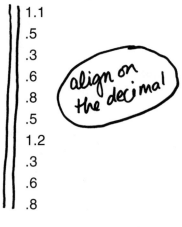

1.1
.5
.3
.6
.8
.5
1.2
.3
.6
.8

French
Italian
German

To indent, you can use the pilcrow (¶) or a small box to indicate a 1-em space (a space that's the same size as the capital letter M). In the old days of movable type, an em-space or em-quad was a standard measurement; although the standard has been replaced, the notation remains. Here are examples of each of these marks.

¶ In the beginning

☐ In the beginning

Exercise 3: Copyediting Marks

Instructions: Now that you've mastered copyediting marks, you're almost ready to tackle a simple manuscript. First, however, complete the following exercise by making the correct copyediting marks.

Delete	rfrequently
	ham and and eggs
Close up	nation wide
Delete and close up	worldywide
Insert the correct letter	editr
Lowercase	chairman of the Board
	CHAIRMAN OF THE BOARD
Capitalize	mexico
Italics	The Economist
Boldface	as soon as possible
Transpose the first two words	the Place period at the end.
Spell out	9 of the soldiers
New paragraph	
Hard hyphen	seventy- seven
Soft hyphen	develop- ment
Stet—let it stand	The news is very bad.

Align	black
	    blue
	red
	    yellow
	  green

Exercise 3 Answers

Delete	ℊfrequently
	ham ~~and~~ and eggs
Close up	nation⌒wide
Delete and close up	world⌒y⌒wide
Insert the correct letter	edit͓r
Lowercase	chairman of the ⱡBoard
	ⱡCHAIRMAN OF THE BOARD
Capitalize	mexico
Italics	The Economist (ital)
Boldface	as soon as possible .
Transpose the first two words	⁀the Place⁀ period at the end.
Spell out	(9) of the soldiers
New paragraph	¶
Hard hyphen	seventy-̄seven
Soft hyphen	develop⌒ment
Stet—let it stand	The news is ~~very~~ bad. (stet)
Align	‖black blue ‖red yellow ‖ green

Exercise 4:
More Practice

Instructions: Exercise 4 has two parts. In A, make the correct editing marks in the following lines and paragraph. The answers follow. If you aren't comfortable using copyediting marks, review the preceding sections. It's all right to have to verify an occasional mark, but you must master the basics before you can proceed with B.

A.   Follow the line-by-line instructions and check your answers.

1. Change to all caps.   Practice in marking copy

2. Change to caps and lowercase (initial caps).   PRACTICE IN MARKING COPY

3. Change to italics.   Practice in Marking Copy

4. Mark for caps and small caps, centered.   Practice in marking copy

5. Mark for lowercase italics, flush right.   PRACTICE IN MARKING COPY

6. Mark for boldface, flush left.   Practice in Marking Copy

Answers

1. Practice in marking copy   PRACTICE IN MARKING COPY

2. PRACTICE IN MARKING COPY   Practice in Marking Copy

3. Practice in Marking Copy (*ital*)   *Practice in Marking Copy*

4.]Practice in marking copy[Practice in Marking Copy

5. PRACTICE IN MARKING COPY] (*ital*)   *practice in marking copy*

6. [Practice in Marking Copy   **Practice in Marking Copy**

Exercise 4, continued

B. Read the paragraph through quickly and then use editing marks to carry out the instructions. Remember to mark within the text.

Line 1—Mark a 1-em paragraph indent. Transpose the letters to correct the spelling error.

Line 2—Delete the repeated word.

Line 4—Delete *the field of*. Add the word *writing* after *educational*.

Line 5—Delete the three extra words.

Line 7—Delete the repeated letters and close up the space.

Line 9—Correct the spelling error.

Line 10—Mark a 1-em paragraph indent. Transpose the letters to correct the spelling error.

Line 11—Delete the *al* from *educational* and mark to close the word up to its comma.

Line 13—Delete the italics from *issue*.

Line 14—Add an *s* to *field*.

Line 15—Lowercase the letters of the last word.

1. Educators had better mind their own langauge

2. if they are going to to move toward a solution

3. rather than compound the problem. The prize for

4. dubious achievement in the field of educational

5. went to a vacuous display of Pennsylvania college

6. professor for a vacuous display of word spinning

7 that seemed to be more representatative of the

8. prose we encounter every day than a national

9 record for educational gobbledyggok.

10. Jargon is a problem in our own patr of the field

11. of educational, and it is commented on by the

12. reviewers of the four books on instructional

13. theory discussed in this *Highlights issue*. In

14. most field, it is the words that help to make

15. the specialists SPecial.

Exercise 4 Answers

Line 1—Mark a 1-em paragraph indent. Transpose the letters to correct the spelling error.

Line 2—Delete the repeated word.

Line 4—Delete *the field of*. Add the word *writing* after *educational*.

Line 5—Delete the three extra words

Line 7—Delete the repeated letters and close up the space.

Line 9—Correct the spelling error.

Line 10—Mark a 1-em paragraph indent. Transpose the letters to correct the spelling error.

Line 11—Delete the *al* from *educational* and mark to close the word up to its comma.

Line 13—Delete the italics from *issue*.

Line 14—Add an *s* to *field*.

Line 15—Lowercase the letters of the last word.

1. Educators had better mind their own langauge

2. if they are going to to move toward a solution

3. rather than compound the problem. The prize for

4. dubious achievement in the field of educational writing

5. went to a vacuous display of Pennsylvania college

6. professor for a vacuous display of word spinning

7. that seemed to be more representatative of the

8. prose we encounter every day than a national

9. record for educational gobbledyggok.

10. Jargon is a problem in our own part of the field

11. of educational, and it is commented on by the

12. reviewers of the four books on instructional

13. theory discussed in this *Highlights issue*. In

14. most field it is the words that help to make

15. the specialists Special.

Exercise 5:
Advice for Editors

Instructions: Use editing marks to correct the following sentences, and then check your answers against the key. Each sentence highlights a particular problem. Although only one solution is given for each sentence, some variations will certainly be correct. Just be sure that you corrected the problem identified in the solution and that you didn't introduce new errors or change the meaning.

1. Catch all mispellings and tpyos.

2. No sentence fragments. Fix run-on sentences they're hard to read.

3. The cause of the problems in many sentences are subject-verb disagreement; subject and verb has to agree in person and number.

4. A pronoun must agree with their antecedent.

5. Catch unclear pronoun reference. For example, correct the copy when the pronouns this and that are used loosely; careful readers confused by this.

6. Working carefully, dangling participles and all misplaced modifiers need correction.

7. You dislike finding fault, but when one sees careless shifts of pronoun case, he or she can't help complaining.

8. If you have done your job as copyeditor, you improved the copy by removing unnecessary verb tense shifts.

The Copyeditor's Guide to **Substance**&*Style*

Exercise 5, continued

9. Use the semicolon properly, always use it where it's appropriate; and never where it's not appropriate.

10. Reserve the apostrophe for it's proper use, and omit it when its not needed.

11. Avoid commas, that are not necessary but be sure to put a comma between the two parts of a compound sentence.

12. Avoid un-necessary hyphens.

13. Nonparallel construction is faulty, undesirable, and don't permit it.

14. Do not leave in words that are not necessary.

15. Strike out redundant tautologies.

16. If you go over your work a second time, you will find on going over it that a great deal of repetition can be avoided by going over your work and editing again.

17. Smothered verbs are an addition to wordiness; when possible, attend to the improvement of clarity by the replacement of nouns with verbs.

18. In most technical writing, the passive voice is to be avoided.

19. Watch for good word use; steer clear of incorrect forms of verbs that have snuck into the language.

Exercise 5 Answers

1. Catch all mis**s**pellings and ty~~o~~ps.

2. ~~No~~ Don't use sentence fragments. Fix run-on sentences^;^ they're hard to read.

3. The cause of the problems in many sentences ~~are~~ **is** subject-verb disagreement; subject and verb ~~has~~ **have** to agree in person and number.

4. A pronoun must agree with ~~their~~ **its** antecedent.

5. Catch unclear pronoun reference**s**. For example, correct the copy when the pronouns _this_ and _that_ are used loosely**;** careful readers **are** confused by ~~this~~ **such usage**.

6. Working carefully**,** **to correct** dangling participles and all misplaced modifiers ~~need~~ ~~correction~~.

7. You dislike finding fault, but when ~~one sees~~ **you** careless shifts of pronoun case, ~~he or she~~ **you** can't help complaining.

8. If you ~~have done~~ **did** your job as copyeditor, you improved the copy by removing unnecessary verb tense shifts.

9. Use the semicolon properly^:^ always use it where it's appropriate**,** and never where it's not appropriate.

The Copyeditor's Guide to **Substance**&_Style_

Exercise 5 Answers, continued

10. Reserve the apostrophe for its proper use, and omit it when its not needed.

11. Avoid commas that are not necessary but be sure to put a comma between the two parts of a compound sentence.

12. Avoid unnecessary hyphens.

13. Nonparallel construction is faulty, undesirable; ~~and~~ don't permit it.

14. ~~Do not leave in~~ Remove unnecessary words that are not necessary.

15. Strike out ~~redundant~~ tautologies.

16. If you go over your work a second time, you will ~~find on going over it that~~ avoid much ~~a great deal of~~ repetition ~~can be avoided by going over your work and editing again.~~

17. Smothered verbs ~~are an~~ addition to wordiness; when possible, ~~attend to the~~ improvement ~~of~~ clarity by ~~the~~ replac~~ement of~~ing nouns with verbs.

18. In most technical writing, avoid the passive voice ~~is to be avoided.~~

19. Watch for good word use; ~~steer clear of~~ avoid incorrect forms of verbs that have crept, ~~snuck~~ into the language.

COPYEDITING:
Working With Text

The more you edit, the easier it becomes. Although at first you may feel that there are too many things to remember, most of the rules and shortcuts eventually become automatic. Don't be overwhelmed. Even experienced editors don't expect to catch every mistake the first time they go through a manuscript. Most editors plan to work through a manuscript at least twice; they want to make three passes if possible.

While you are honing your editing skills, you may want to approach a manuscript by doing one task at a time. For example, devote the first reading to purely mechanical points like spelling, sentence structure, and punctuation. On the second pass, pay more attention to grammar and style issues. The third time through, focus on content: Check to see that the piece reads well and that you have respected the author's basic intent and style. During this whole process, but especially during the last pass, you must concentrate. Good editing demands careful attention.

When you get a manuscript, always check to see that the pages are numbered. If they're not, number them in sequence, beginning with the title page. If you add pages during editing, give them the number of the preceding page plus a, b, c, and so on—for example, 10a, 10b, 10c—and note this number on the preceding page ("p. 10a follows"). If you delete a whole page, mark it with a diagonal line the length of the page. Leave the page in place so that the keyboarder or author won't look frantically for a "missing" piece of paper or see text on screen and with no corresponding manuscript.

Whether you edit in pencil (red or black) or ink depends on whether the material needs to be photocopied or faxed. Ink is better for copies or faxes, but since it's hard to change the marks once they're made, consider editing first in pencil and then going over the marks in ink once you're sure they're correct.

To prevent needless queries from an author, keyboarder, or proofreader, put a check over an unusual spelling or usage. The check means that you have verified the rarity.

Zelinska

quark

Take care of the manuscript; make sure that there's a protection copy (paper or electronic file) of anything you send in the mail. Even courier services occasionally lose things.

Don't write vertically on the page. If you must create a maze of insertions and deletions or if your handwriting is illegible, rekey the page; if you rekey, proofread. Similarly, don't print in block letters; distinguish between caps and lowercase. Don't use a capital letter when you want lowercase. Remember that someone will have to interpret your changes. The easier you make this task, the less the probability of error.

One trick of the editorial trade is to examine layout (the appearance of the piece) and format (indentions, headings, lines, etc.) in a separate pass through the copy. Do all main heads look the same? Are subheads consistently formatted? Are all the paragraphs similarly indented? Are lists consistent, or do some start with 1. and others with 1)? Do all the tables have the same format, or do they vary unnecessarily? It's almost impossible to check layout format as you edit; you'll overlook too many inconsistencies if you try to do too much at once.

When the manuscript you need to edit is as short as the one in Exercise 6, it helps to read it through before you make a mark on the page. Such a cursory reading gives you a sense of the author's approach and the content of the piece. The title, appropriately enough, is "Copyediting." For all its typos and omissions (introduced solely for the exercise), the text clearly describes both the copyediting function and your role as copyeditor.

Don't be discouraged if this exercise took you a long time. Aim for accuracy, not speed. The exercises in this book require more work and more marks than an ordinary manuscript. Remember also that you'll gain speed with practice.

On average, an experienced copyeditor can edit about five pages of double-spaced text an hour. It will take longer to edit a poorly written manuscript or one with extensive references, footnotes, or tables.

Novice copyeditors often assume that their job is not done until the manuscript is perfect. But the publications world is driven by deadlines, which make this goal somewhat unrealistic. Often, copyeditors must set priorities, making a manuscript as good as it can be in the time allotted. Journalists and proposal editors are especially pressed and can seldom give a manuscript more than one reading. You'll catch about 75 percent of the errors on one pass. By slowing down and being very careful or by choosing to ignore certain issues, you can probably raise that figure to 80 percent. The trade-off here is time (or money) versus thoroughness; the choice depends on the situation.

It helps if you can put a manuscript aside for a little while and make a final pass later. Ideally, another editor should look over the work when you finish; another pair of eyes will always find some error that managed to slip by.

Exercise 6: Copyediting

Instructions: Copyedit this article. Pay attention to matters of consistency and to careless errors the author and keyboarder made in preparing this draft. Fix nonparallel constructions; at least query content problems. Watch for grammatical problems and unnecessary passive voice. Use proper editorial marks to show changes. Take as long as you want and try to catch all the errors. Use a dictionary to choose among alternative spellings.

This piece has several headings; decide whether they're main headings or subordinate headings. Distinguish between them by calling main headings *A-heads* and subordinate headings *B-heads*. Put *A* or *B* in a circle next to each one. (The paragraphs have been numbered to make it easy for you to check your editing against the answer key.)

Copy-Editing

1. Copyediting, sometimes called copyreading, is one of the final steps in the editorial process. To copyredit means to bring a Manuscript in line with good English usage; make it sytlistically consistent; and, by making minor minor modifications, to enhance it readability. Let us consider of these functions in turn.

2. English Usage. In the English language, there are no absolute rule of grammar, only practices of good usage which are collated and standardize by recognized experts who produce Grammers, dictioneries, and style books. Therefore, the aim of the copy editor is for reasonable, not absolute correctness? English sas a living language is continually changing. A construction that was "bad in grand fathers day may be permitted today and become "Good" tomorrow. A case in in point is the practice of not ending a sentence with a preposition. Today, only the real purists among grammarians insist

---

The Copyeditor's Guide to **Substance&Style**

on following that practice ABSOLUTELY. Avoiding a preposition at the end of a often causes it to be prim, stodgy and stilted. A pertinant old chestnut is credited to Winston Churchills. When he was with confronted with the rule, he wanted to know if would be supposed to say: "That is something up with which i will not put." Many semicolloquial but very communicative verbs include prepositions. "Put up with", of course, one of them.

3. Another example of change in usage concerns the split infinitive—an infinative with a word, usually an adverb, inserted between "to" and and the rest of the verb. Split infinitives that are awkward, stilted, and unneccessary should be avoided. however, should transferring the word or splitting an infinitive cause a sentence to be ambiguous, that sentence should either be left as is or recast.

4. The copyeditor must be attentive about various other points, including confusion in the sequence of tenses; lack of agreement in number between subject and verb; and use of pronouns whose antecedents are not well established. These require a vigilant eye. The primary purpose of the copy in making a manuscript grammatical is to clarefy menaning, not to make the language reach the language reach a given standard of grammatical "purity. Therefor, effectiveness of communication is more important than considerations of grammar. Some authors employ a style that in colloquial to the point of infringing on good usage, although there doubt as to meaning never. For a copyeditor to try to "clean up" a manuscript of such an author is a violation of the author intent and integrity. as an artist. Other writers use a truncated or staccatto style that does not conform to the

Exercise 6, continued

conventions of sentence structure. Here again the copy editor does not interfere or tamper with the authors basic.

5. <u>Consistant Style.</u> This function of copyediting concerns such questions such as spelling, punctuation, the use of hyphens, quotation marks, and italics. Every manuscript willrequire some corrections of this kind. Probably no author scrutinizes the manuscript with the same care as a copyeditor, because the author's interest main is content. And some authors, even those who turn in highly acceptable copy, are weak in spelling and the fine points English usage. It is the copyeditors job to be proficient in these matters. Don't be too hesitant or too lazy to look up questionable points or those you don't know. In fact, if you study you're style book, your eye will be come more alert to things in manuscript that should be corrected.

6. Readability. This function does not refer to the overall reability of the manuscript; it should be assume that judgement on this point was made when the manuscript was excepted. The copyeditor checks certain details to see whether minor modifications would bring about improvement in communication. The details which should be checked are the first sentence or paragraph, to see that the lead is a good one; the conclusion to see that the piece adds up well; and paragraphing and sentence structure through out the paragraphing and sentence structure.

7. The copyeditor should also watch for overly involve sentences. The simply inserting a period and a subject to make two sentences out one will sometimes enhance readability without cramping or changing the writer's stile.

Exercise 6, continued

There are some writers, even good ones, who are addicted to the "There is" or "There Are" construction. Forms of the verb "to be" are usually weak in a sentence. such sentences may be reconstruct so as to bring foreward a stronger very verb. Part of the copyeditor's job is to check quotations for accuracy.

Copyright

8. It is important also to make sure that no infringements of copy right willl be involved in prnting quotations.

Marking

9. In reading and marking both copy and proof, the editor use a number of standard copyeditor's marks, a kind of shot hand understood by editor's and printer's alike. You should become familiar with these marks as quickly can. Fascimile pages showing edited copy appear in most style books, in many dictioneries, and in grammar texts.

10. Meaning: In all copyediting, be sure not to change in anyway the content of an article or to modify the authors ideas or style. The temptation of the neophite is to make too many changes in copy. Use your pencil sparingly and have sound reasons for every mark you make and you'll be a good copyeditor.

(Adapted from *Editing the Small Magazine* by Rowena Ferguson. Reprinted with permission.)

Exercise 6 Answers

Here's a key to the exercise; explanations and some other editing solutions begin below, and then follow parallel to the marked key.

Heads

The first style decision you had to make in this exercise was how to treat the title, *Copyediting*, used here as a noun. The one-word form shown is accepted by many dictionaries. The main thing to remember is to be consistent in your treatment of words.

To mark the head, *Copyediting*, print a capital *A* next to the head, and circle the letter, so that it won't be set: Ⓐ. Because you're already looking at heads, find *English Usage* at the beginning of the second paragraph. This head is subordinate to the first, in that *English Usage* is a topic subsumed by that A-level head. Mark *English Usage* with a *B*, and circle the letter. *Consistent Style*, *Readability*, *Copyright*, *Marking*, and *Meaning* also are B-level heads, to be marked accordingly. As a copyeditor, you may or may not be responsible for adding design specifications, such as paragraph indents, italics, or run-in heads. However, you'll always be expected to mark the level of heads, so that whoever does the formatting can see how many levels there are.

Paragraph 1: Fix the obvious typographical errors; remember to mark them with delete symbols and close-up hooks, as necessary. Note the unnecessary capital letter and the spacing error. Next, fix the nonparallel construction (two phrases in a series of three contained the word *to*; the middle item didn't). Either insert *to* in the second phrase as shown or delete it from the third (*modifications*, *enhance its readability*). Then take out the doublet or repeated word. Doublets are easy to miss, although they are less common now that word processing systems beep their outrage when a word appears twice in succession. To correct the last sentence of the paragraph, insert the word *each* or delete the word *of*. Also replace *functions*, which doesn't convey the proper nuance. Copyediting is a function; these three items are aspects, phases, aims, or parts of the job.

Paragraph 2: *English Usage*. You've already marked the head level. Make *rule* plural to agree with its verb, *are*. Use a caret and close-up hooks to attach the *s* to *rule*. You need the same sort of insertion to attach a *d* to *standardize*. Change

Exercise 6 Answers, continued

(A) Copy Editing

1. Copyediting, sometimes called copyreading, is one of the final steps in the editorial process. To copyedit means to bring a Manuscript in line with good English usage; make it stylistically consistent; and, by making minor ~~minor~~ modifications, to enhance its readability. Let us consider each of these ~~functions~~ aspects in turn.

(B)

2. English Usage. In the English language, there are no absolute rules of grammar, only practices of good usage ~~which~~ that are collated and standardized by recognized experts who produce Grammars, dictionaries, and style books. Therefore, the aim of the copy editor is ~~for~~ reasonable, not absolute, correctness; English as a living language is continually changing. A construction that was "bad" in grandfathers day may be permitted today and become "good" tomorrow. A case in ~~in~~ point is the practice of not

which to *that* to introduce the restrictive clause, one that limits the meaning of the clause that precedes it. (For a discussion of restrictive clauses, see Chapter 9.) The rest of the sentence contains mechanical (capitalization) errors. Especially note, however, the presence of the serial comma after *dictionaries*. You may delete this comma or leave it in: The use or omission of serial commas is a style decision. Whatever decision you make here you must follow consistently throughout the manuscript.

Then you must decide how to treat *copy editor*. In *Webster's Third New International Dictionary*, it appears as two words, but the distinction between *copyediting* and *copy editor* seems odd. Sometimes, consistency rules as it does here. Therefore, we made *copyeditor* one word. In the same sentence, the word *for* becomes extraneous if you insert a comma to set off the phrase in apposition (explaining *reasonable*). The single comma after *reasonable* is incorrect. Appositives are usually (but not always) set off by commas (see Chapter 10). The sentence wasn't a question, so replace the question mark with a period. Note that, when you delete the *s* at the beginning of *as*, you don't need to delete the space; a simple delete symbol suffices at the beginning of a word.

Add a closing quotation mark after the word *bad* or underscore or italicize such usage. However you handle emphasis within a manuscript, be sure to do it consistently for similar uses, such as the complementing word *good*. *Grand fathers* needs close-up hooks and an apostrophe. For the apostrophe, be sure to place your caret carefully, so that the apostrophe will end up before the *s* and not after it.

The next sentence contains a doublet. The *real purists* sentence has a whole word capitalized. Lowercase *ABSOLUTELY* by using the slash with a "hat" that continues to the end of the word.

Note that a word was omitted. Use a caret to insert it, and insert the serial comma, if that's your chosen style.

The *chestnut* phrase carries the uncommon meaning of an old joke or story and is unnecessary to the sense of the text. Nor does it contribute to the paragraph. Because the accompanying sentences are somewhat wordy anyway, edit a little more heavily.

> Winston Churchill, when confronted with the rule, asked whether he should say, "That is something up with which I will not put."

Exercise 6 Answers, continued

ending a sentence with a preposition. Today, only the real purists among

grammarians insist on following that practice ~~ABSOLUTELY~~. Avoiding a

preposition at the end of a *sentence* often causes it to be prim, stodgy, and stilted.

~~A pertinant old chestnut is credited to~~ Winston Churchill. When ~~he was~~

~~with~~ confronted with the rule, *asked whether he should* ~~he wanted to know if would be supposed~~

~~to say,~~ "That is something up with which I will not put." Many semicolloquial

but very communicative verbs include prepositions. "Put up with",

of course, *is* one of them.

3. Another example of change in usage concerns the split infinitive—an

infin*i*tive with a word, usually an adverb, inserted between "to" and

~~and~~ the rest of the verb. Split infinitives that are awkward, stilted, and

unnecessary should be avoided. however, should transferring the word

or splitting an infinitive cause a sentence to be ambiguous, that sentence

should either be left as is or recast.

Carefully note all the marks in this passage, especially the delete symbol and close-up mark at the end of *Churchills*, and the comma after *say*. A direct quotation is usually preceded by a comma, not a colon, unless the citation is long (an extract) and block-indented rather than marked with quotation marks.

As for changing *i* to *I*, remember that, except for obvious typos (which this one is), you should leave quoted material alone. Some journals and newspapers follow a "don't-embarrass-your-contributor" policy and readily admit to changing quotations. As a rule, however, it's best to get permission before making such changes, which can have legal and ethical ramifications.

For consistency, delete the italics and put the phrase *put up with* in quotation marks. If you chose to italicize *bad* and *good* earlier, italicize this phrase as well. Just be sure that you treat emphasis in the same way throughout the piece. Complete the paragraph by adding *is*; carefully place a caret at the appropriate place in the line.

Paragraph 3: The first sentence contains a doublet and an em-dash notation. Automatically marking dashes and hyphens to prevent any misunderstanding is a good habit. The next sentence contains a serial comma that should be retained or deleted, depending on the choice you made earlier, and an extra letter.

The last sentence in the paragraph contains two errors: *However* needs an initial capital letter, and the word *either* needs to be moved so that the *either* and the *or* are followed by similar constructions.

> ...that sentence should be either left as is or recast...
> ...that sentence should either be left as is or be recast...

Paragraph 4: Persons are not *attentive about*; they are *attentive to*, or, perhaps better, *they attend to*. The semicolons in this sentence can be replaced by commas; the general rule is to use semicolons to separate elements in a series when there is interior punctuation or when the elements are long. In this sentence, the items are relatively short, and the distinction is not crucial. Delete *in number*; the phrase is redundant. The only thing subject and verb agree on is number. *Pronoun* needs an *s* with close-up hooks (because the *s* goes at the end of the word).

Exercise 6 Answers, continued

4. The copyeditor must be attentive ~~about~~ to various other points, including

confusion in the sequence of tenses, lack of agreement ~~in number~~ between

subject and verb, and use of pronouns whose antecedents are not well

established. These problems require a vigilant eye. The primary purpose of the copy editor

in making a manuscript grammatical is to clarify meaning, not to make

~~the language reach~~ the language reach a given standard of grammatical

"purity. Therefore effectiveness of communication is more important than

considerations of grammar. Some authors employ a style that in colloquial

to the point of infringing on good usage, although there is doubt ~~as to~~ in

meaning never For a copyeditor to try to "clean up" a manuscript of such

an author is a violation of the author's intent and integrity as an artist. Other

writers use a truncated or staccato style that does not conform to the

conventions of sentence structure. Here again the copy editor does not

interfere or tamper with the author's basic # style,

The next sentence contains a pronoun without an antecedent: What does *these* refer to? The nearest plural noun is *antecedents*, which are not what the sentence is about. *Problems* will work, although other words, such as *points* or *issues*, will do as well.

Complete the word *copyeditor* so the following sentence has meaning. Delete the doublet. To complete the sentence, note that *purity* has a beginning, but not an ending, quotation mark. You could just as easily delete the beginning quotation mark as add an ending one; the difference is a subtle shift in emphasis.

The next sentence has only one spelling error: *therefore* needs an *e*. The misspelling in the following sentence is easy to correct, but the last phrase requires a little thought. Some rewriting would be helpful, but with *is* and a transposition, the sentence does makes sense.

> Some authors employ a style that is colloquial to the point of infringing on good usage, although the meaning is never in doubt.

Author needs an *'s* twice in the next sentence (in the first case, because of the transposition), and there is an extra period. *Staccatto* requires a delete symbol and close-up hook.

In the last sentence of the paragraph, add an apostrophe to form the possessive for *author* and add a word to complete the thought.

Paragraph 5: For the head, *Consistant Style*, which you have already marked with a circled *B*, correct the misspelling, delete the underscore, and delete part of the space following the period.

The text, again, is discussing an aspect, not a function; the other problems are obvious, except perhaps for the addition of *and*. The key reflects one possible treatment of the items in a list; the sentence might be even clearer if semicolons were used:

> This aspect of copyediting concerns such questions as spelling; punctuation; and the use of hyphens, quotation marks, and italics.

Delete one of the two spaces at the beginning of the next sentence. You may remember that, when typewriters were a state-of-the-art publishing tool, people were told to add two spaces after a sentence. There is no longer any need to mark for

Exercise 6 Answers, continued

5. Consistent Style. ~~Consistant Style,~~ This ~~function~~ _aspect_ of copyediting concerns such questions

such as spelling, punctuation, _and_ the use of hyphens, quotation marks,

and italics. Every manuscript will require some corrections of this kind.

Probably no author scrutinizes the manuscript with the same care as a

copyeditor, because the author's ~~interest main~~ main interest is content. And some

authors, even those who turn in highly acceptable copy, are weak in

spelling and the fine points _of_ English usage. It is the copyeditor's job to be

proficient in these matters. _Copyeditors should_ ~~Don't~~ be _neither_ too hesitant or too lazy to look up

questionable points or those _they_ ~~you~~ don't know. In fact, ~~if you~~ _copyeditors who_ study ~~you're~~ _their_

style book ~~your eye~~ will be come more alert to things in manuscript's that

should be corrected.

Ⓑ 6. Readability. This ~~function~~ _aspect_ does not refer to the overall readability of the

manuscript; it should be assumed that judgment on this point was made

Exercise 6 Answers, continued

additional space after end-punctuation. Spacing features are already programmed into the typefaces used in electronic files (except for monospaced fonts like Courier).

The errors in the *Every* and *Probably* sentences are obvious and easily corrected. Note the apostrophe in *author's*. In the next two sentences, the errors are also quite clear, but the last three sentences of the paragraph are choppy, with a change in person. Up to this point, the whole manuscript has been in the third person; copyeditors do this, and then they do that. *You* has not been used until now. To make the text consistent, edit the sentence into the third person.

> Copyeditors should be neither too hesitant nor too lazy to look up questionable points or those they don't know. In fact, copyeditors who study their style books will become more alert to things in manuscripts that should be corrected.

The other corrections in the sentences are mechanical.

Paragraph 6: You've already marked *Readability* with a circled B.

Readability isn't a function either; edit to *aspect* or something similar. Of the next three misspellings, only *judgement* warrants comment: American dictionaries list both *judgment* and *judgement*. The first is being overtaken by the second, but most U.S. editors still prefer judgment.

The next sentence has a smothered verb (*would bring about improvement readily* becomes *would improve*). *Which should be checked* is a restrictive clause, limiting the meaning of *details*. Use the word *that* to introduce the clause, and don't set it off with commas. Last, you need to make the elements in the sentence parallel.

Paragraph 7: The first two sentences contain simple errors. Be sure that you made your marks correctly. Then look at the third sentence; deleting *There are* produces a much stronger sentence. The rest of the corrections here are straightforward.

The last sentence (about checking quotations) doesn't belong in this paragraph or in a section called *Readability*. As a matter of fact, it may not even belong in this text, because it isn't mentioned in the lead or first paragraph of this exercise, the

The Copyeditor's Guide to Substance&Style

when the manuscript was *ac*~~ex~~cepted. The copyeditor checks certain

details to see whether minor modifications would ~~bring about~~

improve~~ment in~~ communication. The details *that* ~~which~~ should be checked

are the first sentence or paragraph, to see that the lead is a good one;

the conclusion, to see that the piece adds up well; and *the* paragraphing

sentence structure through out ~~the paragraphing and sentence~~ *to see that the parts work well together.*

~~structure.~~

7. The copyeditor should also watch for overly involve*d* sentences. ~~The~~

simply inserting a period and a subject to make two sentences out *of* one

will sometimes enhance readability without cramping or changing the

writer's style. ~~There are~~ some writers, even good ones, ~~who~~ are addicted

to the "There is" or "There Are" construction. Forms of the verb "to be"

are usually weak in a sentence. such sentences may be reconstruct*ed*

one that discussed *English usage*, *stylistic consistency*, and *readability*. That paragraph didn't say a word about *Copyright* (or about the following sections, *Marking* and *Meaning*).

One of the rules of good writing is that a lead paragraph outlines what the text intends to discuss or prove. There should be no surprises for the reader. As a copyeditor, you can only point out such a discrepancy, either to the author or to your supervisor. You shouldn't rewrite, unless given permission to do so. Therefore, write a note in the margin or on a query sheet to explain the problem.

You've already marked the B-level head, *Copyright*.

Paragraph 8: The editorial corrections in this paragraph are mechanical.

Marking. This head, now labeled *B*, may not belong in the piece either, as the query notes.

Paragraph 9: Note that deletion of the words *and proof* changes the meaning of the first phrase. As a copyeditor, you should probably query rather than delete this phrase, but you know that the editor doesn't normally see a proof, but rather works on the copy earlier in the production cycle. Otherwise, the corrections in the sentence are fairly mechanical. Be sure to fix the change in person also.

Paragraph 10: *Meaning*. Here's another B-level head that, according to the lead paragraph at least, doesn't belong. Aside from the misspelled words and the spacing errors, you need to fix the change in person throughout the paragraph, especially the imperative in the last sentence. The solution in the key shifts the meaning somewhat, but without the imperative there's no good way to capture the injunction of the original.

Check the key to make sure you understand all the marks and the reasons for them. If anything is unclear to you, review Chapter 3.

Exercise 6 Answers, continued

~~as~~ to bring for~~e~~ward a stronger ~~very~~ verb. Part of the copyeditor's job

is to check quotations for accuracy.

Move ok.?

¶

B **Copyright** ⊙

8. It is important *also* to make sure that no infringements of copy right will

be involved in pr~~i~~nting quotations.

These sections are not mentioned in lead paragraph. Add an explanation or delete?

¶

B **Marking** ⊙

ok as edited?

the

9. In reading and marking ~~both~~ copy ~~and proof~~, the editor's use a number of

standard copyeditor's marks, a kind of shot hand understood by editor's

Editors

and printer's alike. ~~You~~ should become familiar with these marks as

as possible

quickly ~~can~~. Fas~~c~~imile pages showing edited copy appear in most style

a

books, in many diction~~g~~ries, and in grammar texts.

editors should

B 10. Meaning/ In all copyediting, be sure not to change in any way the content

of an article or ~~to~~ modify the author's ideas or style. The temptation of the

Copy editors should *their*

neoph~~i~~te is to make too many changes in copy. ~~Use your~~ pencil sparingly and

have sound reasons for every mark ~~you make and you'll be a good copyeditor.~~

The Copyeditor's Role

What do copyeditors do? First and last, they determine the author's meaning and clarify it where possible. They never change the meaning; where the meaning is ambiguous, they query. They bring problems or issues to the attention of the author or their supervisor. They attempt to make a manuscript be all that the author meant it to be.

What sorts of problems do copyeditors look for?

- Errors in grammar, punctuation, spelling, and sentence structure: basically, departures from the widely accepted rules of the English language.
- Style decisions dictated by the choice of a style manual: treatment of numbers, capitalization, abbreviations, certain types of punctuation, and so on.
- Formatting inconsistencies: head levels, tables, figure captions.
- Style problems in the larger sense: wordiness, nonparallel construction, poor word choice, and excessive use of the passive voice.
- More complex issues: bias, sexism, inaccuracies, inconsistencies, misquotations, libel, illegality (use of copyrighted material without permission).

This description is by no means exhaustive; copyeditors may perform different functions in different organizations.

Copyediting Tasks

The following section contains a list of copyediting tasks that should help you focus your efforts for each pass through the manuscript. This list is fairly extensive; not all the entries apply to every manuscript. Someone, probably your editing manager, supervisor, or client, should examine each project and tell you the level of effort required and time allowed.

The editor's checklist at the end of this chapter contains all the points discussed here. Such a checklist eliminates the need for sometimes confusing verbal instructions and provides a record for both the editor and the manager or client. Use the checklist or make your own to organize your editing assignments. Note that the first three bullets apply if you are editing on hard copy. If you are editing electronically, they can be replaced by a single bullet indicating whether or not you are to track your edits.

Procedures required on all jobs

- Print neatly and legibly.
- Use standard editing marks in the body of the manuscript, not proofreading marks in the margin.

Light copyedit

Any copyeditor always addresses the points listed below. Notice that rewriting and reorganization are not included. Copyediting is a limited function; the checklist helps restrain copyeditors from doing too much. You may be asked to point out, but not rewrite, awkward, turgid, confusing sections. You may also be asked to point out, but not fix, major organizational problems:

1. Correct spelling, grammar, and punctuation.

2. Eliminate inconsistencies in capitalization, compounding, number style, abbreviations, and alphabetical or numerical sequence.

Standard copyedit

For specific jobs, you may be assigned any or all the tasks listed here, but any copyeditor always addresses the first two points:

1. Correct spelling, grammar, and punctuation.

2. Eliminate inconsistencies in capitalization, compounding, number style, abbreviations, use of italics or underscores, and alphabetical or numerical sequence.

3. Check heads in text against table of contents.

   Not all manuscripts have a table of contents, nor do they necessarily require one. However, if there is a table of contents, its entries must match the text headings exactly. If you find a discrepancy and can't determine which version—text or table of contents—is correct, query the author.

4. Make table of contents.

   Copyeditors are sometimes asked to compile a table of contents or a list of tables or figures after editing. If you have this task, find out from your supervisor or client how detailed the table of contents should be. Then list the titles and headings exactly as they appear in the text. An easy way to differentiate A- and B-heads is by indenting:

   > Introduction
   >> Background
   >> Method
   >> Experiments

5. Mark end-of-line hyphens.

   A hyphen can appear at the end of a line for two reasons: when an unhyphenated word is broken because it's too long to fit on a line (soft hyphen) and when a hyphenated word is broken at the hyphen (hard hyphen) for the same reason.

   Before the class was dismissed for the day, the
   professor outlined for us the process of calci-   (*soft hyphen*)
   fication.

   or

   I was pleased that he had improved his self-   (*hard hyphen*)
   image by cultivating good work habits.

6. Format tables consistently, following required style. Ensure parallelism within and among tables.

   The best way to ensure parallelism within and among tables is to look at them together, apart from the text. With the tables side by side on your desk, compare their format. Are the titles set up the same way? Do the headings match, or are some caps and lowercase and some all caps? Are there rules in some but not in others? If you have specifications for the tables, were they followed? If not, make the tables consistent.

   Looking at all the tables together increases your efficiency. You don't have to remember what the earlier ones looked like; you simply compare them.

   Be sure that the title reflects the material in the table accurately. Check all math; query if your answers deviate from the author's.

7. Check parallelism throughout the text. Make elements in a series parallel.

   Most copyeditors instinctively want to fix parallelism problems. (See Chapter 8, Parallelism.)

8. Make list format(s) consistent. (See Chapter 8, Parallelism.)

9. Check for clear pronoun antecedents; if missing or too far away, add or move the correct nouns as near as possible to the pronouns, or rewrite the sentence as needed.

   Agreement of pronouns and their antecedents gives rise to many questions. Patterns that are acceptable in speech aren't always acceptable in writing,

The Copyeditor's Guide to **Substance***&***Style**

although authors may state (and rightly) that the meaning is clear. From a grammatical point of view, however, the noun that a pronoun is meant to replace is often not clear; in these cases, clarification by the author or the editor is essential. (See Chapter 7, Pronouns.)

10. Eliminate passive constructions where appropriate; try to replace with active voice.

    Some authors are especially fond of the passive voice (in which the subject of the sentence isn't the doer of the action, but rather is acted upon). Although passive voice has a clearly defined place in the language, the passive voice is less forceful than the active. Notice that the checklist says to replace with active voice *whenever appropriate*. The active voice isn't always appropriate, nor is it possible to rephrase every sentence to accommodate the active voice. (See Chapter 6, Active and Passive Voice.)

11. Eliminate smothered verbs and break up noun strings.

    This item deals with word choices; smothered verbs are those buried in a sea of nouns, like *make reference to* instead of *refer* or *make a study of* instead of *study*. Noun strings, on the other hand, are just that: nouns used as modifiers, as in *District employee residency law requirement*. What does this phrase mean? After three readings, you're still not sure. Smothered verbs and noun strings obscure meaning; eliminate both, except in technical or scientific writing where noun strings are sometimes part of the idiom and can't be replaced without loss of meaning. (See Chapter 12, Concise Language.)

12. Shorten and clarify excessively long sentences.

    This straightforward injunction asks you to eliminate wordiness and, where possible, to prefer the plain word. Simple language isn't always preferable, but it often is. (See Chapter 12, Concise Language.)

13. Eliminate sexist language.

    Whenever possible, you should replace nouns and pronouns of gender with neutral, nonsexist terms: *Salesman* becomes *salesperson*, *newspaperman* becomes *journalist*, and so on. (See Chapter 7, Pronouns, for more on avoiding sexist language.)

14. Eliminate the first person as instructed.

Authors sometimes refer to themselves in the first person. If your client or supervisor decides that this usage is unacceptable, you have several options. The simplest is to eliminate certain phrases: "I believe the economy will soon see an upswing" becomes "The economy will soon see an upswing" or "It is likely that the economy will soon see an upswing." Changing first person to third person may be necessary, but it can lead to awkward phrasing: "The author believes the economy will soon see an upswing." Even if you are instructed to eliminate first person in the text, it may still be appropriate in the front matter, so the checklist leaves room for that exception.

15. Eliminate the second person as instructed.

Use of the second person can make sentences shorter and easier to read, but some clients may wish to eliminate it. Bear in mind that imperative sentences may not use the pronoun "you," but they are still written in the second person. "Pick up the hammer" implies the subject "you." To eliminate the second person, such a sentence will need to be changed to "The worker should pick up the hammer" or to passive voice: "The hammer is picked up."

16. Explain unfamiliar acronyms and abbreviations at first mention.

Technical writing especially is full of such shortened forms. As a rule, use the complete form at first mention, with the acronym or abbreviation in parentheses following it. In subsequent references you can use the shortened form alone, or you may wish to employ the long form occasionally. In a book-length manuscript, you may be instructed to explain acronyms at first mention in each chapter or section.

17. Make sure all referenced material (tables, charts, illustrations, footnotes, etc.) follows its first callout.

The existence of every table, chart, or footnote must be noted in text before the referenced item appears. The first text reference is termed a *callout*. Often, with revisions or editing, paragraphs are moved or merged, and callouts get scrambled. To associate callouts with their figures quickly and accurately, copyeditors should note the first mention of each table, chart, or footnote (*T.1* or *fn 1*, for example) in the margin or else use a highlighter to mark the item. Always circle such notations, so no one incorporates your notes into the text by mistake.

18. Check cross-references for accuracy and consistency.

If the text refers the reader to appendix A for information or an explanation, you must verify that there is indeed an appendix A and that appendix A contains what was promised. If the author cites Smith 1986 in the text, be sure the reference list also contains this citation. The spelling of the author's name and the date of publication must match exactly. (See Chapter 13, Citations and References.)

Checking references is best done as a separate step. It can be time-consuming, but if reference citations are inaccurate or incomplete, the author risks being thought careless. However good the content, it will not stand up to scrutiny if the references are sloppy. This is one of the most valuable tasks a copyeditor performs for an author. It's a rare manuscript that doesn't contain a few inconsistencies between text citations and the reference list.

19. Put footnotes and bibliography in consistent form, using the appropriate style.

Arrange references, bibliography, and footnotes according to the specified format (style). Style manuals give extensive rules for the treatment of these subjects. (See Chapter 13, Citations and References.)

20. Check for missing information in notes/bibliography. Query or research and supply.

While you're styling the references, you may spot places where information is missing. For example, an entry may cite a journal article but not give the page numbers for the article. You may be asked simply to insert a query ("page numbers?") or to do the research to locate the missing information. Obviously, if you need to do research, you'll need to allot more time to this step.

21. Check math in tables and problems. Check answers to questions in exercises.

Checking simple math is a basic copyediting function. If you are working in a technical field, you may be expected to have the subject area expertise to check more complex math, such as equations. Checking the answers to questions in exercises will not usually require specialized knowledge; the text should supply the answers.

22. Eliminate redundant portions, or query but do not eliminate.

Both items 22 and 23 fall in a gray area between copyediting and substantive editing. Some clients include eliminating redundancy in the copyeditor's function. If not, you may point out redundancy in a query ("This point has been made twice above. Is it necessary here?").

23. Rewrite verbose or awkward sections, or query but do not rewrite.

   Like item 22, this is a judgment call. No two people will always agree on what constitutes an awkward or verbose section. The more you work with a particular author, client, or supervisor, the more judgment you will be able to exercise regarding what calls for a bit of rewriting.

Formatting tasks

1. Number pages sequentially throughout manuscript or sequentially within chapters or sections.

   No manuscript should ever be without page numbers. In the early stages, consecutive numbers are simple and practical. Once the manuscript is laid out, front matter is normally paginated with Roman numerals. The text may be numbered consecutively or by chapter; a designer usually makes that decision.

2. Mark head levels, e.g., A, B, C, etc., or 1, 2, 3, etc.

   Distinguishing head levels is a key copyediting skill. You should be able to fit the headings into a mental outline, with a clear hierarchy of main heads, subheads, sub-subheads, and so on. Your client or supervisor will instruct you on how to mark the heads. Be sure to circle the marks so that they will not be typeset.

3. Mark em dashes and en dashes (versus hyphens). Mark end-of-line hyphens to be deleted or retained.

   Few authors distinguish hyphens from en dashes, so you will need to mark the latter.

4. Ensure that referenced matter (tables, illustrations, footnotes, etc.) follows its first callout.

   Some publications require authors to submit tables and figures separately from text. You may be asked to insert them following their callouts, or you may simply highlight the callout so the person who does the layout can place them appropriately.

Editorial Checklist

Job Number: _____   Style Guide: _____

Project Manager/Editor: _____   Dictionary: _____

Procedures required on all jobs
- ☐ Print neatly and legibly. Use ___ dark black pencil; ___ erasable red pencil; ___ other.
- ☐ Use standard editing marks in the body of the manuscript, not proofreading marks in the margin.

Light copyedit
1. ___ Correct grammar, spelling, and punctuation.
2. ___ Eliminate inconsistencies in capitalization, compounding, number style, abbreviations, use of italics/underscores, and alphabetical and numerical sequence.
3. ___ Other

Standard copyedit
- ☐ Compile an alphabetical list of all words about which you have made a choice of treatment, e.g., consistency in hyphens, caps, abbreviations, etc.
- ☐ Make a list of queries to the author/client and return with job.
1. ___ Correct grammar, spelling, and punctuation.
2. ___ Eliminate inconsistencies in capitalization, compounding, number style, abbreviations, use of italics/underscores, and alphabetical and numerical sequence.
3. ___ Check heads in text against table of contents. ___ Make the same; ___ query.
4. ___ Make the table of contents.
5. ___ Format tables consistently, following required style. Ensure parallelism within and among tables.
6. ___ Check parallelism in the text. Make elements in a series parallel.
7. ___ Make list format(s) consistent. ___ See attached examples.
8. ___ Check for clear pronoun antecedents.
9. ___ Eliminate passive constructions where appropriate.
10. ___ Eliminate noun strings (3 or more nouns used as modifiers).
11. ___ Shorten and clarify excessively long sentences.
12. ___ Eliminate sexist language.
13. ___ Eliminate the first person. ___ Throughout; ___ except for the preface/foreword.
14. ___ Eliminate the second person.
15. ___ Explain acronyms and abbreviations at first mention in the text. ___ In each chapter/section.
16. ___ Call out in the margin the first citation of referenced matter (tables, illustrations, etc.).

17. ___ Check all cross references for accuracy and consistency.
18. ___ Put footnotes and bibliography in consistent format. ___ Use_____ style; ___ see attached examples
19. ___ Check for missing information in notes/bibliography. ___ Query; ___ research and supply.
20. ___ Check math in tables and problems. ___ Check answers to questions in exercises.
21. ___ Eliminate redundant portions. ___ Query, but do not eliminate.
22. ___ Rewrite verbose or awkward sections. ___ Query, but do not rewrite.
23. ___ Other

Formatting tasks
1. ___ Number pages. ___ Sequentially throughout; ___ within chapters/sections.
2. ___ Mark head levels. ___ A, B, C, etc. ___ 1, 2, 3, etc.
3. ___ Mark em dashes and en dashes (versus hyphens). ___ Mark end-of-line hyphens to be deleted or retained.
4. ___ Ensure that referenced matter (tables, illustrations, footnotes, etc.) follows its first callout.

Exceptions:_____
_____

Read-behind checklist
1. ___ Review editing checklist and instructions.
2. ___ Review editor's style sheet.
3. ___ Check head levels; check heads against the table of contents.
4. ___ Read the editing for sense.
5. ___ Read editor's queries; resolve as many as possible and delete those from the query sheet.
6. ___ Check style decisions against manual.
7. ___ Check callouts for all art and footnotes, and check sequence of footnotes.
8. ___ Compare all art to text descriptions.
9. ___ Pull art and notes; compare for consistency of treatment.
10. ___ Check lists for consistency.
11. ___ Spot-check math, if possible.
12. ___ Print out final query list on a sheet with a boldface/centered head: Query Sheet
13. ___ Send feedback memo to editor.

Read-behind checklist

At EEI Communications, a senior editor reviews each copyeditor's work, following the steps on this part of the checklist. We call this step read-behind editing. A review by a second set of eyes is extremely valuable to ensure that the manuscript is as correct as possible. If you are working alone and have no one else to do a read-behind, try to allow enough time to go through these steps yourself—if possible, a day or so after you've completed your copyediting.

1. Review editing checklist and instructions.

2. Review editor's style sheet.

3. Check head levels; check heads against the table of contents.

4. Read the editing for sense.

5. Read editor's queries; resolve as many as possible and delete those from the query sheet.

6. Check style decisions against manual.

7. Check callouts for all art and footnotes, and check sequence of footnotes.

8. Compare all art to text descriptions.

9. Pull art and notes; compare for consistency of treatment.

10. Check lists for consistency.

11. Spot-check math, if possible.

12. Print out final query list on a sheet with a boldface/centered head: EEI Communications Query Sheet.

    Substitute your own organization's name for EEI Communications.

13. Send feedback memo to editor.

    If you read behind another copy-editor's work, make notes of what that person has done well in addition

Sample Feedback Memo

Dear XXXX,

Thank you for your work on the Smith manuscript. We particularly appreciate your making time to fit this rush job into your schedule. You also caught several factual discrepancies that would have been embarrassing had they made it into print!

For future reference, please note that reference callouts in text should be alphabetical—for example, "(Jones, 1999; Matthews, 2001; Williams, 1998)."

Also, please be sure to use serial commas when editing in Chicago style. You caught some, but not all. (I realize you're more accustomed to working in AP style, which doesn't use serial commas.)

Thanks again!

The Copyeditor's Guide to **Substance**&*Style*

to things that need improvement. Like queries, feedback should be tactfully phrased. If you receive feedback, take it as constructive criticism and use it to improve your skills.

Heavier, more substantive editing, rewriting, and related tasks

This section concerns more substantive tasks than those normally assigned to a copyeditor, although you may be instructed to do some of the tasks listed here, such as numbers 1 and 2.

1. Check math, numbers, problems, answers to questions in exercises.

2. Check descriptions of tables in text against information in tables themselves.

3. Review whole manuscript for sentences, paragraphs, portions that can be eliminated.

4. Add or delete heads and subheads as necessary.

5. Check organization and reorganize if necessary.

6. Rewrite awkward, turgid, or confusing sections.

7. Review logic of arguments; look for weak points.

8. Write transitions.

9. Write summaries for chapters, sections, or the entire document.

10. Check accuracy of content (editor is expected to be familiar with subject).

SUBJECTS AND VERBS:
They *Will* Agree

5

A sentence has two parts: a subject and a predicate. The subject, in the form of a noun or pronoun, identifies what the sentence is about, and the predicate contains a verb—an action word (*run*) or a description of a state of being (*is*). Most nouns, pronouns, and verbs in the English language have singular and plural forms. The subject determines whether the verb should be singular or plural; agreement means that a singular subject takes a singular verb and a plural subject takes a plural verb. How could anything so straightforward cause difficulty?

Many factors combine to obscure the relationship between a subject and its verb. Inverted sentences and collective nouns tend to mask their subjects; prepositional phrases coming between a subject and verb confuse the issue. Here are some basic rules.

1. The following pronouns take singular verbs.

anybody	every	no one
anyone	everybody	one
each	everyone	somebody
either	neither	someone
	nobody	

   <u>Each</u> of the projects <u>is</u> done.

   <u>Neither</u> of us <u>likes</u> pistachios.

   <u>Anyone</u> who wants to come <u>is</u> welcome.

   One pronoun missing from this list is *none*, because *none* can take either a singular or a plural verb, depending on the context. When *none* means *not*

The Copyeditor's Guide to **Substance**&*Style*

one, use a singular verb; when it means *not any*, use a plural verb. In most cases, either is correct, but read closely.

None of the apples is big enough.

None of the apples have been washed.

2. Plurals of Latin and Greek words take plural verbs.

criteria are   media are

curricula are   phenomena are

data are

Some newspaper styles specifically cite *data* and *media* (meaning the press, TV, etc.) as singular, because their traditional singular forms (*datum* and *medium*) no longer appear in that usage. *Criteria, phenomena,* and *curricula* are all plural, and most styles treat them as plural, although you may see these words used (erroneously) as if they were singular.

3. *A number of* takes a plural verb; *the number of* takes a singular verb. Don't try to extend this rule to other nouns; it works only for *number*.

A number of people were at the craft fair.

The number of commitments we have prevents us from accepting your kind invitation.

4. A compound subject takes a plural verb.

Blue and gold are her favorite colors.

Vanity and stupidity mark his character.

5. A compound subject joined by *or* takes a verb that agrees with the subject closest to the verb.

Supplies or money was always lacking.

Money or supplies were always lacking.

Adjustments or questions concerning your bill do not relieve you of late-payment charges.

Pay attention to euphony when editing. If the plural verb "sounds" or "reads" better, transpose the order of the subjects, as shown in the *supplies or money* sentence.

6. Correlative expressions are used in pairs (*either...or* and *neither...nor*) and follow rule 5.

    Either the children <u>or the dog is</u> always clamoring for attention.

    Neither his brother <u>nor his parents were</u> willing to lend him any more money.

7. Some subjects appear compound but aren't. Prepositional phrases such as *in addition to*, *as well as*, or *along with* don't affect the number of the verb.

    <u>Vanity</u> as well as stupidity <u>marks</u> his character.

The real subject here is *Vanity*, which is singular. Note that this sentence could also have commas.

    Vanity, <u>as well as stupidity</u>, marks his character.

8. Nouns that are plural in form but singular in meaning usually take singular verbs. Here are some examples; when in doubt, consult your dictionary.

    Bad <u>news travels</u> fast.

    <u>Physics is</u> required of all chemistry majors.

The following words are regularly treated as singular.

aesthetics	measles
astronautics	mumps
economics	news
genetics	physics
linguistics	semantics
mathematics	

And the following words, all plural in form, are regularly treated as plural.

blue jeans	slacks
pants	suds
scissors	trousers

9. Some nouns can take either singular or plural verbs. A few nouns that end in *ics*, such as *athletics*, *acoustics*, and *statistics*, are considered singular when referring to an organized body of knowledge and plural when referring to qualities, activities, or individual facts.

<u>Statistics is</u> challenging at all levels.

<u>Statistics prove</u> that women live longer than men.

<u>Acoustics is</u> recommended for all third-year students.

The <u>acoustics</u> in the theater <u>are</u> very good.

A collective noun defines a group that is thought of or functions as a unit. Collective nouns, when singular, require a singular verb; when a collective noun is made plural (*team*, *teams*), the noun requires a plural verb. Here are some examples of singular collective nouns.

army	crowd	herd	orchestra
audience	den	jury	platoon
band	faculty	league	public
chorus	family	majority	quartet
class	flock	membership	staff
clergy	gang	mob	team
community	government	navy	variety
council	group		

Ask yourself whether the group in question is functioning as a unit in the sentence: The group must behave as a group.

The <u>team refuses</u> to practice in the rain.

The <u>jury decides</u> whether a defendant is innocent or guilty.

In the first example, the team is unanimously rebelling against getting wet. In the second one, the jury's decision must be unanimous. The jury must behave as a group, so the verb must be singular.

Note, however, that a singular collective noun that clearly refers to members of a group as individuals requires a plural verb.

The <u>faculty have been assigned</u> to various committees.

All the members of the faculty are not on several committees; each member of the faculty has been assigned to one committee, or perhaps two. Look at another example.

The <u>orchestra are going</u> to their homes after the performance.

The members of the orchestra don't all live in the same place; they're going in different directions, so the plural verb is necessary. If the plural noun seems awkward (and it often does), insert *members of* before (or *members* after) the collective noun.

The <u>faculty members</u> have been assigned to various committees.

The <u>members of the orchestra</u> are going to their homes after the performance.

Collective nouns do have plural forms: The plural of *flock* is *flocks*. When such nouns are plural, you must use a plural verb.

Many <u>flocks</u> of birds <u>fly</u> south about the first of October.

Here are some sentences to test what you've learned about subject-verb agreement. Work the following exercise and check your answers.

Exercise 7: Subject-Verb Agreement

Instructions: Select the correct word to fill in the blanks. Fix anything else that's wrong (spelling, punctuation, incorrect word, etc.).

1. The Stars and Stripes _____ (was, were) raised at Iwo Jima.

2. There _____ (is, are) many a good shell to be found on that beach.

3. More than one argument _____ (was, were) cited by the defense attorney.

4. One of the unhappy children who _____ (comes, come) from that
   troubled family _____ (is, are) being treated for depression.

5. What kind of dietary restrictions _____ (does, do) your patients have?

6. Each of my children _____ (has, have) _____ (his, their) own
   strengths and weaknesses.

7. The data we have gathered from our samplings _____ (shows, show)
   that the voters, especially those in the Midwest, _____ (needs, need)
   to be reassured about recent changes in the tax laws.

8. Information about housing units that _____ (has, have) recently been
   released can be ordered from the Center.

9. So few consumer goods _____ (is, are) produced there that the standard
   of living remains low.

10. The media _____ (is, are) present in force outside the courtroom.

11. Mothers Against Drunk Driving, an organization of concerned citizens, _____ (is, are) soliciting funds to support _____ (its, their) efforts to influence legislation.

12. There _____ (is, are) fewer tickets available than there were last year.

13. The list of participants _____ (was, were) arranged in alphabetical order.

14. Steak as well as sausages _____ (was, were) served at the barbecue.

15. Imposition of restrictions on smoking, together with efforts aimed at educating the public, _____ (promise, promises) us a less polluted environment.

16. A number of résumés _____ (was, were) received at the office today.

17. The number of persons being treated at the clinic sometimes _____ (prevents, prevent) us from completing our billing on time.

18. To move into a new house and to make new friends _____ (requires, require) a great deal of effort.

19. Whether the House will pass the bill and whether the president will veto it _____ (remains, remain) to be seen.

20. The complexity of the problem and the need to keep pace with technology _____ (presents, present) the company with many difficult choices.

Exercise 7 Answers

1. The Stars and Stripes <u>was</u> raised at Iwo Jima.

   One flag, familiarly called the Stars and Stripes, was raised.

2. There <u>is</u> many a good shell to be found on that beach.

   The subject of the sentence is *shell*, not *there*. The *there is* (or *it is*) construction is usually unnecessary. Prose is much tighter without it. You can thus edit one step further.

   Many a good shell is to be found on that beach.

3. More than one argument <u>was</u> cited by the defense attorney.

   More than one argument is the complete subject, which is logically plural. But what's really under discussion in this sentence is one presentation (which included arguments).

4. One of the unhappy children who <u>come</u> from that troubled family <u>is</u> being treated for depression.

   The subject of the main clause is one, so the main verb, *is*, is singular. In the subordinate clause, you have to determine the antecedent of *who* and make the verb agree with that word. The antecedent, of course, is *children*. It helps to pretend that the sentence starts with the of phrase.

   Of the unhappy children who come from that troubled family, one is being treated for depression.

   You needn't actually edit this way; just do the mental exercise to determine the correct verb form.

Exercise 7 Answers, continued

5. What kind of dietary restrictions <u>do your patients have</u>?

   The sentence is a question, and the subject follows the verb. The subject is *patients*, and therefore the verb must be plural. If this kind of sentence confuses you, turn it around.

   <u>Your patients do have</u> what kind of dietary restrictions.

6. Each of my children <u>has his</u> own strengths and weaknesses.

   You know, of course, that *each* is the subject and that *each* takes a singular verb.

   <u>Each</u> of my children <u>has</u> strengths and weaknesses.

   You may delete the pronoun because it is not necessary to show possession. If it is necessary, the pronoun must agree in number with its antecedent. Perhaps the parent in the sentence has only sons, in which case *his* is correct. Suppose, however, that this person has a child of each gender; then what should you use? Editors and society generally have been wrestling with this problem for several years, and the use of *their* in this case has become widespread. But *their,* a plural pronoun, can't refer to a singular antecedent. Sidestep the problem if you can. Here are some other solutions.

   Each of my children has (<u>individual/particular/specific</u>) strengths and weaknesses.

   (<u>Both/All</u>) my children have <u>their</u> strengths and weaknesses.

7. The data we have gathered from our samplings <u>show</u> that the voters, especially those in the Midwest, <u>need</u> to be reassured about recent changes in the tax laws.

   The word *data* is generally recognized as grammatically plural and thus requires a plural verb, but some journalistic style guides specify *data* as singular. If your organization relies on one of these guides, by all means use a singular verb, but remember that not everybody agrees. The subject of the subordinate clause is *voters*, which also needs a plural verb.

8. Information about housing <u>units that have recently been released</u> can be ordered from the Center.

   At first glance, it appears that *information* was released. Structurally and grammatically, however, the *units* have been released. The antecedent of *that* is *units*, so you need the plural verb. This sentence actually came from a directive issued by the Department of Housing and Urban Development; units were indeed released for occupancy, not information.

   Suppose for a moment that *information* was released. Here is a rewrite of the sentence that reflects this fact.

   > Information that has been recently released about housing units can be ordered from the Center.

   Here, the antecedent of *that* is *information*, and the singular verb is correct. Everything depends on the context. But what about this sentence?

   > Order information from the Center about <u>housing units that have been recently released</u>.

   Now the antecedent is *units*, and the plural verb is correct.

9. So few consumer <u>goods are produced</u> there that the standard of living remains low.

   The subject of the sentence is *goods*, which demands a plural verb.

10. The <u>media is</u> present in force outside the courtroom.

    Media is singular in a journalistic context, indicating news periodicals, television, radio, and other journalistic reporters and outlets.

11. <u>Mothers Against Drunk Driving</u>, an organization of concerned citizens, <u>is</u> soliciting funds to support <u>its</u> efforts to influence legislation.

    The subject is one organization, soliciting as a group. The pronoun *its* also must agree with the singular antecedent.

12. There <u>are</u> fewer <u>tickets</u> available than there were last year.

    Invert the sentence to find the subject. You may want to delete the words *there are*. Much depends on the flow of the rest of the paragraph, and it's hard to decide when the sentence is out of context.

13. The <u>list</u> of participants <u>was</u> arranged in alphabetical order.

    The subject of the sentence is *list*, which is singular.

14. <u>Steak</u> as well as sausages <u>was</u> served at the barbecue.

    Steak...was served. The intervening prepositional phrase doesn't affect the number of the verb

15. <u>Imposition</u> of restrictions on smoking, together with efforts aimed at educating the public, <u>promises</u> us a less polluted environment.

    The subject of the sentence is *imposition*. The intervening words don't change the number of the verb.

16. <u>A number</u> of résumés <u>were</u> received at the office today.

    A number of takes a plural verb; the sense of the sentence is that many résumés were received.

Exercise 7 Answers, continued

17. <u>The number of</u> persons being treated at the clinic sometimes <u>prevents</u> us from completing our billing on time.

    The number of takes a singular verb.

18. <u>To move</u> into a new house <u>and to make</u> new friends <u>require</u> a great deal of effort.

    A compound subject joined by *and* (two infinitive phrases, *to move* and *to make*) requires a plural verb.

19. <u>Whether</u> the House will pass the bill <u>and whether</u> the president will veto it <u>remain</u> to be seen.

    This sentence contains another compound subject joined by *and* (*Whether… and whether*), so you need a plural verb.

20. The <u>complexity</u> of the problem <u>and</u> the <u>need to</u> keep pace with technology <u>present</u> the company with many difficult choices.

    You need a plural verb to agree with the compound subject—*The complexity* and *the need*.

    _____

In summary, subject-verb agreement isn't a simple topic; subjects hide among prepositional phrases or on the "wrong" side of the verb. As an editor, you must always be alert to hidden subjects. For more practice, continue on to Exercise 8.

Exercise 8: More Subject-Verb Agreement

Instructions: Select the correct words to fill in the blanks. Fix anything else that's wrong.

1. One or the other of you _____ (is, are) lying.

2. When snow, rain, or sleet _____ (falls, fall), the traffic becomes unbearable.

3. When family or friends _____ (comes, come) to call, my cat always runs and hides.

4. Neither the fox nor the hounds _____ (was, were) in sight.

5. Neither the King nor the Parliament _____ (controls, control) the loyalties of the barons.

6. The Cardinals _____ (is, are) a team that _____ (is, are) coming on in this year's race for the pennant.

7. No one but you and two of my friends _____ (knows, know) what I've put in the will.

8. The schools in which the after-school care centers are located _____ (is, are) shown on this map of the county.

9. None of the elevators _____ (is, are) accessible to people in wheelchairs.

The Copyeditor's Guide to Substance&Style

Exercise 8, continued

10. Most of the voters in this area _____ (is, are) conservative.

11. She is one of those students who _____ (plays, play) too much and _____ (works, work) too little.

12. Ask one of the parents who _____ (understands, understand) the system to help you.

13. One of my favorite meals _____ (is, are) ham and eggs.

14. Neither she nor her children _____ (has, have) ever forgiven her father.

15. A variety of solutions _____ (was, were) proposed at the meeting yesterday.

16. A directory of editorial resources, including publications firms and hotlines staffed by various English departments, _____ (was, were) produced on the laser printer.

17. One of the food service supervisors _____ (was, were) working on the floor for the first time in over ten years.

18. Each of the students was asked to report _____ (their, the, his or her) findings to the class.

19. Neither Bill nor Karen _____ (has, have) finished _____ (his, her, their, the) assignment.

20. Neither of the two teachers who _____ (was, were) on the board last year _____ (is, are) willing to continue.

Exercise 8 Answers

1. One or the other of you ___*is*___ (is, are) lying.

2. When snow, rain, or sleet ___*falls*___ (falls, fall), the traffic becomes unbearable.

3. When family or friends ___*come*___ (comes, come) to call, my cat always runs and hides.

4. Neither the fox nor the hounds ___*were*___ (was, were) in sight.

5. Neither the King nor the Parliament ___*controls*___ (controls, control) the loyalties of the barons.

6. The Cardinals ___*are*___ (is, are) a team that ___*is*___ (is, are) coming on in this year's race for the pennant.

7. No one but you and two of my friends ___*knows*___ (knows, know) what I've put in the will.

8. The schools in which the after-school care centers are located ___*are*___ (is, are) shown on this map of the county.

9. None of the elevators ___*are*___ (is, are) accessible to people in wheelchairs. (The plural is preferable, but *is* would be correct, too.)

10. Most of the voters in this area ___*are*___ (is, are) conservative.

The Copyeditor's Guide to **Substance**&*Style*

Exercise 8 Answers, continued

11. She is one of those students who _play_ (plays, play) too much and _work_ (works, work) too little.

12. Ask one of the parents who **understand** (understands, understand) the system to help you.

13. One of my favorite meals _is_ (is, are) ham and eggs.

14. Neither she nor her children _have_ (has, have) ever forgiven her father.

15. A variety of solutions _were_ (was, were) proposed at the meeting yesterday.

16. A directory of editorial resources, including publications firms and hotlines staffed by various English departments, _was_ (was, were) produced on the laser printer.

17. One of the food service supervisors _was_ (was, were) working on the floor for the first time in over ten years.

18. Each of the students was asked to report _their_ (their, the, his or her) findings to the class.

19. Neither Bill nor Karen _has_ (has, have) finished _the_ (his, her, their, the) assignment.

20. Neither of the two teachers who _were_ (was, were) on the board last year _is_ (is, are) willing to continue.

ACTIVE AND PASSIVE VOICE:
Who's Doing What

6

Verbs convey action in one of two ways—active or passive voice. If the subject of a sentence performs the action of the sentence (*John caught the ball*), the verb is in the active voice. If the subject receives the action (*The ball was caught by John*), the verb is passive.

Active voice tends to be more forceful and less wordy than passive. The passive voice always has a helping verb and often contains the prepositional phrase *by* someone or something.

Some editors automatically remove all passives. You can, however, carry your dislike of the passive voice to extremes. The passive has its place and in some cases may even be preferred. If the emphasis is on the thing done, rather than on the doer, for example, use the passive voice. Here are some examples.

> Medea <u>killed</u> her children.

> The children <u>were killed</u> by Medea.

The first sentence emphasizes Medea. The second emphasizes her children, the victims.

> He <u>told</u> me to get out.

> I <u>was told</u> to get out.

The second sentence is much less forceful than the first. The passive voice here allows you to make a statement in a more tentative way than the active. When you read the passive, the emotional content is diminished.

Editors want each sentence to carry its own weight, to tell clearly who did what to whom. Intentionally or not, the passive voice often obscures the doer: No one takes responsibility for the action. Layers and layers of passives in a manuscript make it difficult to determine accountability (or guilt). Events seem to take on a life of their

The Copyeditor's Guide to Substance&Style

own, with no one acting or reacting. In committees and representative bodies, bills are discussed, laws are passed, rumors are circulated, and no names are mentioned. The passive can guarantee anonymity. Sometimes this anonymity is inadvertent; at other times it's exactly what the writer intends.

The passive does have its place. In technical or scientific material, the actor (or researcher) may be unimportant: The emphasis is on the mice that were fed saccharin and whose deaths were observed. It may be best to leave such passives alone and focus on the procedures and the results themselves, unless you can edit to emphasize the mice: "The mice ingested…, measurable tumors appeared…, the mice died."

Further, scientific writers are accustomed to reading the passive and tend to continue using it because it sounds so familiar—and "professional"—to them. Making sentences such as the following active would be difficult and likely result in an awkward, possibly inaccurate revision.

> Adenisine and augite, the essential minerals, are usually found in the proportion of 3 adenisine to 1 augite.

The rhythm of the language or the flow of a paragraph may lend itself to the passive. Think twice before you automatically excise it. Editing requires weighing alternatives: Where does the emphasis belong, on the act or the results? Would making the verb active require you to guess at or lead you to possibly misconstrue the true subject of the sentence? Do Exercise 9 with these considerations in mind. Remember that in the active voice, the subject is doing the acting. In the passive voice, the subject is being acted upon.

Exercise 9:
Active vs. Passive Voice

Instructions: Change the following sentences from passive to active voice if appropriate. (There may be more than one correct way to rephrase each.) You may have to add a subject to do the acting, and you should also fix any other editorial problems you see.

1. The regulation was mainly written by the lobbyist.

2. Consideration is being given to your proposal.

3. A national network of technical assistance providers will be organized.

4. Publications have been developed to address changes in regulations.

5. Since that time, changes have been issued to amend the original publications.

6. A series of technical seminars was sponsored by the Training and Development Office.

Exercise 9, continued

7. Management of the Credit Department will be the responsibility of Ms. Bellamy.

8. Implementation of the guidelines will be carried out by the new staff members.

9. It can be reasonably expected that the program will not be evaluated until 1999.

10. The Attorney General's Office and its representatives are going to be called upon to give its opinion.

11. When a member is to be dropped from the union rolls, he will be notified by the appropriate authority.

12. Recommendations by the Zoning Commission for waivers may be disapproved by the Board of Supervisors.

13. The date of entry into the school system will be shown on the transfer form.

Exercise 9 Answers

[handwritten: The lobbyist wrote most of]

1. ~~The regulation was mainly written by the lobbyist.~~

   The lobbyist wrote most of the regulation.

   You didn't have to add a subject because the prepositional phrase by *the lobbyist* named the subject for you.

[handwritten: We are]

2. ~~Consideration is being given to~~ *[ing]* your proposal.

   We are considering your proposal.

   Here you needed to add a subject. The context normally dictates your choice; lacking a context, you could have picked any reasonable noun or pronoun.

[handwritten: The company will organize — providers of]

3. A national network of technical assistance ~~providers will be organized.~~

   The company will organize a national network of technical assistance providers.

   This sentence also required you to add a subject. In addition, you should at least consider eliminating the noun string as we've done. However, if *technical assistance providers* is commonly understood by your audience, don't change it.

[handwritten: The agency]

4. Publications ~~have been~~ developed to address changes in regulations.

   The agency has developed publications to address changes in regulations.

   This sentence seemed to have an official sound; hence, we used the more official subject (*agency*), although the word *we* certainly makes sense as well. If it isn't clear from the context who or what developed the publications or issued the changes, you must leave the sentence alone.

The Copyeditor's Guide to **Substance**&*Style*

Exercise 9 Answers, continued

5. Since that time, ~~changes~~ *the agency* have been issued to amend the original publications.

Since that time, the agency has issued changes to amend the original publications.

This sentence seemed to follow the last one. In this exercise, you have the leeway to add a subject; in a manuscript with no author guidance, you might have to leave the passive alone for lack of a subject.

6. ~~A~~ *The Training and Development Office* series of technical seminars was sponsored by the Training and Development Office.

The Training and Development Office sponsored a series of technical seminars.

The office that sponsors the series should be the subject.

7. ~~Management~~ *Ms. Bellamy* of the Credit Department will be the responsibility of Ms. Bellamy.

Ms. Bellamy will be responsible for managing the Credit Department.

Here, replacing some of the nouns with verbs produces a more forceful sentence.

8. 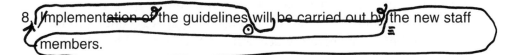 Implementation of the guidelines will be carried out by the new staff members.

The new staff members will implement the guidelines.

As you see, removing the passive voice and correcting wordiness noticeably shorten the sentence.

9. It can be reasonably expected that the program will not be evaluated until 1999.

   This sentence is perhaps best left alone or, if the context gives a clue as to who is going to do the evaluating, changed only minimally.

   > A reasonable expectation is that we will not be able to evaluate the program until 1999.

   You may have been tempted to delete *expected* (or *expectation*), but such a revision might not be wise. Apparently, the 1999 date for the evaluation is not yet firm. The two words *reasonably expected* seem to constitute a sort of disclaimer.

   Sentences like this are difficult to handle, and you must always be wary of subtly shifting the meaning.

10. *Congress will call on*
    The Attorney General's Office and its representatives ~~are going to be~~ ~~called upon~~ to give ~~its~~ an opinion.

    > Congress will call on the Attorney General's Office and its representatives to give an opinion.

    We needed to choose someone to do the action. Congress is a likely subject, but it could just as easily be the president or another government agency.

    In this sentence, did you notice that the second *its* didn't have a proper antecedent? Will the Office alone issue an opinion? Not according to the sentence. Some editing is therefore necessary. Another possible version, depending on the context, follows.

    > Congress will call on the Attorney General's Office and its representatives to give their opinions.

Exercise 9 Answers, continued

11. ~~When~~ a member ~~is~~ to be dropped from the union rolls ~~he will be notified by the appropriate authority.~~ *The appropriate authority* *who* *about*

The appropriate authority will notify a member who is about to be dropped from the union rolls.

Avoid the question of whether all the union members are male. Experienced editors develop creativity in sidestepping *he/she*, *him/her* constructions.

12. ~~Recommendations by the Zoning Commission for~~ waivers ~~may be~~ *disapprove* ~~disapproved by the Board of Supervisors.~~ *that the Zoning Comission recommends.* *The Board of Supervisors*

The Board of Suporvioors may disapprove waivers that the Zoning Commission recommends.

This sentence required a little more editing. Other versions are certainly possible. Be sure that the flow of the edited sentence is better than the original and that the relationship among the parts is clearer.

13. ~~The~~ date of entry into the school system ~~will be shown~~ on the transfer form. *Show*

Show the date of entry into the school system on the transfer form.

The date of entry into the school system ~~will be shown on~~ the transfer form.

The transfer form will show the date of entry into the school system.

You can argue that the sentence is best left alone because there's no obvious subject. If the sentence is part of instructions, you can use the imperative, as shown in the first solution. If the text merely describes the information on the form, use the second or third.

Remember to weigh the alternatives carefully before you automatically change passive voice to active. If you want more practice with passive constructions, continue on to Exercise 10.

Exercise 10:
More Active vs. Passive

Instructions: Change passive voice to active. Fix anything else that's wrong.

1. Several unit funds may be centrally administered by one single fund manager.

2. A comprehensive survey will be conducted biennially by each branch of the corporation to identify staffing needs.

3. Operational usage standards for utility vehicles will be established by each office.

4. Locally fabricated training devices will be maintained by the user of the device.

5. All modifications that are proposed will be endorsed by the affected parties.

6. The condition will be validated by a needs assessment team.

The Copyeditor's Guide to **Substance**&*Style*

7. Guidance and budget information is provided by the manager on each level.

8. Centralized purchasing is accomplished for the fund manager by procurement personnel.

9. The sale of alcoholic beverages by ABC stores is controlled by the state.

10. It is the opinion of this board of inquiry that the equipment was being used in an unsafe manner by the operators.

11. By using computers, much time can be saved by editors.

12. The plan was approved by the committee, but only after six hours of acrimonious debate had been held.

13. The directive was sent down by company headquarters. All reports were to be done in triplicate by the staff.

14. Reference is made to your letter of May 24, and our answer is in the affirmative.

Exercise 10 Answers

1. Several unit funds may be centrally administered by one single fund manager.

   A single fund manager may administer several unit funds.

2. A comprehensive survey will be conducted biennially by each branch of the corporation to identify staffing needs.

   Each branch of the corporation will conduct a biennial comprehensive survey to identify staffing needs.

3. Operational usage standards for utility vehicles will be established by each office.

   Each office will establish operational usage standards for utility vehicles.

4. Locally fabricated training devices will be maintained by the user of the device.

   Users will maintain locally fabricated training devices.

Exercise 10 Answers, continued

The affected parties

5. All modifications that are proposed will be endorsed by the affected parties.

The affected parties will endorse all proposed modifications.

6. The condition will be validated by a needs assessment team.

A needs assessment team will validate the condition.

The manager on each level

7. Guidance and budget information is provided by the manager on each level.

The manager on each level provides guidance and budget information.

do

8. Centralized purchasing is accomplished for the fund manager by procurement personnel.

Procurement personnel do centralized purchasing for the fund manager.

controls

9. The sale of alcoholic beverages by ABC stores is controlled by the state.

The state controls the sale of alcoholic beverages by ABC stores.

Exercise 10 Answers, continued

10. ~~It is the opinion of~~ this board of inquiry ~~that the~~ equipment ~~was being~~ believes were using the ~~used~~ in an unsafe manner ~~by the operators~~.

   This board of inquiry believes the operators were using the equipment in an unsafe manner.

11. ~~By~~ using computers, much time ~~can be saved by editors~~ Editors can save

   Editors can save much time by using computers.

12. ~~The plan was approved by the committee~~ but only after six hours of acrimonious debate ~~had been held~~.

   The committee approved the plan, but only after six hours of acrimonious debate.

13. ~~The directive was sent~~ down ~~by~~ company headquarters. ~~All reports were~~ a directive that required the staff ~~to be done~~ in triplicate ~~by the staff~~.

   Company headquarters sent a directive that required the staff to do all reports in triplicate.

14. ~~Reference is made to~~ your letter of May 24, and our answer is ~~in the affirmative~~. Thank you for yes

   Thank you for your letter of May 24; our answer is yes.

The Copyeditor's Guide to Substance&Style

PRONOUNS:
Case and Number Agreement

7

A pronoun is a word used in place of a noun; using a pronoun allows writers and speakers to avoid repeating the noun. Pronouns change their form (case) depending on their use in a sentence. English has three cases: nominative, objective, and possessive. Anyone who took high school Latin remembers cases; Latin has five. English, as it has evolved, has eliminated Latin's dative and ablative cases, as well as most other case forms—except those for pronouns. English uses the nominative case for subjects of sentences and for predicate nominatives. The objective case is for objects of prepositions and direct and indirect objects of verbs. The possessive case denotes adjectives.

Here are some examples of pronouns in each case.

CASE			
Nominative	**Objective**	**Possessive**	
		(modifying)	(standing alone)
I	me	my	mine
you	you	your	yours
he	him	his	his
she	her	her	hers
it	it	its	its
we	us	our	ours
you	you	your	yours
they	them	their	theirs
who	whom	whose	whose
whoever	whomever		

Nominative Case

Give this message to <u>whoever answers the phone</u>.

Whoever is the subject of the subordinate clause (*whoever answers the phone*) and is in the nominative case.

It was <u>she who was</u> late for school.

The predicate nominative *she* is the antecedent of *who*, which is the subject of the subordinate clause (*who was late for school*). Thus, both pronouns must take the nominative case.

<u>He and his sister</u> are going to camp for two weeks.

The pronoun *He* is part of the compound subject.

Objective Case

Allen Jones is the candidate <u>whom</u> we want to support for the Senate.

Whom is actually the direct object of the verb *support* (we want to support *whom*); as a relative pronoun, *whom* forms a bridge between the two clauses in the sentence.

The race ended in a tie <u>between you and me</u>.

The two pronouns are the objects of the preposition *between*; they must be in the objective case.

He wants to go <u>with Chris and me</u>.

The pronoun *me* is the object of the preposition *with*. In a sentence like this, the correct pronoun case often becomes clearer if you mentally eliminate the preceding noun and conjunction:

He wants to go <u>with me</u>.

In this sentence, *him* is the indirect object of the verb *offered*, the object of the (understood) preposition *to*, so the objective case is correct.

The editor offered him the assignment.

The editor offered the assignment (to) him.

Possessive Case

Whose dog is barking?

The dog is chewing on its bone.

Whose is the possessive form of the relative pronoun *who*, used here to modify *dog*. *Its*, as a possessive, has no apostrophe.

It's is the contraction of *it is*; the apostrophe denotes a missing letter, and this is the only time an apostrophe should be used with *its*. Confusion of *its* and *it's* is quite common, as evidenced by this headline in a major newspaper: "At the top of it's class..."

Do you object to my borrowing your dictionary?

Before a gerund (an *-ing* form of a verb used as a noun), use a possessive pronoun. Although *borrowing* is a verb form, its use here as a noun requires an adjective. *Your* shows possession of the dictionary.

Don't forget that it's mine.

Mine is a predicate adjective, a possessive, representing *my dictionary*.

Most of the time, your ear will tell you which form of the pronoun is correct. The use of *who* and *whom*, however, poses special problems. Maxwell Nurnberg, in his book *Questions You Always Wanted to Ask About English*, offers a workable, nontechnical solution to this problem, best discussed in the context of a sentence.

Give me one example of someone (who, whom) you think was rewarded and not penalized for confessing.

Nurnberg's approach has three steps: First, consider only the words that follow *who* or *whom*. This approach leaves you with

you think _____ was rewarded...

Notice that there's a gap in thought, emphasized here with the underlined space. Fill that gap with either *he* (*she*) or *him* (*her*), whichever is correct and makes sense.

you think he was rewarded...

Replace *he* with *who* (the nominative case). This trick works every time.

Give me one example of someone who you think was rewarded and not penalized for confessing.

Try Nurnberg's formula in Exercise 11.

Exercise 11:
Who and Whom

Instructions: Fill in the blanks with the correct pronoun (*who* or *whom*, unless otherwise specified).

1. They should give a trophy to _____ (whoever, whomever) the coaches choose as the most valuable player.

2. _____ do you think they'll choose to be May Queen?

3. It's not for me to say _____ should be punished for breaking the window.

4. The butler intoned, "_____ may I say is calling?"

5. We'll send a complimentary copy of the directory to _____ (whoever, whomever) responds to the survey.

6. They asked the branch chief _____ on the staff might be the source of the security leak.

7. Senator Janeway is the man _____ we want to nominate.

8. Moreover, we'll sell the house to _____ (whoever, whomever) meets our price.

9. Remember, it doesn't matter _____ you like; it's _____ you know.

Exercise 11 Answers

1. They should give a trophy to <u>whomever</u> the coaches choose as the most valuable player.

    The coaches choose <u>him</u>...

    The correct answer is *whomever*.

2. <u>Whom</u> do you think they'll choose to be May Queen?

    Questions are easier to deal with when you invert them.

    you think they will choose <u>her</u>...

    The answer is *whom*.

3. It's not for me to say <u>who</u> should be punished for breaking the window.

    Who is the subject of the verb *should be punished*.

4. The butler intoned, "<u>Who</u> may I say is calling?"

    In the movies, perfect secretaries and perfect butlers always say, "Whom shall I say is calling?" but this version isn't correct. Apply Nurnberg's rule.

    I may say <u>he</u> is calling.

    Or delete the phrase between the subject and the verb.

    <u>Who</u> is calling?

    Put this way, it becomes clear that *who* is correct.

5. We'll send a complimentary copy of the directory to <u>whoever</u> responds to the survey.

The word *to* may be confusing.

> <u>he</u> responds to the survey

Whoever is the subject of the verb responds and takes the nominative case. The whole clause *whoever responds to the survey* is the object of the preposition *to*.

6. They asked the branch chief <u>who</u> on the staff might be the source of the security leak.

Drop the words between the subject and verb.

> <u>he</u> might be the source

The subject is *who*.

7. Senator Janeway is the man <u>whom</u> we want to nominate.

> we want to nominate <u>him</u>

Obviously, you have to use *whom*.

8. Moreover, we'll sell the house to <u>whoever</u> meets our price.

Whenever a relative pronoun appears to be the object of a preposition, study the sentence carefully. *Whoever* is actually the subject of the subordinate clause, hence, the nominative case. Again, the whole clause is the object of the preposition.

9. Remember, it doesn't matter <u>whom</u> you like; it's <u>whom</u> you know.

> you like <u>him</u>...; you know <u>him</u>

Both clauses require *whom*.

Agreement with Antecedents

Remember that an antecedent is the word to which a pronoun refers; each pronoun should have a clear and immediate antecedent. Grammatically, a pronoun should refer to the closest noun that has the same number as the pronoun. An antecedent should not be much farther away than in the immediately preceding sentence. Here are some simple examples.

> My <u>mother</u> said <u>she</u> would call tonight.
>
> The <u>child whom</u> we hope to adopt is named Elizabeth.
>
> The insurance <u>company</u> dispatches <u>its</u> adjusters whenever disaster strikes.

In these examples, there's only one possible antecedent for each pronoun. Difficulties arise, however, when a pronoun can refer to more than one antecedent.

> <u>Susan</u> is a marvelous dancer and so is her <u>sister</u>. <u>She</u> has the lead in the senior play.

The first sentence in this example is clear, but whom does *she* refer to in the second sentence? Logically, the antecedent is probably *Susan*, but grammatically *she* refers to *sister*.

In the third sentence of the paragraph below, a problem arises with the antecedent of *it*. Logically, it's clear that the orchard was bulldozed, not the day or the sky or any of the other nouns. Grammatically, however, either of those two words could be the antecedent of *it*. To make the sentence correct as well as clear, *it* should be replaced by *the orchard*.

> There was a large walnut <u>orchard</u> behind our <u>house</u>. At <u>dusk</u>, the <u>trees</u> would be silhouetted against the <u>sky</u>. One summer <u>day</u>, however, <u>it</u> was bulldozed to make room for a car dealership.

Theoretically, the antecedent of a pronoun shouldn't be an idea. What is the antecedent of *this* in the following sentence? *Everyone would agree with this.* Not *idea*, but the concept that an antecedent shouldn't be an idea, is the antecedent. Such usage is common in spoken English but not always acceptable in careful writing. Here are a few more examples.

> My son plays football, <u>which</u> upsets his grandmother.
>
> Only 10 persons have turned in the assignment; <u>this</u> is unacceptable.
>
> Our son got second place in the science fair; <u>this</u> made us very proud.

In each of these examples, the pronoun refers to an idea; football doesn't upset Grandmother, but the fact that her grandson plays does. If the sentence is perfectly clear, many editors leave such constructions alone, especially if changing them makes the sentence awkward or unnecessarily wordy.

We should make another point in this discussion of antecedents: An antecedent must be a noun, not a possessive adjective.

> In <u>Professor Walker's</u> class, <u>he</u> discusses Renaissance comedy.

What's the antecedent of *he*? It can't be *Professor Walker's*; that phrase functions as a possessive adjective. The sentence therefore has to be rewritten; here are two options.

> In the class Professor Walker teaches, he discusses Renaissance comedy.

> Professor Walker discusses Renaissance comedy in his class.

To repeat the rules, (1) a pronoun needs a clear antecedent, and (2) the pronoun must agree with its antecedent in number, gender, and person. A plural pronoun can't refer to a singular antecedent, nor can a feminine pronoun refer to a masculine antecedent. Adhering to these rules isn't as easy as it seems. Consider the following examples.

1. The <u>restaurant</u> has added eclairs and fruit tarts to <u>its</u> dessert menu.

2. The <u>employees</u> voiced <u>their</u> protests.

3. Everyone entered <u>her</u> office and turned on <u>her</u> computer.

4. <u>Each dancer</u> bowed as <u>she</u> left the stage.

5. <u>Each cadet</u> must present <u>his</u> rifle for inspection.

6. <u>Everyone</u> should buy <u>their</u> color TV here.

Certainly, no one can object to the first two examples, but look at the third. Many people speaking informally use *their*, not *her*, in this instance. But *their* is plural and shouldn't be used with the singular antecedent everyone. Without digressing into a long discussion on neutral language, note that in bygone days the generic *he* encompassed men and women, as in the following examples.

> <u>He</u> who hesitates is lost.

> <u>He</u> who laughs last laughs best.

The Copyeditor's Guide to **Substance**&*Style*

Many newsrooms are responding to the convergence of print, broadcast, and electronic media by embracing a team-based approach to reporting— an approach antithetical to the traditional view of <u>the reporter</u> as a loner who researches, writes, and takes full credit for <u>his</u> own stories.

This solution is no longer considered acceptable, and the best way to solve the problem is to make the antecedent plural or to recast the statement (if you can). But do not rewrite famous and historical quotations or sayings! That is "hypercorrection," and copyeditors should steer clear of it.

Hypercorrection: He or she who hesitates is lost.

Hypercorrection: Those who laugh last laugh best.

Improved: Many newsrooms are responding to the convergence of print, broadcast, and electronic media by embracing a team-based approach to reporting—an approach antithetical to the traditional view of <u>reporters</u> as loners who research, write, and take full credit for <u>their</u> own stories.

In the numbered examples 4 and 5 on page 100, remember that *his* or *her* alone is fine if the context shows clearly that persons of only one sex are involved. So if example 5 is referring to cadets at an all-male military school, *his* is correct. But many cadets at West Point and the Air Force Academy are women; you still may need to recast the sentence, depending on the context.

Example 6, which came from an advertising campaign, should be recast to avoid the problem.

Everyone should buy a color TV here.

All of the sentences in the following exercise are comprehensible when spoken but less acceptable in careful writing. The context will often direct you to the antecedent, but in complex sentences or technical writing that contains passives, you should either query the author or, if the author is not available, leave the usage alone.

Because so much ambiguity can exist even in writing that is neither complex nor technical, you should always be alert to antecedent problems. Identifying them can be tricky, however, because spoken and written usage in English diverge. Understanding a sentence's meaning doesn't normally justify ambiguity. If antecedents are unclear, fix those you can and query those you can't. With these injunctions in mind, do Exercise 12.

Exercise 12: Pronoun-Antecedent Agreement

Instructions: Correct the following sentences and make sure that each pronoun has one clear, appropriate antecedent. Some sentences are correct but can be improved.

1. In any gathering they attended, John always monopolized the conversation; this annoyed his wife.

2. The person who cooks doesn't do the dishes, which seems to be fair to me.

3. We decided to vacation in Europe; this seemed like a good idea at the time.

4. We bought take out food at the Chinese restaurant, which was very expensive and tasted terrible.

5. Julie was accepted at Princeton, which greatly pleased her grandfather.

6. This army travels on their stomach.

7. Anyone can do it if they try.

8. Just before Christmas, everyone is running around spending their money.

9. Theirs is a friendship spanning three generations, which is most unusual.

10. Don't drink and drive; this could be hazardous to your health.

The Copyeditor's Guide to **Substance**&*Style*

Exercise 12 Answers

The context or the flow of a particular paragraph often dictates the choice of words or the form of the sentence. Sometimes, trying to eliminate ambiguity leads to a wordier, more awkward sentence. In each case you must decide whether the revision is in fact an improvement. Only some of the possible alternatives for the following sentences are listed here.

1. In any gathering they attended, John always monopolized the conversation; this *habit* annoyed his wife.

   This sentence is clear as it stands, but you can also add the noun *habit*.

   Alternative: In any gathering they attended, John always monopolized the conversation; this habit annoyed his wife.

2. The person who cooks doesn't do the dishes *; this division of labor* which seems to be fair to me.

   The person who cooks doesn't do the dishes; this division of labor seems fair to me.

   The antecedent of *which* is an idea, not the preceding noun. Thus for formal writing you need to add a noun and repunctuate the sentence. For informal writing, you could break the sentence after *dishes* and treat the rest as an aside.

   Alternative: The person who cooks doesn't do the dishes—which seems fair to me.

3. We decided to vacation in Europe; *the trip* this seemed like a good idea at the time.

   Again, the sentence is clear as it stands, but you could also change *this* to *the trip*.

   Alternative: We decided to vacation in Europe; the trip seemed like a good idea at the time.

4. ~~We bought~~ *The* take-out food at the Chinese restaurant / ~~which~~ was very expensive and tasted terrible.

The take-out food we bought at the Chinese restaurant was very expensive and tasted terrible.

Alternative: We found the take-out food from the Chinese restaurant both expensive and unappetizing.

5. Julie ~~was~~ *'s* accept~~ed~~ *ance* at Princeton / ~~which~~ greatly pleased her grandfather.

This sentence is clear, but alternatives are also possible.

Alternatives: Julie's acceptance at Princeton greatly pleased her grandfather.

The fact that Julie was accepted at Princeton greatly pleased her grandfather.

6. This army travels on ~~their~~ *its* stomach.

This army travels on its stomach.

7. Anyone *who tries* can do it ~~if they try~~.

Anyone who tries can do it.

Exercise 12 Answers, continued

8. Just before Christmas, everyone is running around spending ~~their~~ money. [*their* crossed out, "g" written above]

   Just before Christmas, everyone is running around spending money.

   Eliminating the possessive adjective doesn't affect the meaning here.

9. Theirs is a friendship spanning three generations, ~~which~~ is most unusual. [*such a bond* written above *which*]

   Alternatives: Theirs is a friendship spanning three generations; such a bond is most unusual.

   Trying to compress the two clauses leads to a slight shift in meaning.

   Their friendship, which spans three generations, is most unusual.

10. Don't drink and drive; this could be hazardous to your health. [*combination* written above, inserted after *this*]

    Don't drink and drive; this combination could be hazardous to your health.

    _____

The following exercise puts antecedent problems into the sort of material that might appear in an advertisement or brochure.

Exercise 13:
Unclear Antecedents

Instructions: Read through the following exercise, noting pronoun problems. Circle each pronoun; make sure each has a clear antecedent and query any other problems. Most readers will find this piece comprehensible, although ungrammatical.

The first site plan in this series illustrates the most common layout for a neighborhood shopping center. They are one-story units averaging 600 feet and having six to eight stores which are usually constructed in suburban areas.

The best example of this kind of layout is the Marwick model, which is a tribute to his architectural prowess in this field. If you look at it, you will note that the drug and grocery stores are at either end. The others are in the middle. Loading docks are at the rear of these. This is as it should be, because no matter how effective your management program is, tenants are careless about their trash, and it will always be there, and that is an eyesore.

The Copyeditor's Guide to **Substance**&*Style*

Exercise 13, continued

This model has easy ingress and egress and convenient, close parking spaces. Marwick takes care to build his centers so that handicapped persons can park there and use them. They do not, however, block delivery service routes to the rear of the building.

A word about drive-in banks—this tenant will pay high rents when they are interested in locating in a good center. The advantage is that they will bring people to your center. It will cause traffic snarls, though, especially on paydays, so you should plan ahead and consider building it on the end.

If you use the Marwick and other models as guides as you are planning, you will find that it will help you to avoid these problems.

The first site plan in this series illustrates the most common layout for a

neighborhood shopping center. (They) are one-story units averaging 600 feet *square feet?*

and having six to eight stores (which) are usually constructed in suburban

areas.

can a model be a tribute?

The best example of this kind of layout is the Marwick model, which is a tribute

Is Marwick an architect, a builder, or a developer?   *what field?*

to (his) architectural prowess in (this) field. If you look at (it) you will note that the

end of what?   *which others?*   *of what?*

drug and grocery stores are at either end. The (others) are in the middle. Loading

docks are at the rear of (these). (This) is as (it) should be, because no matter how

effective your management program is, tenants are careless about their trash,

where?

and It wlll always be (there), and (that) Is an eyesore.

to what?

This model has easy ingress and egress and convenient, close parking spaces.

Marwick takes care to build his centers so that handicapped persons can park

where? centers or spaces?

(there) and use (them). (They) do not, however, block delivery service routes to the

rear of the building.

Exercise 13 Answers, continued

singular — referring to a plural antecedent

A word about drive-in banks—(this) tenant will pay high rents when (they) are

interested in locating in a good center. The advantage is that (they) will bring

people to your center. (It) will cause traffic snarls, though, especially on paydays,

end of what?

so you should plan ahead and consider building (it) on the <u>end</u>.

If you use the Marwick and other models as guides as you are planning,

you will find that (it) will help you to avoid those problems.

PARALLELISM:

A Delicate Balance

8

Put simply, parallelism means that parts of a sentence similar in meaning are similar in construction. To achieve parallelism, writers and editors balance a word with another word, a phrase with another phrase, an infinitive with another infinitive, and so on.

Poets and public speakers use parallel construction extensively.

> We <u>cannot dedicate</u>, we <u>cannot consecrate</u>, we <u>cannot hallow</u> this ground.

> I come <u>to bury</u> Caesar, <u>not to praise</u> him.

Here are some guidelines for parallel construction.

1. A noun and an infinitive aren't parallel.

> The duties of the proposal manager were <u>the coordination</u> of the production and <u>to write</u> the executive summary.

> The duties of the proposal manager were <u>to coordinate</u> the production and <u>to write</u> the executive summary.

It's better to say *to coordinate* than to introduce another smothered verb (*the writing of*).

2. A gerund and a noun aren't parallel.

> You may earn extra credit by <u>writing</u> a report or the <u>submission</u> of a completed reading list.

> You may earn extra credit by <u>writing</u> a report or <u>submitting</u> a completed reading list.

Using two gerunds (*writing* and *submitting*) makes the sentence parallel.

The Copyeditor's Guide to **Substance**&*Style*

3. A gerund and a noun aren't parallel.

    My daughter was less interested in her <u>homework</u> than <u>daydreaming</u>.

    My daughter was less interested in <u>doing her homework</u> than in <u>daydreaming</u>.

    Doing parallels *daydreaming*.

4. A noun and a clause aren't parallel.

    The training director is responsible <u>for planning</u> the curriculum and <u>that the courses should run smoothly</u>.

    The training director is responsible for <u>planning</u> the curriculum and <u>ensuring</u> that the courses run smoothly.

5. Items in a list should be parallel. Here, they are not.

    The preflight checklist included the following:

    - Secure the outside doors,

    - All luggage must be stowed under the seats and not in the aisles,

    - All seats must be in the upright position; and

    - that the flight attendants should be seated.

Not only must all the elements in a list begin with the same part of speech, but the beginning capitalization and ending punctuation must also be consistent. You can correct the example as follows.

    The preflight checklist included the following directions:

    - <u>Secure</u> the outside doors.

    - <u>Stow</u> all luggage under the seats and not in the aisles.

    - <u>Place</u> all seats in the upright position.

    - <u>Tell</u> the flight attendants to sit down.

All items now begin with a capital letter and verb and end with a period. The list is thus parallel.

Lists can be numbered or lettered, bulleted, or simply displayed. A manuscript can contain more than one type of list without being inconsistent. Numbering a list usually implies that the sequence of items conveys some information: the list is chronological or in order or importance, for example. Even in bulleted or displayed lists, the items should be in some kind of order. If they are simply random, consider alphabetizing them.

> These are some of the toys that were strewn on the living room floor:
>
> blocks
>
> dolls
>
> marbles
>
> plastic dishes
>
> stuffed animals

6. An article or a preposition that applies to a series must be used either before the first item or be repeated before each item.

> The objectives were to cut off the enemy's supply routes, demoralize the population, and to support the existing government

Add the word *to* before the second phrase or delete it from the third to make this sentence parallel.

> The objectives were <u>to cut off</u> the enemy's supply routes, <u>to demoralize</u> the population, and <u>to support</u> the existing government.
>
> The objectives were to <u>cut off</u> the enemy's supply routes, <u>demoralize</u> the population, and <u>support</u> the existing government.

7. Correlative expressions (*both…and, not only…but also,* and *either…or*) must be followed by the same construction.

> Either you must follow the doctor's advice or bear the consequences.

The Copyeditor's Guide to **Substance***&Style*

Either you must follow the doctor's advice or <u>you must</u> bear the consequences.

Not only must you fill out your form correctly, but also pay your taxes.

Not only must you fill out your form correctly, but <u>you must</u> also pay your taxes.

Both the Senate and House of Representatives agreed to the postponement.

Both the Senate and <u>the</u> House of Representatives agreed to the postponement.

These general rules govern parallel construction. Most of the time, your ear will guide you. Parallelism pleases; the lack of it jars.

To summarize, parallel construction helps clarify meaning by imposing similar grammatical construction on parts of a whole. Parallelism can also emphasize ideas (or a relationship between them) and can keep complicated sentences from being unnecessarily confusing. Exercises 14 and 15 will give you practice in imposing parallelism.

Exercise 14: Parallelism

Instructions: Correct these sentences as necessary to make them parallel.

1. James likes to read, to swim, and playing soccer.

2. When you finish the test, check it for errors and that your name is at the top.

3. You will be advised when a court date is either set or the charges are dropped.

4. Not only did she scream at the children constantly, but she would also hit them.

5. Her Christmas list included a set of skis, a pair of boots, and money.

6. In this workshop, we will discuss the following topics:

   The importance of location in commercial development

   The elements that determine location

   What about utilities?

   Requirements for parking

   Planning fringe space

7. Either he should give up or try harder.

8. The successful applicant should present a professional image, impeccable credentials, and should have a minimum of six years of supervisory experience.

9. This retirement community offers the advantages of a secure building, the presence of a congenial staff, transferring to a medical facility if necessary, and giving your loved ones peace of mind.

10. Building networks of knowledgeable people is important, and it is equally important to build networks of information.

Exercise 14 Answers

The answers we give in the following key aren't the only possibilities; they're simply the ones that occurred to us.

1. James likes to read, to swim, and ~~playing~~ <u>to</u> soccer.

   James likes to read, to swim, and to play soccer.

   Alternative: James likes reading, swimming, and playing soccer.

   Three infinitives or three gerunds solve the problem.

2. When you finish the test, check it for errors and <u>see</u> that your name is at the top.

   When you finish the test, check it for errors and see that your name is at the top.

   Making both parts into imperatives seems the best solution.

3. You will be advised ~~when~~ <u>either that</u> a court date ~~is either~~ <u>has been</u> set or <u>that</u> the charges ~~are~~ <u>have been</u> dropped.

   You will be advised either that a court date has been set or that the charges have been dropped.

   Remember that what follows *either* must also follow *or*; thus, the word *that* is repeated.

The Copyeditor's Guide to **Substance**&*Style*

Exercise 14 Answers, continued

4. Not only did she scream at the children constantly, but she ~~would~~ also hit them.

   Not only did she scream at the children constantly, but she also hit them.

   If you want to convey the repetitiveness of the action, you should use the conditional (*would*) in both clauses:

   Not only would she scream at the children constantly, but she would also hit them.

5. Her Christmas list included ~~a set of~~ skis, ~~a pair of~~ boots, and money.

   Her Christmas list included skis, boots, and money.

   The word *money* doesn't lend itself to descriptors as the other terms do, so each word in the series needs to stand alone.

6. In this workshop, we will discuss ~~the following topics~~ *commercial development:*

   ~~The importance of~~ location ~~in commercial development~~

   ~~The elements that determine location~~

   ~~What about~~ utilities

   ~~Requirements for~~ parking

   ~~Planning~~ fringe space

Each item in this list needs to begin and end similarly and still make sense. The best way to approach such a list is to put the topic (*commercial development*) in the lead sentence.

> In this workshop, we will discuss commercial development:
>
>> Location
>>
>> Utilities
>>
>> Parking
>>
>> Fringe space

Notice the combination of the first two elements: Both discussed a facet of location. This solution proposes no ending punctuation. Some style guides recommend internal and ending punctuation, and some don't. Nor is it essential that each item in the list begin with a capital letter. However, the elements (including their punctuation and capital letters) must be consistent among themselves. And although one publication may have several kinds of lists that may vary in style according to their complexity, the capitalization and punctuation (or lack of it) should be consistent within each type.

7. ~~Either~~ he should give up or try harder.

> He should either give up or try harder.
>
> **Alternative:** Either he should give up or he should try harder.

8. The successful applicant should ~~present~~ have a professional image, impeccable credentials, and ~~should have~~ a minimum of six years of supervisory experience.

The successful applicant should have a professional image, impeccable credentials, and a minimum of six years of supervisory experience.

9. This retirement community offers the ~~following~~ advantages ~~of~~ a secure building, ~~the presence of~~ a congenial staff, transfer~~ring~~ to a medical facility if necessary, and ~~giving your loved ones~~ peace of mind. *for your loved ones*

   This retirement community offers the following advantages: a secure building, a congenial staff, transfer to a medical facility if necessary, and peace of mind for your loved ones.

10. *It is important to* ~~Building~~ networks of knowledgeable people *both* ~~is important~~, and ~~it is equally important to build~~ networks of information.

    It is important to build both networks of knowledgeable people and networks of information.

Examples like this from the advertising world require a slightly heavier edit to make them parallel.

To summarize, parallel construction helps clarify meaning by imposing similar grammatical construction on parts of a whole. Parallelism can also emphasize ideas (or a relationship between them) and can keep complicated sentences from being unnecessarily confusing. Lack of parallelism strikes a sour note for listeners or readers and diminishes effectiveness. Exercise 15 will give you more practice in parallelism if you wish.

Exercise 15:
More Problems with Parallelism

Instructions: Correct the following sentences.

1. The boss told him to do his work and not going about undermining morale.

2. Neither his disgrace nor whatever prison term he gets will make any difference to his loving family.

3. The chief road engineer discussed the causes as well as giving the ramifications of the drainage problem on the project.

4. No matter what he does or all the ways he tries, he still has trouble understanding math.

5. Jack is an intern who is bright, personable, and has potential.

6. Keep your feet flat on the ground, your eye on the ball, and don't swing too soon.

7. Visiting family can be pleasant, but to spend a whole vacation that way can be hard on everyone.

8. Children have to learn to ask nicely instead of going around making demands.

9. Established services needed enhancement and other services needed to be added.

The Copyeditor's Guide to **Substance**&*Style*

Exercise 15 Answers

1. The boss told him to do his work and not ~~going~~ about undermining morale.

   The boss told him to do his work and not go about undermining morale.

2. Neither his disgrace nor ~~whatever~~ **his possible** prison term ~~he gets~~ will make any difference to his loving family.

   Neither his disgrace nor his possible prison term will make any difference to his loving family.

3. The chief road engineer discussed the causes as well as ~~giving~~ the ramifications of the drainage problem on the project.

   The chief road engineer discussed the causes as well as the ramifications of the drainage problem on the project.

4. No matter what he does or ~~all the ways~~ **how hard** he tries, he still has trouble understanding math.

   No matter what he does or how hard he tries, he still has trouble understanding math.

5. Jack is a~~n intern who is~~ bright, personable, and ~~has potential~~ **promising** intern.

   Jack is a bright, personable, and promising intern.

Exercise 15 Answers, continued

6. Keep your feet flat on the ground, ^keep^ your eye on the ball, and don't swing too soon.

    Keep your feet flat on the ground, keep your eye on the ball, and don't swing too soon.

7. Visiting family can be pleasant, but ~~to~~ spend^ing^ a whole vacation that way can be hard on everyone.

    Visiting family can be pleasant, but spending a whole vacation that way can be hard on everyone.

8. Children have to learn to ask nicely instead of ~~going around making~~. demand^ing^s.

    Children have to learn the art of asking nicely instead of demanding.

9. Established services needed enhancement and other services needed to be added.

    Established services needed to be enhanced and other services needed to be added.

MODIFIERS:
They Dangle, Squint, and Get Lost

9

A modifier is a word, phrase, or clause that adds descriptive detail to another word, phrase, or clause. Modifiers can be adjectives, adverbs, appositives, or clauses.

Adjective:	The <u>chattering</u> bird hopped swiftly across the grass.
Adjectival phrase:	<u>Pale with fright</u>, Hansel and Gretel cowered in the corner.
Adverb:	She looked <u>hopefully</u> through the employment ads.
Adverbial clause:	<u>Although her work is</u> good, she needs to improve her attendance.
Appositive:	John Wilkes Booth, <u>the brother of Edwin Booth</u>, shot Lincoln.
Clause:	The dress <u>that she chose</u> made her look older.

Restrictive and Nonrestrictive Clauses

The last example points to another characteristic of certain modifiers: They can be either restrictive (essential) or nonrestrictive (nonessential). A restrictive modifier limits the meaning of a term; without the modifier, the sentence could be ambiguous or could have a different meaning. Restrictive modifiers aren't set off by commas. Here are some examples.

The restaurant <u>that we went to</u> was very crowded.

The clause restricts *restaurant* to the one in which we ate.

Scrooge was a man <u>who hoarded money</u>.

The clause restricts the meaning of *man*.

The play <u>that I love best</u> is "Twelfth Night."

The clause restricts *play* to the one I love best, as opposed to all others.

Nonrestrictive modifiers are parenthetical in meaning. They add information but aren't crucial to the sentence; such modifiers are set off by commas.

> Ernest Hemingway<u>, who wrote many books,</u> committed suicide.

> The proposal<u>, which was 100 pages long,</u> was delivered on time.

The length of that proposal had no bearing on whether it was delivered on time, but if it had, that information would be essential—restrictive.

> The <u>proposal that was 100 pages long</u> was delivered on time.

The implication is that another proposal, of a different length, was delivered late.

Generally speaking, the word *that* introduces a restrictive clause, and the word *which* introduces a nonrestrictive one. Although the *which/that* distinction may be disappearing, especially in spoken English, it's technically correct. In Britain, *which* is used for both kinds of modifying clauses, and formal and informal British writing reflects that fact.

If you aren't sure whether a modifier is restrictive or nonrestrictive, consider the context. If you're still in doubt, then query or leave the construction alone. Some modifiers can function either way; in such cases you have to determine the intended meaning. Look at these examples

> <u>Older persons who take many different kinds of medication</u> are susceptible to cross-reactions.

> Older persons<u>, who take many different kinds of medication,</u> are susceptible to cross-reactions.

The modifier in the first sentence is restrictive; only certain older persons—those who take many kinds of medications—are susceptible to cross-reactions. The second sentence, however, says that all older persons are subject to cross-reactions because they all take many different medications.

> <u>Americans whose diets are composed of 30 percent fat</u> are prone to heart disease.

> Americans<u>, whose diets are composed of 30 percent fat,</u> are prone to heart disease.

The restrictive modifier in the first sentence here limits *Americans* to just those whose diet is rich in fats. The second sentence says that Americans in general are prone to heart disease; the fact that they eat too much fat is additional information.

The Copyeditor's Guide to **Substance**&*Style*

Exercise 16: Restrictive and Nonrestrictive Modifiers

Instructions: In the following sentences, decide whether modifiers are restrictive or nonrestrictive. Correct the sentences as necessary by adding or deleting commas or changing *which* to *that*.

1. This is the house which he rents.

2. A van is the type of automobile which caterers prefer.

3. The river which used to be full of salmon was polluted.

4. The report which I compiled and sent to you should help.

5. The report on editing and grammar which you did for the style guide should help everyone write better.

6. Mark wrote a poem about fall which was printed in the school newspaper.

7. The river which ran through the city was lined with marinas.

8. The veil which had been in the family for three generations was made of ivory lace.

9. Our offices which are located on Canal Street are easily accessible by bus.

10. The university which he attends has an excellent physics department.

Exercise 16 Answers

1. This is the house ~~which~~ *that* he rents.

   This is the most likely solution.

2. A van is the type of automobile ~~which~~ *that* caterers prefer.

   This clause is restrictive, and so *that* is correct. *That* could also be omitted; the sentence would then be elliptical, with *that* understood.

3. The river‸which used to be full of salmon‸was polluted.

   In the absence of a context, the most likely meaning is nonrestrictive.

4. The report ~~which~~ *that* I compiled and sent to you should help.

   Alternative: The report which I compiled and sent to you should help

5. The report on editing and grammar ~~which~~ *that* you did for the style guide should help everyone write better.

6. Mark wrote a poem about fall‸which was printed in the school newspaper.

7. The river ~~which~~ *that* ran through the city was lined with marinas.

   Alternative: The river which ran through the city was lined with marinas.

   Either way could be correct. In the first solution, there's apparently only one river. The second solution implies that there's another river close by that doesn't run through the city.

The Copyeditor's Guide to Substance&Style

Exercise 16 Answers, continued

8. The veil‸which had been in the family for three generations‸was made of ivory lace.

   Alternative: The veil ~~which~~ that had been in the family for three generations was made of ivory lace.

9. Our offices‸which are located on Canal Street‸are easily accessible by bus.

10. The university ~~which~~ that he attends has an excellent physics department.

If you'd like more practice on restrictive and nonrestrictive modifiers before you proceed, continue on to Exercise 17. If you can easily distinguish between restrictive and nonrestrictive modifiers, continue on to misplaced modifiers.

Exercise 17: Restrictive and Nonrestrictive Clauses

Instructions: Decide whether the relative clauses in the following sentences are restrictive or nonrestrictive and correct if necessary.

1. The child who pulled the sword out of the stone was crowned king.

2. People who live in glass houses shouldn't throw stones.

3. David Harvey who is my agent is on vacation.

4. The table which I found at the flea market is an antique.

5. The exposé which John wrote has been sent off to a publisher.

6. John's book which has been accepted for publication will probably go through several printings.

7. My Bible which burned in the fire had been in the family for many years.

8. Foods which contain artificial sweetener may be a health hazard.

The Copyeditor's Guide to **Substance**&*Style*

Exercise 17 Answers

1. The child who pulled the sword out of the stone was crowned king.

2. People who live in glass houses shouldn't throw stones.

3. David Harvey ‸who is my agent‸ is on vacation.

4. The table ~~which~~ *that* I found at the flea market is an antique.

5. The exposé ~~which~~ *that* John wrote has been sent off to a publisher.

6. John's book ‸which has been accepted for publication‸ will probably go

   through several printings.

7. My Bible ‸which burned in the fire‸ had been in the family for many years.

8. Foods ~~which~~ *that* contain artificial sweetener may be a health hazard.

Misplaced Modifiers

A word or phrase placed next to a word that it can't sensibly describe is called a dangling modifier. Copyeditors must be particularly alert to placement of modifiers, or absurdities will slip into print.

Dangling modifiers often appear at the beginning of sentences. Look at these humorous examples.

> <u>Running</u> for the bus, <u>his hat</u> fell off.

> <u>Hissing</u> furiously, <u>the boy</u> removed the kitten from the tree.

However, dangling modifiers needn't be at the beginning of a sentence. They can also appear in the middle, where they seem to function ambiguously: They can modify either the preceding phrase or the following one. Here are some examples.

> While <u>she</u> hesitated <u>with gun poised he</u> attacked.

> The judge <u>said Friday</u> the probationary <u>period is over</u>.

Who has the gun? A small detail, to be sure. Did the judge make the statement on Friday or does the probation end on Friday? As the sentences stand, no one knows. Some grammarians call these problems squinting modifiers.

Other modifiers are misplaced; they stand near a word other than the one the writer or speaker intended them to describe. Adverbs such as *almost, merely, even, nearly, hardly, only*, and *just* are especially easy to misplace.

Look what happens when you misplace one of these adverbs.

> I was just asking for a small favor.

As written, I seem to be saying that I didn't mean it: I was just asking, or hoping. But is that what I really meant? Or did I mean this:

> I was asking for just a small favor.

(The favor I asked for was small.)

The same sleight of hand can be performed with *only*. Consider the following sentence:

> He said that he loved me.

Add the adverb *only* in different places and see how the meaning changes.

> <u>Only he said</u> that he loved me.
>
> He <u>only said</u> that he loved me.
>
> He <u>said only</u> that he loved me.
>
> He said that <u>only he loved</u> me.
>
> He said that <u>he only loved</u> me.
>
> He said that <u>he loved only</u> me.

Each of these sentences conveys a different nuance, a variation on the theme. With that fact in mind, check the placement of adverbs carefully.

Spoken and written English diverge in the placement of modifiers. A spoken sentence that's incorrect may be perfectly comprehensible. But a written sentence needs to be correct, because the reader has more time to contemplate it.

Modifiers add enormously to the richness of the language, but they must be judiciously placed. Not all misplaced modifiers are funny; some are simply clumsy. In any case, careful editing is necessary.

If you want more practice with problem modifiers, turn to Exercises 18 and 19.

Exercise 18: Problem Modifiers

Instructions: Rewrite or edit the following sentences to eliminate the dangling, squinting, and misplaced modifiers. Without a context, it's hard to know exactly which noun or pronoun to use; simply remember that many variations are possible, depending on the rest of the paragraph.

1. Watching from the wings, the orchestra played the overture.

2. After reading the book, the train arrived at its destination.

3. While taking a nap, the cat jumped up on Julie and began to purr.

4. Thinking about her mother, who struggled to feed and clothe them, her eyes filled with tears.

5. To test well on vocabulary, good books must be read.

6. Yesterday I saw a man skiing down the mountain with one leg.

7. The semester passed very quickly, studying for comps and writing my dissertation.

The Copyeditor's Guide to **Substance**&*Style*

Exercise 18, continued

8. Seen off the coast of southern Italy only once before, two Italian sailors reported a large UFO about two miles out to sea.

9. When only a child, Mozart's father presented him at the Austrian court.

10. Short on hope, our patience wears thin; lacking in faith, our courage wanes.

11. Being new in the production department (7 months), it was assumed that this was a more technical class.

12. To be in fashion, your colors should be kept bold, and skirts should be kept long.

13. Described as the most polluted river in the country, you should hold your breath as you drive along the banks.

14. Jogging in the hot sun, her energy began to flag.

15. Cute and playful, you will find that this puppy will entertain you for hours.

Exercise 18 Answers

1. **As(?) ~~ed~~** Watching from the wings, the orchestra played the overture.

    As (?) watched from the wings, the orchestra played the overture.

    Someone or something other than the orchestra is watching; it could be a soprano or a murderer. Query the author unless you are certain from context you can supply the correct noun or pronoun.

2. **I finished** After reading the book, the train arrived at its destination.

    After I finished reading the book, the train arrived at its destination.

    Whether to put the corrected clause at the beginning or the end of a sentence depends on the flow of the paragraph, as well as on your personal preference. Note that what comes first in the sentence does, however, receive the greater emphasis.

3. **As Julie was** ~~While~~ taking a nap, the cat jumped up on ~~Julie~~ **her** and began to purr.

    As Julie was taking a nap, the cat jumped up on her and began to purr.

    Alternative: The cat jumped up on Julie, who was taking a nap, and began to purr.

    The second solution turns the dangling modifier into a nonrestrictive clause.

4. **When she thought** ~~Thinking~~ about her mother, who struggled to feed and clothe them, her eyes filled with tears.

    When she thought about her mother, who struggled to feed and clothe them, her eyes filled with tears.

    The context should tell you whether she often thought about her mother or whether this was a particular instance. If you wish to emphasize that she

The Copyeditor's Guide to **Substance** *&* **Style**

Exercise 18 Answers, continued

often thought of her mother, you could replace the word *filled* with *would fill*. Note how the meaning shifts.

> When she thought about her mother, who struggled to feed and clothe them, her eyes would fill with tears.

If the writer is describing an isolated incident, use *as* to begin the introductory clause.

> As she thought about her mother, who struggled to feed and clothe them, her eyes filled with tears.

5. ~~To~~ *If you want* test well on vocabulary, ~~good books must be read.~~ *you must read*

> If you want to test well on vocabulary, you must read good books.

In this instance, it's probably best to cast the sentence into the second person. Of course, any number of other versions are possible, as long as you eliminate the dangling modifier.

6. Yesterday I saw a *one-legged* man skiing down the mountain ~~with one leg.~~

> Yesterday I saw a one-legged man skiing down the mountain.

The misplaced modifier consists of a phrase that needs to be moved closer to the noun it modifies. Here the phrase becomes an adjective or unit modifier (i.e., both parts of the hyphenated word modify the noun).

7. The semester passed very quickly *as I* stud~~ying~~ *ied* for comps and ~~writing~~ *wrote* my dissertation.

> The semester passed very quickly as I studied for comps and wrote my dissertation.

Exercise 18 Answers, continued

8. *a UFO had been*

~~Seen~~ off the coast of southern Italy only once before, two Italian sailors reported a large UFO about two miles out to sea.

> Two Italian sailors reported a large UFO about two miles out to sea; a UFO had been seen off the coast of southern Italy only once before.

The best way to edit this sentence is to create two independent clauses. Watch the antecedents.

9. *Mozart was* *his*

When only a child, ~~Mozart's~~ father presented him at the Austrian court.

> When Mozart was only a child, his father presented him at the Austrian court.

As originally written, *him* refers to *father*, because *Mozart's* is an adjective and can't be an antecedent.

10. *If we are* *if we*

~~Short~~ on hope, our patience wears thin; ~~lacking in~~ faith, our courage wanes.

> If we are short on hope, our patience wears thin; if we lack faith, our courage wanes.

11. Being new in the production department (7 months), ~~it was~~ *I* assumed that

class

this was ~~a~~ more technical ~~class~~.

> Being new in the production department (7 months), I assumed that this class was more technical.

In the absence of context, you can use any number of nouns or pronouns.

Exercise 18 Answers, continued

12. To be in fashion, your colors ~~should be kept~~ *keep* bold and skirts ~~should be kept~~ *your* long.

    To be in fashion, keep your colors bold and your skirts long.

    We used the imperative to revise this example. The subject, then, is *you* (understood); the construction of the sentence is now parallel as well.

13. *As you drive along the banks of that river* Described as the most polluted ~~river~~ in the country, you should hold your breath, ~~as you drive along the banks.~~

    As you drive along the banks of that river, described as the most polluted in the country, you should hold your breath.

    The independent clause could go at either end.

14. *As she* ~~Jogging~~ *ed* in the hot sun, her energy began to flag.

    As she jogged in the hot sun, her energy began to flag.

    Alternative: Her energy began to flag as she jogged in the hot sun.

    The emphasis you want to convey determines the version you choose.

15. ~~Cute and playful~~ you will find that ~~this~~ puppy will entertain you for hours.

    You will find that this cute, playful puppy will entertain you for hours.

    This example reminds us that a dangling modifier needn't translate into a complete clause.

    _____

    If you want more practice with problem modifiers, continue on to Exercise 19.

Exercise 19: More Problem Modifiers

Instructions: Eliminate the dangling and misplaced modifiers in the following sentences.

1. Having a large family, her house is always cluttered.

2. He found my wallet walking by the river.

3. The CEO spoke to the vice president with a stern voice.

4. These regulations were developed to adapt to new conditions last week.

5. Sale of alcoholic beverages is regulated by the state in public restaurants.

6. Taking cues from nature, the bombardier beetle can produce an explosion of boiling-hot liquid by using enzymes, which are an organic catalyst.

7. Puffing on his pipe, the article was attacked by the editor.

8. He found the ring exposed by the waves walking on the beach.

9. FareStart provides job training and placement for homeless men and women in the food service industry.

The Copyeditor's Guide to **Substance**&*Style*

Exercise 19 Answers

1. *Because she has*
   ~~Having~~ a large family, her house is always cluttered.

   Because she has a large family, her house is always cluttered.

2. He found my wallet *as he was* walking by the river.

   He found my wallet as he was walking by the river.

3. The CEO spoke to the vice president with a stern voice.

   With a stern voice, the CEO spoke to the vice president.

4. These regulations were developed *last week* to adapt to new conditions ~~last week.~~

   These regulations were developed last week to adapt to new conditions.

5. *The state*
   ~~the~~ Sale of alcoholic beverages is regulated ~~by the state~~ in public restaurants.

   The state regulates the sale of alcoholic beverages in public restaurants.

6. *In nature,*
   ~~Taking cues from nature,~~ the bombardier beetle can produce an explosion of boiling-hot liquid by using enzymes, which are an organic catalyst.

   In nature, the bombardier beetle can produce an explosion of boiling-hot liquid by using enzymes, which are an organic catalyst.

7. Puffing on his pipe, the ~~article was~~ *editor* attacked ~~by~~ the *article* ~~editor.~~

   Puffing on his pipe, the editor attacked the article.

8. He found the ring exposed by the waves *while* walking on the beach.

   While walking on the beach, he found the ring exposed by the waves.

9. FareStart provides job training and placement for homeless men and women in the food service industry.

   FareStart provides job training and placement in the food service industry for homeless men and women.

A spoken sentence that's perfectly comprehensible may still be incorrect. Placement of modifiers can convey nuance; there's often no right or wrong answer. Some versions are simply better than others—they read or sound better, or they suit the context better.

PUNCTUATION: 10
The Pause That Clarifies

Most of the punctuation questions that copyeditors confront are matters of style rather than grammar. We assume that anyone who is interested in copyediting is beyond explanations of the basic functions of punctuation marks.

Periods

The trend today is to omit periods in abbreviations and acronyms such as IRA, NATO, IRS, ACTION, and PTA. Using periods in these cases is a style decision; consult your style manual.

Periods (or dots) form an ellipsis (...), indicating that a word or words in a quotation have been omitted. If the part of the quotation that's omitted is in the middle of a sentence, use three dots.

> "One nation...with liberty and justice for all."

If the citation contains punctuation at the point where you're stopping the citation, include the punctuation.

> "Four score and seven years ago...a new nation...."

If the omission is at the end of the sentence, use four dots (i.e., three dots followed by a period).

> "To thine own self be true...."

If words are omitted from the beginning of a quote, the tendency is to omit the ellipsis and replace it with a capital letter. Some styles use brackets to tell the reader that what's inside the brackets wasn't in the original quotation, but most styles simply substitute the capital for the lowercase letter.

> "And justice for all."

> "[A]nd justice for all."

Commas

Style manuals differ on whether or not to use the serial comma—the comma that precedes the final conjunction in a series.

> He ate three hamburgers, two ears of <u>corn, and a</u> banana split.

> I didn't know whether to vacation in Mexico, <u>Spain, or</u> Ecuador.

Some journalistic styles, notably *Associated Press* and other styles that follow it, omit the serial comma in the interests of saving space.

> He ate three hamburgers, two ears of <u>corn and a</u> banana split.

> I didn't know whether to vacation in Mexico, <u>Spain or</u> Ecuador.

For clarity, these styles retain the serial comma if any of the elements in the series includes a conjunction.

> Additional funds were allocated for equipment, research <u>and development, and</u> salaries.

Use a comma in the following constructions.

Compound sentences. Unless the sentence is extremely short, use a comma between two independent or main clauses (those that express a complete thought) joined by *and*.

> She was angry <u>and</u> so was I.

> She left to go shopping at the mall<u>, and I began to weed the garden</u>.

Appositives. Appositives are nouns that explain, repeat, or stand in the same position as other nouns; appositives are also set off by two commas. Consider these two sentences.

> <u>David, our accountant</u>, is on vacation.

> David, <u>our accountant is on vacation</u>.

In the first example, David and the accountant are the same person; our accountant is an appositive. In the second, you're telling David that the accountant is on vacation. David is a noun of direct address.

The Copyeditor's Guide to **Substance**&*Style*

Because they define or limit the meaning of the noun, restrictive appositives don't use commas (just like other restrictive phrases and clauses).

> The poet Longfellow was born in Maine.
>
> Henry the Eighth had six wives.
>
> Oscar the Grouch is a character on *Sesame Street*.

Parenthetical words, phrases, or clauses. These items simply add information. You can remove them without changing the essential meaning of a sentence.

> His strategy, however, backfired.
>
> In fact, he asked his father for a loan.
>
> To my chagrin, the professor read my paper to the class.
>
> Time management techniques, as we have said, are based on a clear understanding of priorities.
>
> There are six persons, if you count the project manager, working on the proposal.

Similar or identical verbs and nouns. Use a comma between identical words to prevent misunderstanding.

> What it was, was football.
>
> Who she is, is not your concern.

Missing words. Sometimes words can be replaced by a comma.

> To err is human; to forgive, divine. (omitted: is)
>
> James is in charge of personnel; Mark, of advertising. (omitted: is in charge)

Dates and locations. A comma is usually placed between a day and a year, but this issue shades over into style. In the following examples, note the two commas; both are necessary because the year or the location is really in apposition. Omitting the second comma in either sentence is incorrect.

> I flew to Tokyo on January 4, 1995, and returned 10 days later.
>
> She lives in the Fairfax, Virginia, area.

No comma is used in international or military dates.

> The fleet held maneuvers in the Mediterranean from <u>17 October 1942</u> to <u>2 November 1942</u>.

After introductory (adverbial) clauses and phrases. Unless the introductory phrase is very short, a comma is necessary to indicate the pause in thought.

The comma in the following example provides the necessary break between the dependent and independent clauses.

> Although he had been running competitively for many years, he had never entered the Boston Marathon.

According to many style guides, the comma can be omitted in the following sentence because the introductory phrase is short, it contains no verb, and the sentence is easily understood without the extra mark.

> As part of its marketing strategy, FGH has increased its advertising budget.

Between words or phrases linked by a coordinate or subordinate conjunction, if ambiguity could result from omission. Conjunctions are used to join words, phrases, or clauses. Coordinating conjunctions (*and, but, or, nor,* or *for*) join parts of equal grammatical weight; subordinating conjunctions (*because, if, since, where,* and *when*) join dependent clauses to main clauses.

> The bridesmaid wore a <u>dress</u> trimmed with lace<u>, and pearls</u>.
>
> The bridesmaid wore <u>a dress trimmed with lace and pearls</u>.

In the first sentence, she wore a lace-trimmed dress and a string of pearls. In the second, her dress was trimmed with both lace and pearls.

Between adjectives of equal weight not linked by *and*.

> The cage was filled with <u>angry, snarling</u> lions.
>
> I have to edit two <u>equally technical, 30-page</u> reports.

Both *angry* and *snarling* independently modify *lions*, so a comma is necessary. Both *equally technical* and *30-page* modify *reports*, so a comma is necessary.

> She wore a <u>pale pink</u> dress to the graduation.

Pale modifies *pink*, not *dress*, so these two words shouldn't be separated by a comma.

The Copyeditor's Guide to **Substance**&*Style*

Before and after nonrestrictive clauses.

Persons with disabilities, who still face discrimination, must have an equal chance to succeed in the working world.

The cover, which was designed by our staff, is riveting.

Remember that restrictive clauses don't use commas (see Chapter 9).

Children who have talents should be allowed to develop them.

Miscellaneous. Use commas in the following situations.

1. After exclamations such as *Oh* or *Yes*.

   Oh, dear, what can the matter be?

   Yes, I will go right away.

2. Before *of* when it denotes a place of residence.

   The speaker was Patrick Henry, of Virginia.

3. After digits that denote thousands, millions, billions....

   1,500   33,000   66,000,000

For five-digit numbers, most style guides advocate a comma; for four-digit ones, some styles omit it.

As you edit, watch for comma splices, characterized by the separation of two main clauses by a comma alone, with no coordinating conjunction such as *but* or *and*.

Wrong: I went down to the Lincoln Memorial, it was beautiful at night.

This is also called a run-on sentence, and it requires a conjunction or a semicolon.

I went down to the Lincoln Memorial, and it was beautiful at night.

I went down to the Lincoln Memorial; it was beautiful at night.

Apostrophes

The use of the apostrophe is a complicated issue. Every good style guide contains instructions on how to handle particular situations; dictionaries also offer solutions to issues such as *traveler's checks, user's manual, writer's cramp, teachers college, Teamsters Union,* and *the Court of St. James's.*

Apostrophes show the possessive case of nouns or the omission of a letter or letters. Some styles use apostrophes to denote plural letters, figures, and symbols.

Some styles add *'s* to singular nouns ending in *s* or an *s* sound; others add only an apostrophe, or leave it off altogether, treating the proper noun as an adjective.

the hostess's invitation	Dickens's works
the hostess' invitation	Dickens' works
Charles's house	the Davises' cat
Charles' house	the Davis cat
Congress's resolution	Berlioz's symphony
Congress' resolution	a Berlioz symphony

Plural nouns not ending in *s* or an *s* sound form the possessive by adding *'s.*

children's clothing

men's clothing

women's clothing

The possessive case of plural nouns ending in *s* is formed by adding an apostrophe after the final *s.*

the Adamses' house

the kittens' claws

For the treatment of plural letters, figures, and symbols, check your style manual for specified usage. Most agree on the need for apostrophes in the following examples.

P's and Q's	x's and y's
a's and b's	N's and n's
M.A.'s and Ph.D.'s	

Style guides disagree on the following:

the 1960s	most HMOs pay
the 1960's	most HMO's pay

Colons

A colon is used to introduce, supplement, explain, or add something to a sentence. A complete sentence should precede a colon.

> Only one course was open to the president: to fire the secretary.

> Everything was ready: The audience was in place, the lights were dimmed, and the orchestra began.

Some style guides capitalize the word following a colon if it introduces a complete sentence.

A colon is often used to introduce a list. Again, it should be preceded by a complete sentence.

> We will discuss the following types of problems:
> - Poor planning
> - Sporadic communication
> - Defective parts

Semicolons

Because the semicolon shows a more definite break in thought than a comma does, the semicolon is "stronger."

1. Use a semicolon between independent clauses when the conjunction is omitted.

> I'm going to the pool; I'll be back at 6 o'clock.

> Claire is president of the company; Robin and Andrea, vice presidents.

2. Use a semicolon to separate independent clauses joined by conjunctive adverbs (those used to connect main clauses).

> Being a volunteer at the hospital isn't easy; however, it's challenging and rewarding.

> That child refuses to do any work for the class; therefore, he's failing.

The most common conjunctive adverbs are the following: *accordingly, also, consequently, furthermore, hence, however, moreover, nevertheless, otherwise, still, therefore,* and *thus.*

3. Use a semicolon to separate items in a series when at least one of them already contains a comma.

> This plane will stop in Denver, Colorado; Kansas City, Kansas; Atlanta, Georgia; and Orlando, Florida.

Using commas alone would make this sentence very confusing; semicolons set each unit apart.

Also use a semicolon to separate elements of a series that are too long or complex for commas.

> Parking spaces reserved for persons with disabilities should be as close as possible to building entrances; curbs in the route of travel should have curb cuts or ramps; and all walks should be level.

Quotation Marks

The chief copyediting question with regard to quotation marks is their relation to other kinds of punctuation.

1. Put a comma or period inside the closing quotation mark.

> "I'm leaving now," she said.

> He replied, "See you later."

2. Put a colon or a semicolon outside the closing quotation mark, unless it's part of the quotation.

> The first topic was "Financing a College Education"; the second was "How to Choose a College."

The Copyeditor's Guide to **Substance***&Style*

Those are the rules; at first glance, they don't seem very logical. According to an apocryphal tale, in the old days of movable type, periods and commas would break off, and so they were put inside the quotation marks to protect them. Colons and semicolons didn't break off and so were put outside. That explanation is as good as any other.

Note that some style guides—and British English—distinguish between quoted words and whole sentences or clauses. For example, look at the following.

> She decided to avoid these "friends".

Logically, such a distinction is defensible; grammatically, it isn't, at least in the United States. One of the few hard-and-fast rules of American English is that commas and periods go inside closing quotation marks; semicolons and colons don't.

For question marks and exclamation points, the rules are more complicated. An exclamation point or a question mark goes inside the closing quotation marks if the punctuation was part of the original quotation; otherwise, it goes outside.

> He asked, "Are you afraid?"

> Did you reply, "Yes, I am"?

In the first example, the quotation is indeed a question, so the question mark goes inside the marks. In the second, however, the quotation is a declarative sentence that's part of a question. The question mark isn't part of the original quotation and goes outside the marks.

As for exclamation points, consider these sentences.

> She screamed, "No, never!"

> Some "friend"!

In the second example, the whole sentence is exclamatory, not just the word inside the quotation marks. The exclamation point therefore goes outside the marks.

Parentheses

Parentheses are often used to enclose asides or additional information.

> The results of the survey (see appendix A) demonstrate this dichotomy clearly.

In a list format, a single parenthesis is sometimes used. Many style guides don't permit the single parenthesis in any list format. Some prefer the use of bullets to numbers or letters when no ranking among the elements is intended.

> The flow sheet should include
> - the name of the project,
> - the name of the manager,
> - the deadline for the deliverable, and
> - the specifications.

Such a list presented within a sentence, however, is clearer if two parentheses are used.

> The flow sheet should include (a) the name of the project, (b) the name of the manager, (c) the deadline for the deliverable, and (d) the specifications.

Brackets

Brackets are used to enclose words in a quotation that weren't in the original and to give stage directions in a play, among other things.

> He said, "Once upon a midnight dreary [and here he paused for effect] While I pondered weak and weary,"

> The Ghost: [fading away] Remember what I told you.

Brackets may also be used as parentheses within parentheses.

> (The author also notes [pages 3–6] that Lincoln suffered from depression.)

Authors often use the bracketed word [sic], which means *thus* in Latin, to indicate that they're reproducing the speaker's words exactly, grammatical mistakes, misspellings, and all. Essentially, to use [sic] is to insert a disclaimer.

Hyphens

The use of hyphens and dashes is largely governed by style. In addition to being used to divide a word between syllables at the end of a line, the hyphen (-) is used to form compound words. The first function is self-evident; the second isn't. Many compound words are found in the dictionary: coat-of-arms, make-believe, great-aunt, and so on. Moreover, numbers between twenty-one and ninety-nine are hyphenated. (There's no simple rule for fractions that are spelled out.) Within these rules, however, is an enormous gray area.

Unit modifiers are hyphenated when they precede a noun, but not when they follow the verb as a predicate adjective.

> Garfield is a well-fed cat.

> Garfield is well fed.

In the second example, no noun follows for *well fed* to modify, so it isn't hyphenated. For compounding, it's always wise to check your dictionary. If a word is hyphenated there, it should be hyphenated wherever it's used in a sentence.

Style rules govern hyphens used with prefixes and suffixes. The use of hyphens sends copyeditors to the dictionary and style guide perhaps more often than any other question.

Dashes

Dashes come in two sizes—em-dashes (as in this sentence) and en-dashes. Their names come from typesetting terminology: the em dash is as long as the letter *m* is wide; the en dash is as long as the letter *n* is wide. In most fonts, the en dash is slightly longer than the hyphen. When manuscripts were produced on typewriters, two hyphens were used to represent an em dash. Today, the default setting on most word processing programs automatically converts two hyphens to an em dash. Most styles call for dashes to be "bumped up"—in other words, to have no space between the dash and the words it follows or precedes.

Em-dashes in a sentence show that there's an abrupt change in thought.

> He said—and I think he was wrong—that history would vindicate him.

> Everyone in the class—students and teachers—appreciated the joke.

In the second example, you might be tempted to use commas, because the phrase *students and teachers* is in apposition (explains what precedes it).

> Everyone in the class, students and teachers, appreciated the joke.

Here, however, the commas can be misread as serial commas, so dashes make the meaning clearer.

The main use of en-dashes is in ranges of numbers to indicate *to* or *through*. En-dashes often appear in tables, references, bibliographies, and indexes, but not usually in text except in parenthetical references.

Although style guides vary, most specify the use of en-dashes in these two cases:

1. Use en-dashes when all elements are figures (numerals).

    $15–$20 (note that the $ sign must be repeated; in text, use *from $15 to $20*)

    Public Law 85–1

    pp. 38–45

    chapters 6–12

    John 4:3–6

    1939–45 (in text, *from 1939 to 1945*, unless used as a unit modifier: *the 1939–45 war*)

2. Use en-dashes when all elements are letters (but not words).

    WXYZ–AM–FM–TV

    AFL–CIO

In Exercise 20, apply what you've learned so far. Some of the hyphens shown there should remain as hyphens, and some should appear as em- or en-dashes.

The style issues alluded to in this chapter, especially those relating to apostrophes, commas, and hyphens, are further discussed in Chapter 3.

Punctuation consists of both grammatical rules and style issues, but most marks are governed by the rules found in any grammar book. As an editor, you must know these rules so well that placing punctuation marks is second nature to you. When you have so many other things to think about, proper punctuation must be automatic.

You must know not only what to do, but also why. If you can't give a reason, you won't be able to defend your choices.

The style issues alluded to in this chapter, especially those relating to apostrophes, commas, and hyphens, are further discussed in Chapter 11.

Exercise 20: Punctuation

Instructions: Punctuate the following sentences.

1. Our plans unfortunately suffered a setback

2. Unfortunately our plans suffered a setback

3. Id like a Greek salad with extra feta cheese and coffee

4. If you want to argue with your father not me

5. Thomas Jeffersons home Monticello is located near the town of Charlottesville Virginia

6. Children dont fight like that said Mother

7. On July 4 1776 the members of the Continental Congress signed the Declaration of Independence in Philadelphia

8. We grow eight vegetables in our garden tomatoes peppers lettuce beans cucumbers spinach radishes and carrots

9. Youre free to do as you like however what you propose will cost more money

10. She said I refuse

11. My niece whos visiting from Boston is a vegetarian

12. After the soccer game is over the team is going to Martys to celebrate

13. She slept late on Sunday morning therefore she was late for church

14. My son who refuses to take music lessons plays by ear

15. The secretaries desks were all unoccupied because of the strike

16. He said and I agreed with him that there was no time to lose

17. I didnt feel comfortable calling her Peanuts

18. Fortunately Lee this project wont be due for weeks

19. Did he say I will not go

20. My father always said Theres no fool like an old fool

Exercise 20 Answers

1. Our plans, unfortunately, suffered a setback.

   The word *unfortunately* is traditionally set off by commas. If your style follows current trends and you omit the commas, be sure to omit both of them.

2. Unfortunately, our plans suffered a setback.

   If you choose (or your style dictates) the omission of the comma after *unfortunately*, delete the comma consistently throughout the manuscript whenever there is an introductory adverb.

3. I'd like a Greek salad with extra feta cheese, and coffee.

   The apostrophe, of course, belongs with the contraction *I'd*. The comma after *cheese* can't be omitted; otherwise, you'll have coffee in your Greek salad.

4. If you want to argue with your father, not me.

   Depending on the context, this clause could be a sentence fragment, but it does make sense if you punctuate it as shown here. Both commas are necessary for clarity.

5. Thomas Jefferson's home, Monticello, is located near the town of Charlottesville, Virginia.

   Monticello must be set off by commas because it's in apposition. The apostrophe in *Jefferson's* indicates possession, and the comma after *Charlottesville* shows that *Virginia* is also in apposition.

6. "Children don't fight like that," said Mother.

   This sentence is ambiguous. As a simple declarative sentence, the punctuation shown above is correct. The apostrophe marks the contraction, and the comma goes inside the quotation marks.

But you could read the sentence as an admonition.

"Children, don't fight like that!" said Mother.

Children is set off by a comma because it's a form of direct address; the statement ends with an exclamation point inside the quotation mark because it goes with what was quoted. If the context doesn't tell you which interpretation is meant, query the author.

7. On July 4, 1776, the members of the Continental Congress signed the Declaration of Independence in Philadelphia.

Again, the commas come in pairs. Although the second one is often left out, the omission is incorrect.

8. We grow eight vegetables in our garden: tomatoes, peppers, lettuce, beans, cucumbers, spinach, radishes, and carrots.

The colon is correct here; what precedes it is a complete sentence, and what follows it explains or adds to the statement. Commas are sufficient to separate the items in the series. Remember that the last comma—the one that precedes *and*—can be omitted according to some style guides. And did you count to make sure that eight vegetables were listed?

9. You're free to do as you like; however, what you propose will cost more money.

The apostrophe marks the contraction, and the semicolon precedes the conjunctive adverb *however*, which is also set off by a comma.

10. She said, I refuse!

The exclamation point is part of the quotation, so it goes inside the marks. A comma, not a colon, precedes the quotation.

Exercise 20 Answers, continued

11. My niece whos visiting from Boston is a vegetarian

    The apostrophe marks the contraction for *who is*. If two nieces were visiting at the same time—one from Boston and one from New York—the clause would be restrictive and wouldn't be set off by any punctuation at all.

    > My niece who's visiting from Boston is a vegetarian. My niece who's visiting from New York loves to eat meat.

12. After the soccer game is over the team is going to Martys to celebrate

    The comma after *over* helps clarify a sentence that has an introductory adverbial clause longer than a few words. The apostrophe is necessary to indicate the possessive, whatever sort of place Marty's might be (house, restaurant).

13. She slept late on Sunday morning therefore she was late for church

    The conjunctive adverb *therefore* is preceded by a semicolon and followed by a comma.

14. My son who refuses to take music lessons plays by ear

    Putting commas around the clause (as shown here) makes it nonrestrictive; the information inside the commas becomes almost parenthetical. The implication is that the writer has only one son and that his refusal is not needed to distinguish him from other sons.

    > My son who refuses to take music lessons plays by ear.

    Without commas, the clause is restrictive. The refusal identifies a particular son, the one who refuses to take music lessons, as opposed to the one who doesn't refuse.

15. The secretaries desks were all unoccupied because of the strike

    Indicate the plural possessive with an apostrophe following the *s*.

Exercise 20 Answers, continued

16. He said, and I agreed with him, that there was no time to lose.

    The parenthetical clause *and I agreed with him* needs to be set off by commas. Dashes could be used instead if you prefer. (See the following section.)

17. I didn't feel comfortable calling her "Peanuts."

    Be sure you add the apostrophe and that your closing quotation mark is outside the period.

18. Fortunately, Lee, this project won't be due for weeks.

    Lee is a form of direct address, set off by commas, both of which are necessary, and the apostrophe marks the contraction.

19. Did he say, "I will not go"?

    Here, the question mark goes outside, because it applies to the whole sentence. The quotation itself is a simple assertion.

20. My father always said, "There's no fool like an old fool."

    The direct quotation is preceded by a comma and the period, which applies to the whole sentence, falls inside the closing quotation mark. The apostrophe marks the contraction.

The Copyeditor's Guide to **Substance**&*Style*

Exercise 21:
Hyphens and Dashes

Instructions: According to the preceding rules, should the hyphens in the following sentences be hyphens, em-dashes, or en-dashes? Mark them all as follows.

If the hyphen should remain a hyphen, use ⁻.

If the hyphen should be an em-dash, use ⟋ₘ.

If the hyphen should be an en-dash, use ⟋ₙ.

1. The vice-presidency, he said-and no one contradicted him-is up for grabs in the next election.

2. The entire staff worked on the AFL-CIO report (chapters 6-12).

3. Long-term loans-although in small amounts ($10,000-$20,000)-have provided working capital for the small businesses of the area.

4. For a free copy of Questionnaire 3-C, write to 987-A North Main Street.

5. Is the web-footed, gray-billed platypus olive-green?

1. The vice-presidency, he said—and no one contradicted him—is up for grabs in the next election.

2. The entire staff worked on the AFL-CIO report (chapters 6–12).

3. Long-term loans—although in small amounts ($10,000–$20,000)—have provided working capital for the small businesses of the area.

4. For a free copy of Questionnaire 3-C, write to 987-A North Main Street.

5. Is the web-footed, gray-billed platypus olive-green?

EDITORIAL STYLE:
Manuals and Word Lists

In the editorial sense, style consists of those issues that are not governed by grammar—decisions about which editors may have a choice. Editors must first know the difference between style questions and rules of grammar and then use a manual to resolve style questions: No editor should ever expect to function without a style manual and dictionary.

There is no one universal style manual. Many organizations have developed their own formal or informal style guides to answer questions particular to their situations. For book publishers, the most widely used general style manuals are *The Chicago Manual of Style (Chicago)* and the *United States Government Printing Office Style Manual (GPO)*. In 1994, HarperCollins published the *New York Public Library Writer's Guide to Style and Usage*, written by EEI staff, with the intent of offering a guide for business and technical writers and editors. Newspapers have style manuals as well, such as *The Associated Press Stylebook and Libel Manual (AP), The New York Times Manual of Style and Usage,* and *The Washington Post Deskbook on Style.* Finally, organizations often develop their own style guides, some of which move into wider use. Among these are the *Publication Manual of the American Psychological Association (APA)*; the *American Medical Association Manual of Style (AMA)*; and *The ACS Style Guide*, published by the American Chemical Society. Each is used by numerous publishers in their respective fields.

The GPO Style Manual began as a guide for printers, so many of the questions it treats in detail may seem irrelevant to editors. The focus of the manual has shifted over the years, but it has never lost sight of its origins. A helpful spelling and compounding guide is *Word Division, Supplement to GPO Style Manual,* which was developed to aid printers in breaking words at the ends of lines.

The hallmark of a good copyeditor is consistency in the treatment of these basic elements of style.

abbreviations and acronyms	*U.S.* or *US; V.I.S.T.A.* or *VISTA*
alphabetization	*McBride, Malone* or *Malone, McBride*
capitalization	*Federal* or *federal*
citations	*Smith, Jones, and Scott 1988* or *Smith, Jones, & Scott, 1988* or *Smith et al. 1988*
compounding	*co-worker* or *coworker; vice-president* or *vice president*
italics	"Light in August" or *Light in August*
numbers	*ten apples or 10 apples*
punctuation	*apples, oranges, and bananas* or *apples, oranges and bananas*
spelling	*judgment or judgement*

Abbreviations and acronyms can appear with periods (*M.I.T.*) or without (*NASA*); uppercase (*AM*), small caps (*AM*), or lowercase (*am*); long (*Calif.*) or short (*CA*).

Alphabetization appears to be straightforward, but do you alphabetize word by word or letter by letter (ignoring word breaks)? Does *McBride* precede *Malone*? If no method is specified, you can ask your client or your supervisor, or you can look to see how the index in your style manual is alphabetized and follow its pattern.

Capitalization also appears relatively straightforward, but it isn't. Proper names should always be capitalized. *GPO* capitalizes any term referring to the federal government, the planets, and celestial bodies. But what about terms such as *french-fried potatoes* and *roman numerals*? The same word may be capitalized or lowercase depending on context ("We were driving west" vs. "The United States is the leader of the West").

Citations are governed by style. *APA* and *Chicago*, which are relatively academic guides, list extensive rules for notes and references, while *GPO* has no specific style for citations other than an admonition to be consistent, and *AP* does not mention the topic at all.

Compounding refers to the presence or absence of hyphens in compound words such as *decision maker*, *fire tested*, *vice president*, and *well known*. Each style guide gives detailed (often quite complex) rules on compounding. Note that a word may be compounded differently depending on its use as a noun, verb, predicate adjective, or unit modifier—for example, *run-down* as a noun and unit modifier, but *run down* as a verb and predicate adjective.

Italics may be used used for titles of compositions such as books and magazines, the names of ships and aircraft, and foreign words. The rules differ from manual to manual.

Numbers should always send you to your style guide. When do you use figures and when do you use words? The only general rule is that a number as the first word in a sentence is nearly always spelled out. Special rules govern usage when several numbers appear in the same sentence or paragraph, and style guides diverge widely.

Punctuation rules, especially those dealing with serial commas and introductory colons, also vary among guides. And the appearance of diacritical marks in foreign words (tilde in *mañana*, umlaut in *fräulein*) varies extensively as well.

Spelling refers to the choices you make among correct alternatives (*gray* or *grey*). *Merriam-Webster's Collegiate*, the abridgment of *Webster's Third New International Dictionary*, is the authority for most style guides. Other guides may specify other dictionaries, such as *Webster's New World Dictionary*, favored by several of the journalistic style manuals. If no dictionary is specified, ask your client or supervisor.

GPO contains extensive lists showing spelling, compounding, and capitalization examples. The latest edition of the manual, published in 2000, eliminated many of the odd spellings that used to set *GPO* style apart. *Align*, *gauge*, *subpoena*, and *marijuana* have replaced *aline*, *gage*, *subpena*, and *marihuana*. Nevertheless, some unusual spellings remain; when in doubt, look up the word.

If you edit for an organization that doesn't use a style manual, you may propose creating a house style. It can be as simple as a list of terms that are always used, spelled, and capitalized a certain way, with the statement, "For other style questions, see [title of published style manual]." Creating a more comprehensive house style should be a team effort. Try to ensure that representatives from all departments have input. Not only will the style guide be more complete, but people will be more apt to use it. As style issues arise that aren't covered by the house style, keep a record of them, and be prepared to update the house style periodically.

Style manuals exist to eliminate inconsistencies that can detract from the quality of a publication and distract the reader. If no style manual is specified, compile your own style sheet or word list to help you remember the choices you made and to note those choices for others who may work on the manuscript. As you see words that can be treated in more than one way, write down your choice. Also note each acronym with its equivalent and the page number on which it first appears. That way you can tell at a glance whether a full name has been spelled out before (and how far back in the manuscript). By the time you get to page 222, you won't remember whether the acronym was spelled out on page 17.

The search-and-replace function of word processing software is no substitute for a style sheet; to be able to search, you have to know what to search for. It's very difficult to remember every word or issue about which you made a choice while editing a long manuscript.

There's no one way to compile a style sheet. Some editors prefer to list their choices alphabetically, while others use categories (abbreviations, capitalization, punctuation, and so on). Do whatever works best for you or for the particular manuscript.

A sample style sheet follows. (Abbreviations: n = noun; um = unit modifier; adv = adverb; v = verb)

SAMPLE STYLE SHEET

online		de-fueled	
aboveground	um	Federal	
acid fueling	um	fence line	um,n
air monitoring	um	fieldwork	n
anticorrosion		Former Nike SL-10	
Atterberg limits		Launch Area property	
backup	n	fourth-quarter	um
borehole	n	groundwater	n,um
buildup	n	groundwater-monitoring	um
built-up	um	hard-copy	um
chain link fence		I-55	
city of St. Louis		Incident Number	
cleanup	n	in house	adv
colocated		in-line	um
county of Allegheny		intrasite	
cross-contamination		job site	n
data-qualifying	um	launch pad	um,n
decision making	n	logbook	

SAMPLE STYLE SHEET, continued

low-flow sampling techniques
make-up   n
metals-contaminated   um
Nike site, but Nike Site SL-10
non (close up)
nonfunctioning
off-site   adv
on-site   adv,
                                  um

Orphan Site
post-digestion spike
precleaned
predate   v
pre-operation   n
QA department
reacquire
reanalysis
record-keeping um
re-evaluation
reoccurrence
reuse
runoff   n
semi-annually
site logbook
Site Review
small-arms   um
solid waste   um
standby
startup   n
State
surface water drainages
TACO tier 2 evaluation
TACO Tier 1 Objective
tiedown   n
U.S. Army
washdown   n
wash tub   n
washout   n
wastewater   um
water-level   um
workday   n

workplace
Work Plan

Boiler House
Production Building
Water Treatment Building
Lime House

Numbers
one-nine, 10 up
numerals for measurements

Misc.
order by year for citations, reference
    entries [earliest to most recent]
11 June 1971
DACA27-98-D-0031, Delivery Order
    0008
Engineering Manual 200-1-3,
    *Requirements for the Preparation
    of Sampling and Analysis Plans*
ground fault circuit interrupter
(217) 782-3397
Bange Rd.

terms: italicize
data: plural

Madison County Department of Public
    Works and Sheriff's Department
No Defense Action Indicated
Preliminary Assessment

Acronyms not preceded by The:
TACO
DPCFPD
IEPA
ARDL

Acronyms preceded by The:
USACE
USARC

Also, except in very informal circumstances, you should submit a cover memo with each edited manuscript and keep a copy of the memo yourself. It should explain in both general and specific terms what you've done to the manuscript—the tasks performed (edited for grammar, consistency, and style), the problems encountered, and the major changes made. A query sheet, listing any specific questions, should accompany the cover memo. Questions should be tactfully phrased and clear, both in the memo and in the text (if they appear there as well). A sample memo follows.

SAMPLE COVER MEMO

May 31, 2006

TO: Author

FROM: Editor

RE: Status of AFL–CIO Manuscript

I enjoyed working on your book. Per instructions, I have edited for spelling, punctuation, grammar, and conformity to the style sheet I was given.

Here are my queries:

Page	Paragraph	Query
3	2	Where does the direct quotation end?
20	1	What is the antecedent of it?
25	1	Smith 2004 is not listed in the references.
40	3	Another example would be helpful here.
References		The following references are not cited in the text. Should they be deleted? Abrams 1999; Jane and McAdams 2004; Robertson 2003.

Please call me at 123-4567 if you have any questions or problems with what I have done.

Sometimes the list of queries will be extensive, especially if there are many discrepancies in the citations. The manuscript may return to you after the author has answered the queries. Then you plug the holes, fill in the missing information, and check the changes to see that the author has approved them. In many cases, however, you'll never see the manuscript again; it moves on to the next stage in the production process.

The phrasing of queries will influence how well they are answered. Try to avoid simple "yes-or-no" questions. If, in an effort to get the author to rephrase a sentence more clearly, you ask, "Will readers understand this sentence?" the author may simply respond "Yes." In this situation, it might be better to edit the sentence to the best of your ability, then query "Edit okay? Is this the meaning?" A "yes" answer to this question is just fine; an author who disagrees with your edit is more likely to rewrite the sentence.

After writing your memo and query list, review them. What could be more humiliating than making a typo or a grammatical error here? And remember, this is no place to display your wit. Never be sarcastic or hostile in communicating with an author. Eliminate the pronoun "you," which conveys an accusatory tone. Instead of writing, "On page 77, you say there are 12 candidates for EU membership; here, you say there are 11. Which is correct?" write, "Page 77 says there are 12 candidates for EU membership; this page says there are 11. Which is correct?"

Style guides vary enormously; to help pinpoint the differences among them, the matrix starting on page 168 shows how different guides treat several subjects. This matrix is by no means exhaustive; some of these subjects are extremely complex and don't lend themselves to distillation. Study the matrix and then use it to work Exercise 22.

For a while, you'll have to look everything up, but as you become familiar with a particular guide, you'll learn to make many of the correct choices instinctively. If you've been using one style guide for some time and then have to use a different one, you'll have to go back to looking things up for a while until you shift mental gears.

The Chicago Manual of Style (Chicago) (15th Edition, 2003)	United States Government Printing Office Style Manual (GPO) (2000)

Abbreviations

Gives extensive listing of rules and examples; recommends omission of most abbreviations in running text (except technical matter); general: period in lowercase abbreviations, no period in caps, no preferences for state names.

Gives extensive listing of rules and examples; uses abbreviations to save space and eliminate repetition; uses periods with standard word abbreviations like *St.* and *U.S.*; doesn't use periods with units of measure or state abbreviations; prefers Postal Service abbreviations (*VA*) for state names.

Acronyms

Set in all caps without periods.

Uses acronyms with no periods; extensive list in chapter on capitalization.

Alphabetization

Prefers letter-by-letter method for most books (alphabetize up to the first mark of punctuation), but accepts word-by-word system (alphabetize up to the end of the first word).

Not covered.

Capitalization

Capitalizes proper nouns and trademarks and trade names, titles (except when used alone or in apposition, as in *Seward, the secretary of state*), and some cultural movements, awards, and so on; except in titles of works, doesn't capitalize after a colon if the second clause illustrates or amplifies the first; lowercases all forms of government (*federal*, *state*, and *local*); capitalizes proper (not descriptive) geographic and structural names, including *Capitol* and *Washington Monument*; in titles of works, capitalizes the first and last words and all nouns, pronouns, adjectives, verbs, adverbs, and subordinating conjunctions (e.g., *if*, *as*, *that*) but lowercases articles, coordinating conjunctions, and prefers "down" style of fewer caps; lowercases prepositions unless stressed or used adverbially, adjectivally or as conjunctions; always lowercases *to* and *as*; doesn't capitalize chapter references in text.

Capitalizes proper nouns and trade and brand names, titles of persons before (and sometimes after) the name; capitalizes the first word of a main clause following a colon; capitalizes words relating to the *Federal Government* and governments of the *50 States* (but not localities); capitalizes geographic and structural names, including *Capitol* and *Washington Monument*; capitalizes first and important words in titles; doesn't capitalize chapter references if no title follows.

The Copyeditor's Guide to **Substance**&*Style*

Restricts use of abbreviations to those that are conventional, familiar, and helpful; prefers few in text; spells out abbreviated terms on first appearance, immediately followed by the abbreviation in parentheses, which is used exclusively thereafter; abbreviations accepted as words by *Merriam-Webster's Collegiate Dictionary* can be used without spelling out; Latin abbreviations (*i.e.*) may be used only parenthetically; uses English translations (*that is*) in text; uses periods with Latin abbreviations; doesn't use periods for measures (except *in.*) or capital-letter abbreviations (*APA*); prefers Postal Service abbreviations (*VA*) for states in reference lists.	Provides most entries under individual listings; uses familiar abbreviations or acronyms that should not be placed in parentheses immediately after their full names; recognized groups (*FBI*) may be identified fully at first reference or not at all; follows manual or first-listed abbreviation in *Webster's New World Dictionary* for use of caps and periods, and for abbreviations not listed, uses caps and omits periods; uses *a.m.* and *p.m.*; prefers traditional abbreviations (*Va.*) for state names, except for eight states that are never abbreviated.
Uses acronyms with no periods.	Usually omits periods; see individual listings.
Alphabetizes reference list letter by letter.	Not covered.
Capitalizes proper nouns and trade and brand names, but not names of laws, theories, or hypotheses; capitalizes the first word following a colon in a title and the first word of an independent clause; capitalizes *Day 2*, *Trial 5*, *Figure 2*, but not *chapter 3* or *page 72*; capitalizes the first word, all major words, and all words of four letters or more in titles except in reference list; capitalizes both words of a hyphenated compound in titles; doesn't address items such as government or geography.	Prefers lowercase in general; capitalizes proper nouns and trade and brand names; capitalizes formal titles used immediately before a name; lowercases those that are job descriptions; lowercases words derived from proper nouns that don't depend on the original for meaning (*roman numerals*); lowercases all forms of government (*federal*, *state*, and *local*); capitalizes geographic and structural names, including *Capitol* and *Washington Monument*; in titles of works, capitalizes the first, last, and all major words and prepositions and conjunctions of four or more letters; capitalizes the first word after a colon only if an independent clause follows; if no individual listing, check *Webster's New World Dictionary* and use the lowercase form if given.

The Chicago Manual of Style (Chicago) (15th Edition, 2003)	**United States Government Printing Office Style Manual (GPO) (2000)**

Citations

Sets forth two basic systems: author-date and notes-bibliography. Recommends author-date citations in text for most natural science and social science manuscripts; presents extensive discussions and examples.

Says only that many styles are acceptable; lists some examples.

Compounding

States that most questions are answered by an unabridged dictionary; offers general principles and an expanded table of examples; hyphenates most unit modifiers; doesn't hyphenate most common prefixes (such as *mini*, *non*, *pre*, *post*), except for compounds in which the second element is a capitalized word or numeral, those that must be distinguished from similar words (re-cover), and those in which the second element has more than one word.

Doesn't use hyphens in most words with combining forms, suffixes, and prefixes, including those beginning with *anti*, *multi*, *non*, and *pre*; exceptions include unit modifiers, some prefixes and suffixes (*ex*, *quasi*, *self*), compounds with proper nouns or adjectives, duplicated prefixes, compound numbers, chemical elements, and improvised compounds.

Italic Type

Recommends limited use for emphasis; uses italics for foreign words, except those that have passed into English; key terms at first mention; letters (in some cases); legal case names; genera, varieties, species, and mathematical letters; theorems and proofs; and titles of literary works, periodicals, newspapers, movies, television shows, some musical compositions, and works of art.

Decries overuse of italics and doesn't use for emphasis, foreign words, technical or key terms, or titles of publications (unless specifically requested). Does use italics for letters; indexes. See legal case names (except the v.); genera, species, and varieties; and mathematical symbols, theorems, and proofs.

The Copyeditor's Guide to **Substance**&*Style*

Publication Manual of the American Psychological Association (APA) (Fifth Edition, 2001)	The Associated Press Stylebook and Libel Manual (AP) (2004)
Offers a style; presents an extensive discussion similar to *Chicago*.	Not covered.
Asserts that most questions are answered by the dictionary (*Merriam-Webster's Collegiate* preferred) except technical language questions; for those that aren't, hyphenates "purposefully" for clarity, especially unit modifiers; most common prefixes aren't followed by hyphens; doesn't hyphenate compounds that aren't misleading (*grade point average*).	Uses hyphens to avoid ambiguity; hyphenates unit modifiers, two-thought compounds (like *socio-economic*), some prefixes and suffixes (especially to avoid duplicated vowels and tripled consonants—consult individual entries), compound proper nouns and adjectives; hyphenates modifiers that occur after the verb to be (*He is well-known*) and some numbers and fractions.
Recommends infrequent use; uses italics for [*sic*] and to introduce new technical and key terms; letters as symbols; legal case names in text; genera, species, and varieties; mathematical symbols and algebraic variables; volume numbers in reference lists; words used as examples; and titles of books and periodicals. Doesn't use italics for Greek letters, nonstatistical subscripts, commonly used foreign words, or trigonometric terms.	Italics, emphasis, etc., not listed in the manual; "composition titles" entry recommends quotation marks to set off names of books (except the Bible and reference books, catalogs, and directories), movies, television shows, works of art, poetry, and speeches. Doesn't use quotation marks with names of newspapers and magazines.

Numbers

Spells out whole numbers under 100; treats numbers that are part of the same category the same way within the same paragraph—consistency should rule; expresses fractions less than one in words (*two-thirds*) and sometimes uses figures and words for large numbers starting with million; in scientific and other technical text only, uses figures for physical quantities, decimals, percentages, and (often) money; advises applying the same general rules to ordinal numbers; doesn't allow a sentence to begin with a figure; if the first word of a sentence must be a number, the words must be written out.

Spells out whole numbers under 10; if two or more numbers, one of which is more than nine, appear in a sentence, all numbers in that sentence should be figures, unless the number over nine is a unit of time, money, or measurement; always uses figures for time, distance, money, measures, decimals, and percentages (even those under 10); advises applying the same general rules to ordinal numbers; expresses fractions less than one in words and uses figures and words for large numbers (*3 million*); doesn't allow a sentence to begin with a figure; if the first word of a sentence must be a number, the words must be written out.

Punctuation

Uses the serial comma and the en-dash; gives rules and examples for each mark of punctuation, doesn't use apostrophes with plurals of numbers or letters (*three Rs*), but does with abbreviations (*Ph.D.'s*); adds *'s* to all singular possessives (*Charles's*) except names with more than one syllable with an unaccented ending pronounced *eez* (*Euripides' plays*) and other exceptions. See the complicated discussion at 7.17–7.30.

Uses the serial comma and the en-dash; gives rules and examples for each mark of punctuation, to form the possessive of plural nouns ending in an *s* or *s* sound, adds only an apostrophe (*bosses'*); singular ending in *s* gets apostrophe and *s* (*boss's*).

Spelling

Recommends *Merriam-Webster's Collegiate Dictionary* and *Webster's Third New International*; uses the first spelling; gives general rules for plurals, proper names, compounds, word divisions, special terminology, and foreign words.

Recommends *Webster's Third New International* for words not listed in the manual; contains an extensive spelling list; treats plurals, diacritical marks, geographic names, and transliterations.

Spells out whole numbers under 10; treats numbers that are part of the same category the same way within the same paragraph—consistency should rule; always uses figures for statistical or mathematical functions (1st quartile), time, money, measures, decimals, and percentages (even those under 10) in the abstract of a paper; applies the same general rules to ordinal numbers; expresses fractions less than one in words (one fifth, but two-thirds majority) and uses figures and words for large numbers starting with million; doesn't allow a sentence to begin with a figure; if the first word of a sentence must be a number, the words must be written out.

Spells out whole numbers under 10 and follows that general rule even for two or more numbers in the same sentence; always uses figures for time, money, decimals, and percentages (even those under 10); advises applying the same general rules to ordinal numbers; expresses fractions less than one in words (*two-thirds*) and uses figures and words for large numbers (*3 million*); doesn't allow a sentence to begin with a figure; if the first word of a sentence must be a number, the words must be written out; the one exception is in the case of a year: *1066 was the year....*

Uses the serial comma; doesn't use an apostrophe with plurals of letters or numbers (*three Rs*); briefly discusses punctuation marks.

Doesn't use the serial comma; uses the apostrophe with plurals of a single letter (*three R's*), but not with plurals of numerals or multiple letters; to show possession, adds *'s* to singular common nouns ending in *s* unless the next word begins with an *s* (*the hostess's invitation, the hostess' seat*); adds only an apostrophe to singular proper names ending in *s*; doesn't add an apostrophe to words ending in *s* that are descriptive (*teachers college*); check the listing for each mark.

Recommends *Merriam-Webster's Collegiate Dictionary*—if the word isn't there, use *Webster's Third New International*; uses the first spelling; for compounds, see the dictionary and the manual's table of hyphenation for compound psychological terms (page 91).

Organized like a dictionary; for spelling, style, and usage questions not covered in the manual, consult *Webster's New World Dictionary*; uses the first spelling, unless a specific exception is noted in the manual.

Exercise 22: Style

Instructions: First pick a particular style—*Chicago*, *GPO*, *APA*, or *AP*. Working with the matrix in this chapter, copyedit the paragraph. Don't reword. Finally, check your version against the appropriate key.

Bridge from Town to Suburbs

Samuel Smith, the well known republican senator from the state of New

Illiana, announced today the allocation of $152,000,000.00 in federal funds

to build the long planned Smith bridge at the confluence of the Illiana and

Westering. The bridge will link the city of Inverness with the communities

of Robinwood, Georgeville and Five Corners and will route a badly needed

work force to Inverness's booming shale oil industry.

The Copyeditor's Guide to **Substance**&*Style*

Exercise 22 Answers

CHICAGO STYLE

Bridge from Town to Suburbs

Samuel Smith, the well-known republican senator from the state of New Illiana, announced today the allocation of $152 million ~~,000,000.00~~ in federal funds to build the long-planned Smith bridge at the confluence of the Illiana and Westering. The bridge will link the city of Inverness with the communities of Robinwood, Georgeville, and Five Corners and will route a badly needed work force to Inverness's booming shale oil industry.

GPO STYLE

Bridge from Town to Suburbs

Samuel Smith, the well-known republican senator from the state of New Illiana, announced today the allocation of $152 Million ~~,000,000.00~~ in federal funds to build the long planned Smith bridge at the confluence of the Illiana and Westering. The bridge will link the city of Inverness with the communities of Robinwood, Georgeville, and Five Corners and will route a badly needed work force to Inverness's booming shale oil industry.

Exercise 22 Answers, continued

APA STYLE

Bridge from Town to Suburbs

Samuel Smith, the well-known republican senator from the state of New Illiana, announced today the allocation of $152 million ~~000,000.00~~ in federal funds to build the long-planned Smith bridge at the confluence of the Illiana and Westering. The bridge will link the city of Inverness with the communities of Robinwood, Georgeville and Five Corners and will route a badly needed work force to Inverness's booming shale oil industry.

AP STYLE

Bridge from Town to Suburbs

Samuel Smith, the well-known republican senator from the state of New Illiana, announced today the allocation of $152 million ~~000,000.00~~ in federal funds to build the long-planned Smith bridge at the confluence of the Illiana and Westering. The bridge will link the city of Inverness with the communities of Robinwood, Georgeville and Five Corners and will route a badly needed work force to Inverness' booming shale oil industry.

The Copyeditor's Guide to **Substance**&*Style*

CONCISE LANGUAGE: 12
Or, A Rose by Any Other Name

Prose need not be pedestrian, but it must always be clear. Today, government offices, businesses, and consumer advocates are increasingly emphasizing the use of plain English instead of bureaucratese. Anyone who has ever waded through an insurance form or the instructions for preparing a tax return can only cheer.

This isn't to say that editors should vigorously excise all uncommon or erudite words from manuscripts. As an editor, you must watch nuances in the changes you're proposing. If an unusual word expresses the author's meaning and its everyday variant doesn't, you should respect the author's choice. If the text is awash in jargon and redundancy, however, you must help clarify meaning. Remember that each profession has its favorite words, its particular vocabulary, and its sacred cows. You can edit many of these words to enhance readability or to reach a larger audience and offend no one. But if there is the slightest ambiguity or doubt, either query or leave the words alone.

You'll make many judgment calls in the course of working on a manuscript, but you must always respect the integrity of the author's style. You must also consider the intended audience: A specialist writing for other specialists can use expressions that someone writing for a lay audience can't.

Noun Strings

What's familiarly called jargon often falls into the category of a noun string, a combination of nouns grouped together as if they were adjectives. Many phrases that began as noun strings have passed into common usage: *health maintenance organization* and *sample selection bias*, for example. Other strings, however, defy understanding.

> Oklahoma Natural Gas Company Employee Counseling Program Evaluation Model

> directed energy ordnance neutralization systems development

> physician group practice level quality

> community banking funds transfer risk management

Sometimes nouns and adjectives are strung together.

> Urban American Indian Adolescent Alcohol and Drug Abuse
> Research Center

> Spanish-speaking mental health resource center

Such strings create problems because you don't know until you get to the end of the string exactly what the author is talking about. Even then, you may not be sure. Consider the following example:

> paperwork reduction plan implementation meeting preparation

What seems to be the subject? The very last word? Preparation for what? A meeting.... What's the meeting for? Implementation of a paperwork reduction plan..., but even that phrase can be broken down further. Untie the noun string:

> preparation for a meeting to implement a plan to reduce paperwork

Note that the "untied" string is a few words longer than the original version. In such cases, it's false economy to sacrifice clarity for the sake of shortening the phrase slightly.

One way to attack noun strings is to start from the end and break them into manageable chunks. Wherever possible, turn nouns into verbs and insert prepositions and articles to make the meaning clearer and to define the relationship among the elements. Consider this string:

> computer spreadsheet program advance information

Again, go to the end; the last word is usually the subject of the phrase or clause. So the subject is *information* or rather *advance information*. Then deciphering the noun string becomes easy:

> advance information on spreadsheet programs for the computer

As you can see, noun strings are taxing and often frustrating for both the editor and the reader. Left uncorrected, noun strings obscure meaning and bog down the reader. Remember, though, that your interpretation of an ambiguous phrase may not conform to the author's. Unless you're certain of the meaning, query the author ["Edit okay?"] to be sure that you've correctly interpreted the thought.

Exercise 23:
Unpacking Noun Strings

Instructions: Try to make sense out of the sentences by turning smothered nouns into verbs, creating prepositional phrases, and breaking noun strings apart. For more practice, do Exercise 24.

1. Rapid operational equipment distribution is a strength of the new plan.

2. The plant safety standards committee discussed recent air quality regulation announcements.

3. This paper is an investigation into information processing behavior involved in computer human cognition simulation games.

4. Based on our extensive training needs assessment reviews and on selected office site visits, there was an identification of concepts and issues to constitute an initial staff questionnaire instrument.

5. Pancreatic gland motor phenomena are regulated chiefly by parasympathetic nervous system cells.

6. Diabetic patient blood pressure reduction may be a consequence of renal extract depressor agent application.

7. Corporation organization under state law supervision has resulted in federal government inability as to effective implementation of pollution reduction measures.

8. The end results of the evaluation will be furnished to the automotive parts item manager in the inventory control department.

Exercise 23 Answers

1. Rapid ~~operational~~ equipment distribution is a strength of the new plan. *(edited: "of" added, words rearranged)*

   Rapid distribution of operational equipment is a strength of the new plan.

   Adding a preposition and rearranging the words clarify the sentence enormously.

2. The plant safety standards committee discussed recent air quality regulations announcements about *(edited)*

   The plant safety standards committee discussed recent announcements about regulations on air quality.

   You now have a sentence that clearly delineates the relationship among the various elements.

0. This paper ~~is an investigation into~~ information processing behavior involved in computer human cognition ~~simulation games~~. *(edited: investigates how, is processed, in games where, computers simulate)*

   This paper investigates how information is processed in games where computers simulate human cognition.

   The sentence now flows better and is comprehensible.

4. ~~Based on our~~ extensive training needs ~~assessment~~ review and ~~on~~ selected office site visits, ~~there was an~~ identification ~~of concepts and~~ issues to include in ~~constitute~~ an initial staff questionnaire ~~instrument~~. *(edited: After an, of, we, to include in)*

   After an extensive review of training needs and visits to selected office sites, we identified the issues to include in an initial staff questionnaire.

   Some redundancies are gone now, and the sentence is in the active voice.

Exercise 23 Answers, continued

5. Pancreatic gland ~~motor phenomena~~ are regulated ~~chiefly by~~ parasympathetic nervous system ~~cells.~~ *the chief ors of the Cells of the*

Cells of the parasympathetic nervous system are the chief regulators of the pancreatic gland.

Remove both the passive voice and the noun strings. If, for some reason, you want to leave the sentence in the passive voice, you can still remove the noun strings as shown above.

6. Diabetic patient's blood pressure ~~reduction may be a consequence of~~ renal extract depressor ~~agent application.~~ *may reduce* *Applying a*

Applying a renal extract depressor may reduce a diabetic patient's blood pressure.

This solution eliminates many unnecessary words and pares the sentence down to a simpler, more understandable form.

7. ~~Corporation organization under~~ state law ~~supervision has resulted in~~ federal government ~~inability as to~~ effective~~ly~~ implementation ~~of~~ pollution reduction measures. *Because* *regulates the incorporation procedure, the* *cannot*

Because state law regulates the incorporation procedure, the federal government cannot effectively implement pollution reduction measures.

8. The ~~end~~ results of the evaluation ~~will be furnished to the~~ automotive parts item manager in the inventory control department. *require* *for*

The item manager for automotive parts in the inventory control department will receive the results of the evaluation.

Exercise 24:
Unpacking More Noun Strings

Instructions: Eliminate the noun strings from the following sentences. Also correct any other problems.

1. The project will benefit from computer programs advance information.

2. Your manning-level authorizations reassessment suggestion should lead to major improvements.

3. The regulation offers an explanation of Communication Center operations personnel training.

4. Enforcement of guidelines for new car model tire durability is a Federal Trade Commission responsibility.

5. The main goal of this article is to formulate narrative information extraction rules.

6. Determination of support appropriateness for community organization assistance need was precluded by difficulty in the acquisition of data relevant to a committee activity review.

Exercise 24 Answers

1. The project will benefit from ~~computer programs~~ advance information *on* ~~.~~

   The project will benefit from advance information on computer programs.

2. Your *suggestion to reassess* manning-level authorizations ~~reassessment suggestion~~ should lead to major improvements.

   Your suggestion to reassess manning-level authorizations should lead to major improvements.

3. The regulation ~~offers an~~ explanation *ins the training* of Communication Center operations personnel ~~training.~~

   The regulation explains the training of Communication Center operations personnel.

4. ~~Enforcement of~~ *ring* guidelines ~~for~~ new car ~~model~~ tire durability *on the durability of tires on* ~~is a~~ Federal Trade Commission *to* responsibility *is for* *The*

   The Federal Trade Commission is responsible for enforcing guidelines on the durability of tires on new cars.

5. ~~The main goal of~~ this article *aims* ~~is~~ to formulate *rules to* narrative information ~~extraction rules.~~

   This article aims to formulate rules to extract narrative information.

6. Determin ~~ation~~ *ing* *an* ~~of support~~ appropriate ~~ness~~ *level of support* for community organization *s* ~~assistance need was precluded by~~ *not possible because of* difficulty in ~~the~~ acquisi ~~tion of~~ *ring* *relevant* data ~~relevant to a~~ *for the* committee ~~activity~~ *to* review.

   Determining an appropriate level of support for community organizations was not possible because of difficulty in acquiring relevant data for the committee to review.

Replaceable Words and Phrases

Wherever possible, prefer the simple word. Many writers, especially those whose milieu is highly technical, are afraid to use simple words. Perhaps they fear that, in some readers' minds, simple words mean simple ideas; but simple prose can be lucid and elegant. Delete or replace jargon if you can do so with no loss of meaning. Avoid buzzwords like *to liaise, to interface,* and *to impact.* Eliminate redundancy: Phrases such as *final product, successfully passing* [a test], and *end result* are redundant. Here are some others, with shorter replacements.

- Delete or replace technical jargon and optional terms of art with plainer language if you can do so with no loss of meaning. Reserve for specific, limited contexts words such as *utilize, strategize, reengineering,* and *human capital.*
- Watch out for the casual, confusing expansion of terms beyond their technical meanings, such as *actionable* (which doesn't mean "something you can do"), *virtual* (which can mean either "almost entirely the case" or "true only in theory, not in reality"), and *robust* which can mean anything from "sturdy" to "comprehensive."
- Avoid business-buzzword phrasing that adapts or morphs one part of speech into another, such as *liaise with other departments, incent employees to be more productive, impact the bottom line,* and *transition the company to a new management structure.*
- Eliminate redundancy in phrases such as *successfully passing a test, the end result, at the present time, initiate innovations,* and *final conclusions.*

Here's a list of commonly encountered phrases that can be simplified and clarified:

Instead of	Try
in close proximity	near, nearby, close
is cognizant of	is aware of, knows
disseminate	send, mail, e-mail, issue
expedite	hurry, speed up, rush
in conjunction with	with
with the exception of	except for

Smothered Verbs

Smothered verbs are action words buried in a group of words: *have a need for* instead of *need.* Adverbs also get buried: *in large measure* or to *a great extent* for *largely.*

Exercises 25 and 26 will help you focus on smothered verbs in context. Many of these phrases are so common that we accept them without thinking. Remember that verbs carry the force of the language; eliminating excess words produces a tighter, more forceful sentence. So, usually, does removing the passive voice.

The Copyeditor's Guide to Substance&Style

Exercise 25:
Smothered Verbs

Instructions: Clarify these sentences by changing nouns into verbs. Decide which action the sentence is relating; try to use active verbs to indicate that action. Another exercise on smothered verbs appears in Exercise 26.

1. A modification of the original plan was made by the staff assistant.

2. The elimination of wordy constructions by writers is a desirable feature.

3. The project had become more urgent than ever in that staff cuts made

   it imperative to find a more time-efficient way to accomplish the

   compilation and distribution of the newsletter.

4. The defendant made a confession that he had been in town on Tuesday.

5. Upon court appearance by the defendant, courtroom legal proceedings

   will be effected by the presiding judge.

6. The finalization of the plan was brought about by the committee, but only after 10 hours of discussion had been conducted.

7. The regulation makes it specific that analysis of the data must be conducted by technically qualified personnel.

8. Delivery of all the material must be achieved by the distributor within five working days of receipt of the order.

9. Compilation of the statistical data must reach completion by resource personnel no later than 15 June.

10. The accusation was leveled at the Nuclear Regulatory Commission by the GAO that it succumbed to failure in its attempt to force compliance to the ruling by local power plants.

Exercise 25 Answers

1. A modification of the original plan was made by the staff assistant. *(should: A modified the original plan)*

   The staff assistant modified the original plan.

   The passive served no useful purpose in the original version; the corrected sentence is clearer.

2. The elimination of wordy constructions by writers is a desirable feature. *(should eliminate)*

   Writers should eliminate wordy constructions.

   Cutting through wordy constructions isn't always as easy as it was here, but, as a maxim, the sentence is certainly valid.

3. The project had become more urgent than ever in that staff cuts made it imperative to find a more time-efficient way to accomplish the compilation and distribution of the newsletter.

   The project had become more urgent than ever in that staff cuts made it imperative to find a more time-efficient way to compile and distribute the newsletter.

4. The defendant made a confession that he had been in town on Tuesday.

   The defendant confessed that he had been in town on Tuesday.

5. Upon court appearance by the defendant, courtroom legal proceedings will be effected by the presiding judge. *(When ... appears in court ... begin)*

   When the defendant appears in court, the presiding judge will begin proceedings.

Exercise 25 Answers, continued

6. The ~~finalization of~~ the plan, ~~was brought about by the committee,~~ but only
   after 10 hours of discussion ~~had been conducted.~~

   committee approved

   The committee finalized the plan, but only after 10 hours of discussion.

7. The regulation ~~makes it~~ specific that ~~analysis of~~ the data must be conducted
   by technically qualified personnel.

   The regulation specifies that technically qualified personnel must
   analyze the data.

8. Delivery ~~of~~ all the material ~~must be achieved by~~ the distributor *must* within five
   working days of receipt of the order.

   The distributor must deliver all the material within five working days
   of receipt of the order.

   The last part of the sentence could still be reworked, but this version uncovers
   the verb and removes the passive voice.

9. Compilation of the statistical data ~~must reach completion~~ by *must* resource
   personnel no later than 15 June.

   Resource personnel must compile the statistical data no later than 15 June.

10. The accusation ~~was leveled at~~ the Nuclear Regulatory Commission ~~by~~
    ~~the GAO that it succumbed to failure in its attempt~~ to force compliance to
    the ruling by local power plants.

    GAO

    The GAO accused the Nuclear Regulatory Commission of failing to
    force local power plants to comply with the ruling.

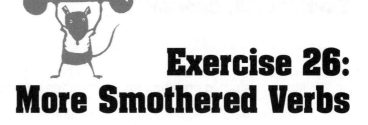

Exercise 26:
More Smothered Verbs

Instructions: Resuscitate the smothered verbs in the following sentences. Correct any other problems you may find.

1. Additional authorization for the administration of the survey by the staff members has emanated from the director of the department.

2. The project manager is vested with the responsibility for the appointment of one individual office to serve as a central focal point to perform coordination functions and provide information to all regional offices about the company's activities.

3. A diagnosis of a recurrent disorder may be made by the patient, but a confirmation should also be made by the physician.

4. The aim of this article is a presentation of a summary overview of the drugs most commonly used in an effort to render treatment and achieve prevention of psychological disorders.

5. The expenditures made by organizations in the provision of services and the administration of programs resulted in a substantial increase in operating costs.

6. Managers got information about resource allocation by direct participation in daily operations, personal observation of the operations, or supervision of the operations.

7. The goal of this research program is the elucidation of the physiological and behavioral correlates of voluntary alcohol consumption by humans through conducting an analysis of animal models.

8. Apathy and withdrawal was a consequence of the dogs' inability as to shock alteration or prevention.

Exercise 26 Answers

The department director has issued

1. ~~A~~dditional authorization for the ~~administration of the survey by the~~ staff
members ~~has emanated from the director of the department.~~ _to administer the survey._

   The department director has issued additional authorization for the
   staff members to administer the survey.

2. The project manager is ~~vested with the~~ responsibilit~~y~~ _(is)_ for th~~e~~ appoint~~ment of~~ _ing_
one ~~individual~~ office to ~~serve as a central focal point to perform~~ coordination~~
functions and ~~provide~~ information ~~to~~ all regional offices about the company's
activities.

   The project manager is responsible for appointing one office to coordinate
   functions and inform all regional offices about the company's activities.

3. ~~A~~ diagnos~~is of~~ a recurrent disorder~~, may be made by the~~ patient~~, but a~~ _Although a_
~~confirmation should also be made by~~ the physician~~,~~ _should confirm the diagnosis._ _may_

   Although a patient may diagnose a recurrent disorder, the physician
   should confirm the diagnosis.

4. ~~The aim of~~ this article ~~is~~ _(is)_ _to_ ~~presentation of a~~ _an_ ~~summary~~ overview of ~~the~~ drugs
most commonly used ~~in an effort~~ to ~~render~~ treatment and ~~achieve prevention~~ _prevent treat_
~~of~~ psychological disorders.

   This article aims to present an overview of drugs most commonly used
   to prevent and treat psychological disorders.

5. ~~The~~ expenditures ~~made by~~ organizations ~~in the provision of~~ services and
the ~~administration of~~ programs ~~resulted in a substantial increase~~ in operating
costs. *Caused operating costs to*

   Organizational expenditures to provide services and administer
   programs caused operating costs to increase substantially.

6. Managers got information about resource allocation by ~~direct~~ participation
in ~~daily operations, personal~~ observation ~~of the operations,~~ or supervision
~~of the~~ operations. *daily*

   Managers got information about resource allocation by participating
   directly in, observing, or supervising daily operations.

7. The goal of this research ~~program~~ is ~~the elucidation of~~ the physiological and
behavioral ~~correlates~~ of voluntary alcohol consumption ~~by~~ humans ~~through
conducting an~~ analysis ~~of~~ animal models. *to clarify* *basis* *in* *by* *zing*

   The goal of this research is to clarify the physiological and behavioral
   bases of voluntary alcohol consumption in humans by analyzing
   animal models.

8. Apathy and withdrawal ~~was a~~ consequence of the dogs' inability ~~as~~ to
~~shock~~ alteration or prevention. *were* *s* *to* *shock.*

   Apathy and withdrawal were consequences of the dogs' inability to
   alter or prevent shock.

Redundancy

Editors should watch for redundancies (tautologies, needless repetitions of an idea) and eliminate them. Many of the catchwords and phrases with which we are so familiar are actually redundant. For example, consider phrases such as these:

serious crisis	future plans
untimely death	important essentials
basic fundamentals	true facts
unconfirmed rumor	final outcome
past history	advance planning

By definition, a crisis is serious. Can facts be other than true? Has there ever been a timely death, except perhaps Attila the Hun's?

Of course, redundancy can occur in whole sentences or paragraphs, not just phrases. If you find yourself haunted by déjà vu while editing, redundancy may be to blame. Some authors use virtually identical phrasing in the introduction to a chapter and in its summary—and those phrases may appear in the intervening text as well. Another common source of redundancy is text that states exactly the same information as presented in a figure or table. Ascertain from your supervisor or client how much leeway you have to attack this problem. You may be authorized to rephrase passages, or you may be limited to querying the author (*The last two paragraphs on page 90 are identical to the first two on page 78. Is this okay?*).

In summary, when you can do so with no loss of meaning, use simple words. Your goal is not to impoverish the language, but rather to free it to communicate. The so-called plain English movement has clarified the language and even generated insurance policies that are readable. Keep your audience in mind, while heeding nuances in meaning.

Each sentence in Exercise 27 contains needless words; in time, deleting them should become almost automatic. Many of the redundancies in this exercise seem commonplace, but they're still repetitious. Some are tautologies, like *new innovations*; some (like *in order to*) are just superfluous. For more practice, do Exercise 28.

How well did you do? Did your second and third passes through the material uncover more problems? Remember that even experienced editors don't find every error the first time. An experienced editor would need about 90 minutes for manuscripts the length of these exercises.

If you found that you were struggling, remember that speed and accuracy come with practice. Try the exercises again later on and you'll probably be pleasantly surprised by how quickly redundancies jump out at you. Good copyeditors develop a sort of radar.

Exercise 27: Redundancy

Instructions: Edit the sentences as needed. Delete redundant words and phrases; uncover smothered verbs and adverbs.

1. The agency seeks new innovations for disseminating standards.

2. We are accumulating the data items that are needed to carry out an evaluation of the situation.

3. We must extend the deadline in order to guarantee delivery.

4. The chairman is currently reviewing the regulation.

5. A question contained on the form concerned the past history of the agency.

6. For the purpose of implementing your request, we need to know the nature of your future prospects.

7. The Department recognizes the general consensus of opinion.

8. The end result of the conference was satisfactory.

9. Headquarters is now in the process of preparing statements regarding policy.

Exercise 27, continued

10. The car you want can be obtained for the price of $15,000.

11. The requirements with respect to recruitment are similar to those used during the previous year.

12. Policy questions frequently arise during the course of complaint investigations.

13. Additional resources are required only in those instances when the data indicate the need to add them.

14. We might lighten the paperwork burden imposed on employees.

15. Emphasis is placed on voluntary compliance.

16. I was asked to review the decision that was reached by the local units.

17. We must focus our attention on clear writing.

18. The litigant has 60 days in which to file an appeal.

19. Members tended to choose the location which was nearest to their home.

20. You may prereserve your seat by calling in advance.

Exercise 27 Answers

1. The agency seeks ~~new~~ innovations for disseminating standards.

   The agency seeks innovations for disseminating standards.

   Innovations are by definition new.

2. We are accumulating the data ~~items that are~~ needed to ~~carry out an~~ evaluation ~~of~~ the situation.

   We are accumulating the data needed to evaluate the situation.

   This sentence contains a smothered verb as well as extraneous words. Why say *carry out an evaluation* when *evaluate* alone is much stronger?

3. We must extend the deadline ~~in order~~ to guarantee delivery.

   We must extend the deadline to guarantee delivery.

4. The chairman is ~~currently~~ reviewing the regulation.

   The chairman is reviewing the regulation.

   The *-ing* form of the verb tells you that the action is in progress, so *currently* is redundant.

5. A question ~~contained~~ on the form concerned the ~~past~~ history of the agency.

   A question on the form concerned the history of the agency.

   Here, two words are unnecessary; if a question is on a form, it is contained there, and all history is past (except for a *medical history*).

The Copyeditor's Guide to **Substance**&*Style*

Exercise 27 Answers, continued

6. ~~For the purpose of~~ To implement~~ing~~ your request, we need to know ~~the~~ ~~nature of~~ your future prospects.

   To implement your request, we need to know your prospects.

   The verb is buried, *the nature of* is unnecessary, and *prospects* are always future.

7. The Department recognizes the ~~general~~ consensus ~~of opinion.~~

   The Department recognizes the consensus.

   This sentence contains a tautology: *Consensus* includes opinion and is general.

8. The ~~end~~ result of the conference was satisfactory.

   The result of the conference was satisfactory.

9. Headquarters is ~~now in the process of~~ preparing statements ~~regarding~~ ~~policy~~.

   Headquarters is preparing policy statements.

   The progressive form of the verb (*is preparing*) makes the phrase *now in the process* redundant. So is *regarding*.

10. The car you want ~~can be obtained for the price of~~ costs $15,000.

    The car you want costs $15,000.

    You can shorten this sentence in several ways without losing any information.

11. ~~The~~ requirements ~~with respect to~~ recruitment are similar to ~~those used during the previous~~ year's. *last*

    Recruitment requirements are similar to last year's.

    If you cut out the redundancy, the meaning is much clearer.

12. Policy questions frequently arise during ~~the course of~~ complaint investigations.

    Policy questions frequently arise during complaint investigations.

13. Additional resources are required only ~~in those instances~~ when the data ~~indicate the need to add~~ them. *support*

    Additional resources are required only when the data support them.

14. We might lighten ~~the~~ paperwork burden ~~imposed on~~ employees.

    We might lighten employees' paperwork burden.

    As a sentence, this version leaves something to be desired; in context, it would be easier to fix. Avoid a discussion of whether paperwork is by definition a burden. The solution presented here assumes that it is.

15. ~~Emphasis is placed on~~ voluntary compliance. *is emphasized*

    Voluntary compliance is emphasized.

    Compliance could be grudging, so *voluntary* is necessary. Without more information it's difficult for an editor to eliminate the passive construction.

Exercise 27 Answers, continued

16. I was asked to review the ~~decision that was reached by the~~ local units'.

    I was asked to review the local units' decision.

    The passive should remain, unless you know who asked.

17. We must ~~focus our attention~~ *concentrate* on clear writing.

    We must concentrate on clear writing.

    Focus our attention has a simpler equivalent.

18. The litigant has 60 days ~~in which~~ to file an appeal.

    The litigant has 60 days to file an appeal.

    The litigant has 60 days to appeal reflects a change in meaning. Filing an appeal is a legal process; appealing is not.

19. Members tended to choose the location ~~which was~~ nearest to their homes.

    Members tended to choose the location nearest to their homes.

    This conservative edit retains the concept of a tendency. A heavier edit results in the following.

    Most members chose the location nearest their homes.

    There's a slight shift in meaning, and only the context will tell you whether this version is acceptable.

20. You may ~~pr~~reserve your seat by ~~calling in advance.~~ *telephone.*

    You may reserve your seat by telephone.

Exercise 28: More Redundancy

Instructions: Prune the redundancy from these sentences.

1. These various different agencies and offices that provide aid and assistance services to individual persons who participate in our program activities that we offer have reversed themselves back from the policy that they recently announced to return to the original policy they followed earlier.

2. The scientific endeavor in general depends on essentially true and fully accurate data if it is to offer any ideas and theories that will actually allow mankind to advance forward into the future in a safe and cautious way.

3. It is probably true that in spite of the fact that the educational environment is a very significant and important facet to each and every one of our children in terms of his or her own individual future development and growth, various different groups and people do not at all support certain tax assessments at a reasonable and fair rate that are required for the express purpose and intention of providing an educational context at a decent level of quality.

4. Most likely, a majority of all the patients who appear at the public clinic facility do not expect specialized medical attention and treatment, because their health problems and concerns often seem not to be of a major nature and can for the most part usually be adequately treated with enough proper understanding and attention by the clinic staff.

5. It is necessary to make special and particular mention of von Willebrand's disease as a consequence of the suggestion inferred from coagulation test results that the possibility exists that there might be a disorder of the platelet.

6. An additional question that was asked in the survey instrument centers around the problem of whether or not the extension of the roles of women to include roles that have been the traditional domain of men will have the effect of leading to an increase or reduction of problems that are related to abusive alcohol usage among women.

Exercise 28 Answers

1. These various ~~different~~ agencies ~~and offices~~ that ~~provide aid and~~ assistance ~~services to individual persons~~ who participate[nts] in our program ~~activities that we offer~~ have reversed ~~themselves back from the policy that~~ they recently announced ^policy^ to return to the original one[.] ~~policy they followed earlier.~~

   The various agencies that assist participants in our program have
   reversed the recently announced policy to return to the original one.

2. The scientific endeavor in general depends on ~~essentially true and fully~~
   accurate data if it is to offer any ~~ideas and~~ theories that will ~~actually~~ allow
   mankind to advance ^safely[.]^ ~~forward into the future in a safe and cautious way.~~

   The scientific endeavor in general depends on accurate data if it is
   to offer any theories that will allow mankind to advance safely.

3. Although school ~~It is probably true that in spite of the fact that~~ the educational environment
   is a ~~very~~ significant ^development factor for^ ~~and important facet to each and every one of~~ our children[,]
   ~~in terms of his or her own individual future~~ development ~~and growth~~ various
   ~~different~~ groups ~~and people~~ do not ~~at all~~ support ~~certain~~ ^the reasonable^ tax[es] ^as necessary^
   ^to provide good schools[.]^ ~~assessments at a reasonable and fair rate that are required for the express purpose and intention of providing an educational context at a decent level of quality.~~

   Although school is a significant development factor for our children,
   various groups do not support the reasonable taxes necessary to
   provide good schools.

The Copyeditor's Guide to Substance&Style

Exercise 28 Answers, continued

4. Most ~~likely, a majority~~ of ~~all~~ the patients ~~who appear~~ at the public clinic ~~facility~~ do not expect specialized medical attention and treatment, because their health problems ~~and concerns~~ often seem ~~not to be of a major nature~~ *minimal* and can ~~for the most part~~ usually be ~~adequately~~ treated ~~with enough proper~~ ~~understanding and attention~~ by the clinic staff.

> Most of the patients at the public clinic do not expect specialized medical attention and treatment because their health problems often seem minimal and can usually be treated by the clinic staff.

5. ~~It is necessary to make special and particular mention of~~ von Willebrand's ~~disease as a consequence of the suggestion inferred from~~ *When* coagulation test *suggest* results ~~that the possibility exists that there might be~~ a disorder of the platelet *be certain to consider* von Willebrand's disease.

> When coagulation test results suggest a platelet disorder, be sure to consider von Willebrand's disease.

6. ~~An additional question that was asked in~~ the survey ~~instrument centers~~ *asked* ~~around the problem of~~ whether ~~or not the~~ exten~~sion~~ *ding* of the roles of women to include ~~roles that have been the~~ traditional *ly the* domain of men ~~will have the~~ *those* ~~effect of leading to an~~ increase or reduc~~tion of problems that are related to~~ ~~abusive~~ alcohol ~~usage among~~ women. *abuse in*

> The survey asked whether extending the roles of women to include those traditionally the domain of men will increase or reduce alcohol abuse in women.

Exercise 29:
Putting It All Together

Instructions: This article on a subject of interest to editors and publishers appeared a few years ago in *The Editorial Eye.* The article has been extensively reworked to introduce errors. The main problems in the text are punctuation, spelling, grammar, and redundancy, but some style decisions have to be made as well. Use a dictionary to verify any unfamiliar spellings.

Read through the exercise before you mark anything. Then concentrate on making the manuscript internally consistent. Be sure to note any general instructions or queries to the author. Also mark heads.

Note how long it takes you to edit the manuscript to your satisfaction. You'll need to make several passes through the text.

The answer key largely reflects the *Eye*'s version, followed by a detailed analysis of what needed to be fixed. (The paragraphs have been numbered to help you compare your corrections with the answer key.)

Fair Use and Copyright: An Unanswered Questions

1. What is copyright? Who owns it? How does an author or publisher obtain

    copy right? What is eligable for copyright protection? How much of a piece

    of work can be quoted or produced again without being considered as an

    infringement on the copyright laws? What affects has new technology

    had upon copyright? Of all these questions, fair use is the largest source

    of constraint for authors and editors.

The Copyeditor's Guide to **Substance**&*Style*

Exercise 29, continued

Fair Use

2. Fair use is the one biggest exception to the copy-right law. That is, whatever the copyright owner decides is a fair quotation or use of the protected material does not create copyright infringement. The current copyright law of recent years recognizes that the printing press is no longer the primary media of communication and fair use now includes phonorecords and reproduction copies, as well as printed material. The law specifies also the legitiment boundaries of fair use "criticism, comment, news reporting, teaching (including multiple copies for use in the classroom, scholarship, or research.

3. It is this phase of the copyright law that is being so troublesome to authors, editors and publishers who get very confused with the details of the law. Exactly just what constitutes fair use? The law is unclear on this point and this point ultimately leaves the problem of its definition up to the owner of the copyright.

Exercise 29, continued

4. For those people who wish to quote the material written by others than themselves, the lack of definition are most definite sources of worry and frustration. The law says that many factors could be considered in determining fair use, including:

• The purpose and characteristics of the use, including whether such use is of a commercial nature or that it is being used for nonprofit purposes in an educational situation.

*   what is the nature or topic of the work that has been copyrighted.

— how much and how substantial a portion used with respect to the

…whole piece is important, too, and last but not least,

— How effective the use is upon the potential market for the work that has been copy righted

5. This means that the use an author besides the original author makes of some copyrighted material is not allowed in any way, shape, or form to compete or diminish the existing market value of the original work. Many publishers believe 250 words to be fair use of copyrighted material-that is material that anyone can use and quote without first obtaining permission

The Copyeditor's Guide to **Substance**&*Style*

Exercise 29, continued

from whomever they should have obtained it from. But now think for a minute, just suppose an author quoted 250 words from a 500 word article. Clearly, this kind of quotation would diminish the value of the original work.

6. Sometimes an author will object to having too little quoted. The chief book reviewer of the Washington Post took recently exception to a publishers' use, in promoting a trashy novel, of just two words from his review of the book, quoted, but not quoted in context. The general unfavorable review had been made to appear like an unqualified rave because of the purpose and character of the publisher's use of the quoted words obviously commercial in its use.

7. A sample of a crosssection of publishers turned up a general consensus for a general policy of a request and requiring permission for anything and everything that is quotable. Most publishers want to know the use of the quoted material will be used, whether the person who wants permission will be charging a fee for the publication that the quoted material will appear in, and whether such use might be in direct competition with the original work. If you want to always be on the safe side, ask permission in writing

in advance of your publication date for anything you want to print again in a work you are publishing.

NEW TECHNOLOGY AND COPYRIGHT

8. A very important recently new amendment to the law, closely related to fair use, has to due with reproduction, xerographic or otherwise, of a copyrighted work. The Copyright Act provide that libraries and Archives may make one copy or phonorecord of a work, and diseminate such single copies under certain particular stringent conditions. The reproduction must be made without any single purpose of commercial advantage, the collections of the library or Archive must be open and available to the public cummunity or available to all persons who are doing research in a specialized field, not just to those who are affiliated with the institution, and the reproduction must include the copyright notice. These rules only apply to unpublished works such as letter, dairies, journals, thesis, and disertations.

9. The Newsletter Association of America contends, in its newsletter Hotline (vol. 6, no. 17) that libraries are abusing this section of the Act. Siting a

report done for the Copyright office, Hotline says that the majority of users

making library photocopies are either unaware of copyright notices or

presume that duplication of copyright materials is permitted for educational

or research purposes." In particular, NAA says that data-bases "use

[copyright] materials without permission, under the guise of abstracts."

10. To fight this abuse of the law, at least one computer based permissions

system has appeared—the Copyright Clearance Center in Salem

Massachusettes. The center is setup, according to its promotional material,

to protect copyright holders from both deliberate and inadvertant infringment.

The center used coded publication registartion forms, quite like those for

copyright registration, to collect royalty fees, and convey permissions on

behalf of it's participating publishers.

11. Another instant of the affect of communication technology are the provisions

in the now current law for paying, under a system of compulsory liscencing,

of certain royalties for the secondary transmission of copyrighted works vie

cable tv.

Background on Copyright

12. The first legislation on copyright was an Act of Parliament passed in Britain in 1907, aimed at preventing scrupulous book-sellers from publishing works without the conscent of the authors. It provided that the author of a book had the soul right of publication for a term of twentyone years, and the penalty for infringement was a penny a sheet. The British Copyright Law was amended and changed in 1801 (the fine went up to three-pence a sheet), and again in 1842.   In 1887 a group of Nations, which was not including the US, ratified the Berne Union copyright convention, which required members of said group to have minimum standards of copyright protection, and applying them equally to all citizens of all the nations that are all represented.

13. In the U.S.A., copyright found its protection in the constitution, Article One, section 1, Clause eight, ratified in 1879. In 1790, seperate legislation on copyright was enacted. The copyright Law was revised and altered again in 1831, 1870, 1909, 1976 and 1978, and the 1978 Law was amended in 1890.

Exercise 29, continued

14. According to The Nuts and Bolts of Copyright a pity booklet published by the copyright Office of the library of congress:

> Copyright is a form of protection given by the laws of the United States…to the authors of original works of authorship" such as literary, dramatic, musical, artistic, and certain other intellectual works.

"Copyright ownership"

15. Only the author or only the persons whom the author has given or assigned the rights to the work may have the opportunity to claim the copyright for that material. Between those other than the author, who may legitimatly claim copyright is an employer who's employees have created a copyrightable work as a result of his or her employment (work for hire); a publisher to whom the author has relinquished the copyright or who has paid the author to create the work; someone who has comissioned a work, such as a sculptor, painting or piece of music, or someone who has asked the author to contribute their work to a collective endeaver such as a motion picture, a translation, or a anthology or as a test or instructional materials. It is

extremely, extremely important to note that the owner of a manuscript, or original sheet music, or a painting, for example is not necessarily the owner of the copyright to those particular works that are copyrightable.

16. To get and obtain copyright protection that protects copyrightable material, the orignator of the original work needs only to attach to it a notice of copyright, the form of which is specified in absolute detail in the copyright law. The notice must contain the symbol or the word "copyright" or the abbrev. "Copr;" the year of publication; and the name of the copyright owner; for example "John Doe 1980". The notice of copyright must appear in a prominant place in the work that is to be protected. This element is something that again is extremely, extremely important in light of the 1978 revision of the revised copyright law wich specifies that any work published after January 1, 1987 without such notice permanently forfiets any and all copyright protection in the U.S. of A. This notice is all that is required to obtain and get the necessary copyright protection. Registration of copyright means filling out a series of forms and to send them with the correct amount of the fee, and with two copies of the work to the Copyright Office at its

Exercise 29, continued

correct location. The copyright owner need not register the copyright with the library of Congress, however, if a law suit should ever araise over the work, the registration is very necessary to prove that ownership belongs to the owner.

The Final Summary In Brief

17. On fair use and reproduction of copyrighted material, the copyright law undoubtedly without a doubt rises more questions that they answer. It does not try or make an attempt to adress sophisticated electronic methods of infringing on copyright and it spells out in more detail than ever before the boundaries of fair use. But it still is not descriptive in the area of fair use, and that section of the Act will continue to confuse and addle authers and publishers and provide fertil ground for legal and impartial, judicial debatable items.

Exercise 29 Answers

Remember to check your marks for correctness.

Format: First, you had to indicate the head level of the title. If this text were part of a larger manuscript, you would ensure that the format of the head levels corresponded to what went before and after. In this exercise, however, only one A-level head appears.

Find the first B-head, *Fair Use*, following the first paragraph. The head is shown flush left, caps and lowercase. Make the other B-heads (*New Technology and Copyright*, *Background on Copyright*, *Copyright Ownership*, and *The Final Summary in Brief*) match this one.

Note that the first paragraph was flush left, but others were indented. You should have marked the paragraph style for consistency. (Sometimes the first paragraph in an article is not indented, however, although the rest of the paragraphs are.) Did you notice that the other indents were inconsistent? Some paragraphs were indented three spaces; others, four. Such format errors may not seem like editorial problems, but they are.

Paragraph 1: The first paragraph contains style questions, redundancies, and misspellings. According to the dictionary, *copyright* is one word. To achieve parallel construction in the third question, substitute *it*. Correct the spelling of *affects* and *eligable*. Note the redundancies: *produced again*, *being considered as*, and *upon*. You might have substituted *confusion* for *constraint*, although the change does affect the meaning slightly.

Fair Use and Copyright:
An Unanswered Questions

1. What is copyright? Who owns it? How does an author or publisher obtain copy right? What is eligable for copyright protection? How much of a piece of work can be quoted or produced again without being considered as an infringement on the copyright laws? What affects has new technology had upon copyright? Of all these questions, fair use is the largest source of constraint/confusion for authors and editors.

Exercise 29 Answers, continued

Fair Use

2. Fair use is the ~~one~~ biggest exception to the copyright law. That is, whatever the copyright ~~owner decides~~ is a fair quotation or use of the protected material does not create copyright infringement. ~~The~~ current copyright law ~~of recent years~~ recognizes that the printing press is no longer the primary media of communication and fair use now includes phonorecords and reproduction copies, as well as printed material. The law ~~also~~ specifies the legitimate boundaries of fair use, as "criticism, comment, news reporting, teaching (including multiple copies for use in the classroom, scholarship, or research.

word ok?

check quote where does quote end?

3. It is this *aspect* ~~phase~~ of the copyright law that is ~~being~~ so troublesome to authors, editors and publishers ~~who got very confused with the details of the law.~~ Exactly ~~just~~ what constitutes fair use? The law is unclear on this point and ~~this point~~ ultimately leaves the problem of its definition ~~up~~ to the owner of the copyright.

Paragraph 2: The first two sentences are relatively straightforward, but the third contains not only a redundancy (*of recent years*); it also lacks a comma (after *communication*). Note the plural *media* instead of the singular that is meant. The last sentence lacks an end quotation mark, about which you must query the author. You're also missing a closing parenthesis, but you can fix that yourself. For the sentence to make sense, you have to do something after *fair use*; add *as* or a colon. Finally, *legitimate* was misspelled and the sentence flows better if *also* precedes *specifies*.

Paragraph 3: Deletions improve the first sentence. Also, add a serial comma after *editors* and change *phase* to *aspect* to clarify the meaning. The last sentence contains repetition of *this point*.

Paragraph 4: Rewriting is necessary to make the first sentence flow better; moreover, the subject of the second clause disagrees with its verb. Both issues are easily resolved. The colon introducing the list, however, needs some support. (A colon must be preceded by a complete sentence.) Did you make the elements of the list consistent? Whether you chose bullets or dashes is immaterial, as long as you don't have both. Also, did you eliminate the redundancy?

4. For those ~~people~~ who wish to quote ~~the~~
   persons
   material written by others than themselves,
   is
   the lack of definition ~~are~~ most definite*ly*
   a source*s* of worry and frustration. The law
   says that many factors could be considered
   the following
   in determining fair use, including:
   what are
   • The purpose and characteri~~stics~~ of the use?
   Is the quotation for
   ~~including whether such use is~~ of a commercial use or
   ~~nature or that it is being used~~ for nonprofit
   purposes in an educational situation?
   • what is the nature or topic of the work ~~that~~
   ~~has been~~ copyrighted.
   to the
   • ~~how much and how substantial a portion~~
   regard
   ~~used with respect to the~~ whole piece is
   ~~important, too, and last but not least,~~
   what will have
   • ~~How~~ effective the use ~~is~~ upon the potential
   market for the work ~~that has been~~ copyrighted.

Paragraph 5: This paragraph begins with a pronoun for which there is no antecedent. *Concept* works, although there are certainly other choices. The rest of the sentence needs tightening. You also need to add *with* after *compete* and then delete extraneous words and clarify meaning by adding a few words. To finish the paragraph, you need to mark the em-dash (*material—that*) and to add a hyphen to the unit modifier *500-word*.

5. This
   concept
   means that the use ~~an author besides~~
   ~~the original author makes~~ of ~~some~~ copyrighted
   material is not allowed ~~in any way, shape, or~~
   with
   ~~form~~ to compete, or diminish the existing market
   value of the original work. Many publishers
   that constitutes
   believe 250 words ~~to be~~ fair use of copyrighted
   material-that is ~~material that~~ anyone can use
   M

Exercise 29 Answers, continued

250 words

and quote, without first obtaining permission.

~~from whomever they should have obtained it~~

~~from~~. But ~~now think for a minute;~~ just suppose

an author quoted 250 words from a 500-word

article. Clearly, this kind of quotation would

diminish the value of the original work.

6. Sometimes an author will object to having

too little quoted. The chief book reviewer of

(ital) the Washington Post took recently exception to

a publisher's use, in promoting a trashy novel,

of just two words from his review of the book,

out of

quoted ~~but not quoted in~~ context. The generally

unfavorable review had been made to appear

~~like~~ an unqualified rave because of the purpose

and character of the publisher's use of the

for purposes

quoted words obviously commercial ~~in its use~~.

(word ok?)

ing

7. A sample of a cross section of publishers

showed

~~turned up~~ a ~~general~~ consensus for a general

policy of ~~a request and~~ requiring permission

for anything ~~and everything~~ that is quotable.

now

Most publishers want to know ~~the use of~~ the

quoted material will be used, whether the

person who wants permission will be charging

Paragraph 6: The title of the newspaper (*The Washington Post*) needs to be marked for italics. The two transpositions (*recently took exception* and *publisher's*) are self-explanatory. The rest of the paragraph needs careful reading and editing.

Paragraph 7: You can replace *sample* with *sampling*, but query the author. *Sampling* seems to make better sense, although it carries the connotation of a formal poll. If *crosssection* is left (it is redundant), it needs to be separated into two words as shown. The next sentence contains nonparallel elements in a series (use *how* to make the first phrase parallel with *whether* in the other two). In the last sentence the person changed for no apparent reason; edit into the third person and recast the sentence.

Exercise 29 Answers, continued

New Technology: Mark and correct the head.

Paragraph 8: Correct the redundancies, misspellings, and punctuation errors in this paragraph. Note the transposition: it fixes a misplaced modifier (*apply only*).

---

a fee for the publication ~~that~~ *in which* the quoted material will appear in, and whether such use might be in direct competition with the original work. ~~If you~~ *Editors and publishers who* want to ~~always~~ be on the safe side ~~ask~~ *should request* permission in writing ~~in advance~~ ~~of your~~ *before the* publication date for anything ~~you~~ *they* want to print ~~again in a work you are publishing.~~

(B) N~~E~~EW TECHNOLOGY AND COPYRIGHT

8. A very important ~~recently now~~ *recent* amendment to the law, closely related to fair use, ~~has to due~~ *deals* with reproduction, xerographic or otherwise, of a copyrighted work. The Copyright Act provide*s* that libraries and ~~A~~rchives may make one copy or phonorecord of a work, and di~~s~~eminate ~~such~~ *this* single cop~~ies~~ under certain ~~particular~~ stringent conditions. The reproduction must be made without any ~~single purpose of~~ commercial ~~advantage~~ *intent*, the collections of the library or ~~A~~rchive must be open and available to the public ~~cummunity~~ or ~~available~~ to ~~all persons~~ *anyone* who ~~are~~ doing research in a specialized field, not just to those ~~who are~~ affiliated with the institution, and the reproduction must include

The Copyeditor's Guide to **Substance**&*Style*

Exercise 29 Answers, continued

the copyright notice. These rules only apply to unpublished works such as letters, diaries, journals, theses, and dissertations.

9. The Newsletter Association of America (NAA) contends, in its newsletter *Hotline* (vol. 6, no. 17) that libraries are abusing this section of the Act. Citing a report done for the Copyright office, *Hotline* says that ~~the majority of users~~ most users making library photocopies are either unaware of copyright notices or presume that duplication of copyrighted materials is permitted for educational or research purposes." In particular, NAA says that data bases "use [copyright] materials without permission, under the guise of abstracts."

Paragraph 9: Add the abbreviation *NAA* to the first sentence, so that its later use in the paragraph is clear. The comma after *contends* is wrong, unless you add another comma after the closing parenthesis. The name of the newsletter needs to be marked for italics both times it appears. *Most* seems stronger here than *majority*. Query the lack of a beginning quote, and delete the hyphen in *data bases*. This term is sometimes found as one word and sometimes two, but it's not usually hyphenated.

10. To fight this abuse of the law, at least one computer-based permissions system has appeared—the Copyright Clearance Center in Salem, Massachusetts. The center is set up, according to its promotional material, to protect copyright holders from both deliberate and inadvertent infringement. The

Paragraph 10: *Computer-based* is a unit modifier and needs a hyphen. Be sure to mark the em-dash also. The next sentence had two misspellings and a misplaced modifier; edit to read *According to its promotional material, the center....* The rest of the paragraph has only straightforward corrections.

Exercise 29 Answers, continued

center used coded publication registration forms, quite like those for copyright registration, to collect royalty fees and convey permissions on behalf of its participating publishers.

Paragraph 11: Edit this paragraph for spelling, punctuation, and redundancy.

11. Another instance of the effect of communication technology is the provisions in the now current law for paying, under a system of compulsory liscencing, of certain royalties for the secondary transmission of copyrighted works via cable tv.

Background on Copyright: Although the subhead is correctly formatted, you should mark the head anyway. (Marking even correct ones in this manner makes it easy to make global format changes later.)

Background on Copyright

Paragraph 12: The misplaced modifier (*passed in Britain in 1907*) needs to be corrected, and the date 1907 must be queried. If the rest of the dates in the paragraph are correct, this one isn't. How to treat *twenty-one* constitutes a style decision; if you're using GPO, the answer is *21*; Chicago specifies *twenty-one*. The rest of the errors in the paragraph are fairly mechanical. Remember, though, that most styles require you to spell out *United States* when it's used as a noun.

12. The first legislation on copyright was an Act of Parliament passed in Britain in 1907, aimed [1709 ?] at preventing unscrupulous book sellers from publishing works without the consent of the authors. It provided that the author of a book had the sole right of publication for a term of twenty-one years; and the penalty for infringement was a penny a sheet. The British Copyright Law was amended and changed in 1801 (the fine went up to three pence a sheet), and again in 1842. In 1887, a group of Nations, which was not including the US,

The Copyeditor's Guide to Substance & Style

ratified the Berne Union copyright convention, which required members of said *the* group to have minimum standards of copyright protection, and applying them equally to all citizens of their all the nations that are all represented.

United States
13. In the U.S.A., copyright found its protection *is* *ed* *by* in the constitution, Article One, section 1, Clause eight ratified in 1879. In 1790, seperate legislation on copyright was enacted. The copyright Law was revised and altered again in 1831, 1870, 1909, 1976 and 1978, and the 1978 Law was amended in 1890.

14. According to The Nuts and Bolts of Copyright *(ital)* a pity booklet published by the copyright Office of the library of congress.

Copyright is a form of protection given by the laws of the United States...to the authors of original works of authorship" such as literary, dramatic, musical, artistic, and certain other intellectual works.

open quote ok?

Paragraph 13: This paragraph contains many problems. Articles of the Constitution are roman (*Article I*). There's a smothered verb (*found its protection*), which is replaced in the edited version with a present passive (present tense because the protection is continuing, passive because the focus is on copyright). Finally, query the dates. Without clarification, it's hard to know whether the edited version changed the meaning.

Paragraph 14: The corrections to this paragraph are fairly mechanical (adjusting spelling, capitalization, and punctuation).

Exercise 29 Answers, continued

Copyright Ownership: Of course, you deleted the quotation marks on the subhead.

Paragraph 15: Fix the subject-verb disagreement in the second sentence, and delete the auxiliary verbs (redundant in this case). The nonparallel constructions need correction, and errors in punctuation and spelling abound.

Copyright ownership

15. Only the author or ~~only~~ the persons to whom the author has given or assigned the rights to the work may ~~have the opportunity to~~ claim the copyright for that material. ~~Between~~ those other than the author who may legitimatly claim copyright ~~is~~ *are* an employer ~~who's~~ *whose* employees ~~have~~ created a ~~copyrightable~~ work as a result of ~~his or her~~ *their* employment (work for hire); a publisher to whom the author ~~has~~ relinquished the copyright or who ~~has~~ paid the author to create the work; someone who ~~has~~ comissioned a work, such as a sculpture *are*, painting or piece of music, or someone who has asked the author to contribute ~~their~~ work to a collective endeavor such as a motion picture, a translation, or a anthology or as a test or instructional materials. It is ~~extremely, extremely~~ important to note that the owner of a manuscript, or original sheet music, or painting, for example is not necessarily the owner of the copyright to ~~those particular~~ *at* works ~~that are copyrightable.~~

The Copyeditor's Guide to **Substance**&*Style*

16. To ~~get and~~ obtain copyright protection, ~~that protects copyrightable material,~~ the originator of the ~~original~~ work needs only ~~to~~ attach to it a notice of copyright, the form of which is specified in ~~absolute detail in~~ the ~~copyright~~ law. The notice must contain the symbol, or the word *copyright,* or the abbreviation *Copr.,* the year of publication; and the name of the copyright owner; for example "John Doe 1980." The notice of copyright must appear in a prominent place in the work ~~that is to be protected.~~ This element is ~~something that again is extremely,~~ ~~extremely~~ important in light of the 1978 revision of the ~~revised~~ copyright law, which specifies that any work published after January 1, 1982, without such notice permanently forfeits any and all copyright protection in the U.S. ~~of A.~~ This notice is all that is required to ~~obtain~~ ~~and~~ get ~~the necessary~~ copyright protection. Registration of copyright means filling out a series of forms and ~~to~~ sending them with ~~the~~ ~~correct amount of the~~ fee, and ~~with~~ two copies of the work to the Copyright Office ~~at its correct location.~~ The copyright owner need not register

abbreviation correct?

(sp)

OK? language of law?

Paragraph 16: The second sentence contains many punctuation problems (the placement of commas and quotation marks) and needs a copyright symbol. Reference to words used as words should be italicized (*copyright, Copr*). Query the abbreviation, as well as the *any and all* phrase that appears later. Note the addition of the commas and the semicolon, all of which are grammatically necessary. The other corrections are self-explanatory.

Exercise 29 Answers, continued

the copyright with the library of Congress,
however, if a law suit should ever arise over
the work, the registration is ~~very~~ necessary
to prove that ownership ~~belongs to the owner.~~

B ~~The~~ Final Summary ~~In Brief~~

The Final Summary In Brief:
You can call it a *Summary* or *In Brief*, but not both.

17. On fair use and reproduction of copyrighted
material, the copyright law undoubtedly ~~without~~
~~a doubt~~ rises more questions ~~that they~~ answer.
It does ~~not~~ try ~~or make an attempt~~ to adress
sophisticated electronic methods of infringing
on copyright and it ~~spells out in more~~ detail more
than ever before the boundaries of fair use.
But ~~it~~ still is not ~~descriptive in the area of~~ fair
use, and the section of the Act will continue
to confuse ~~and addle~~ authers and publishers
and provide fertil ground for legal ~~and impartial,~~
judicial debat~~able items.~~

Paragraph 17: There are antecedent problems (*they* can't refer to *law*, and *It* needs to be explained). Eliminate redundancies and make the other necessary corrections.

224

The Copyeditor's Guide to **Substance** *&* **Style**

CITATIONS AND REFERENCES:
The Supporting Documentation

13

Citations and references are full of editorial style elements: colons, capitals, commas, page numbers, and quotation marks versus italics, among other things. Attention to these details is the test of a good copyeditor. They are time-consuming to edit, and there's no substitute for practice.

Many authors in academic or research fields delegate reference lists to their assistants, who may not be conscious of style guidelines. They may copy references from various electronic sources, each of which follows a different style. The result, while factually accurate, may be a stylistic hodgepodge that cries out for copyediting.

The descriptions in this chapter aren't meant to be exhaustive; they merely point out the kinds of information in references and the sorts of things you must make consistent. To edit references, you must cultivate methodical work habits and attention to detail. It also helps to have a sample format for each type of reference you might encounter.

You'll rely heavily on a style guide or style sheet to work on references. When you edit them, be alert for missing information or inconsistencies; you can't edit references mechanically and simply impose the proper format.

As intimidating as editing references seems to a beginning editor (and even to experienced ones), the job gets easier as you learn the patterns of the different types of references. A given style will treat all journal articles, all chapters of a book, all conference proceedings in a given way. You'll still need to refer to the style guide from time to time, but you'll learn where to look when you have a question, and you'll learn what questions to ask.

The format of in-text citations (including footnotes or endnotes) and of the citations themselves (capitalization, punctuation, and word order) are determined by the style manual. Academic or research-oriented guides such as *The Chicago Manual of Style* (*Chicago*) and the *Publication Manual of the American Psychological Association* (*APA*) deal extensively with citations. Conversely, *The United States Government Printing*

Office Style Manual devotes only one page to citations, saying merely that many styles are acceptable, and the *Associated Press* and other journalistic guides ignore the subject, as citations are not a feature of newspapers or popular magazines.

Many journals or publishers have their own preferred style for references. A house style sheet or manual with examples of each sort of reference—journal, book, chapter, report, single author, multiple author, corporate author, and so on—is indispensable.

References must contain certain kinds of information, although each style presents the information differently. Essential facts are the name of the author or authors, the title, the date of publication, and the publishing data (i.e., the city of publication, publisher, or title of the journal or book in which the work appeared). For references from the Internet, the date the reference was accessed is useful, since references may not remain posted indefinitely. The purpose of such details is to allow readers to verify or obtain information. Authors often write extensively on a particular subject, and each publishing fact is important to distinguish one reference from another.

Citations

Although traditional footnotes haven't disappeared altogether, most trade books and nonscientific journals now put the notes at the end of each chapter or together at the end of the book (*endnotes*). Moreover, many style guides have adopted the author-date style of citation exclusively.

When the author-date system is used, the details of publication are relegated to a reference list at the end of the book or article. The reference list contains only works cited in the text; additional sources may be listed in a bibliography or supplemental readings section.

As an alternative to the author-date system, some scientific journals list all references in a numbered, alphabetized reference list and insert the number of the reference in parentheses or brackets in the text whenever the references is cited. If any references are added, deleted, or moved, many of the citations must be renumbered.

Here are some examples of in-text citations in various styles:

> Before proceeding with a discussion of our findings, it is helpful to examine the conclusions of previous researchers in the field (Adams and Taylor 1986; Cormier 1987; Mickle 1985). [*Chicago*]

> Before proceeding...in the field (Adams & Taylor, 1986; Cormier, 1987; Mickle, 1985). [*APA*]

Before proceeding...in the field (1, 3, 6). [*Council of Biology Editors Style Manual*]

Note that *Chicago* uses no punctuation between the author's name and the date in text, whereas *APA* does. Note also that both *Chicago* and *APA* list multiple citations alphabetically.

As a copyeditor, you're expected both to put the references in the proper format according to the manual used and to check the citations in text against the references to see that they match. For instance, if the text says that the Mickle reference dates from 1985 and the reference list says 1986, you should try to verify the date and make the appropriate change or query the author about the discrepancy. A query is necessary if *Mickle 1985* is not listed in the references, if it is in the references but is not cited in the text, or if it is spelled *Mickel* in the references. If you're dealing with numbered citations, query any that are missing from the text.

As a manuscript goes through various revisions, references invariably suffer. Text gets shifted and references get misnumbered, misplaced, or even dropped. Check references at the end of every revision cycle, even if you have checked them before. Such a review is a form of insurance—and it's essential for heavily referenced material that has been extensively edited.

Checking in-text citations against the references should be the last step in the editing cycle. It's virtually impossible to edit and cross-check references at the same time. As you encounter each reference, put a check mark next to it or highlight it. In electronic files, you may search for parentheses.

References

Most academic style guides devote at least one long, detailed chapter to the treatment of references. Note that while you are copyediting references, you will change the capitalization of titles to fit your style guide, but you should not change the punctuation of titles. For example, if your style calls for serial commas but the title does not use them (*The Differences among Cats, Dogs and Horses*) you may not insert a serial comma. Nor may you change spelling, such as British spellings to U.S. spellings (*haematoma* vs. *hematoma*).

Here are two formats for books cited in a reference list or bibliography.

Tuchman, Barbara. *The Guns of August* (New York: Dell Publishing Co., 1962). [*Chicago*]

Tuchman, B. 1962. *The guns of August*. New York: Dell. [*APA*]

The most obvious difference in these two citations is the placement of the date. Also, in the second case, the author's first name and the publisher's name are abbreviated. The capitalization style differs; some styles use initial caps, and some prefer sentence-style capitalization—in which only the first word of a title or subtitle is capped (unless it contains proper nouns). Some styles separate parts of the reference with commas, some use only initials of authors, some use no space between initials, and so on.

A citation to a chapter in a book or to a revised or subsequent edition of a book must reflect the chapter or edition. The format might then be as follows.

> Stoughton, Mary. "Why Edit?" In Linda B. Jorgensen, ed.,
> *Stet Again! More Tricks of the Trade for Publications People*
> (Alexandria, VA: EEI Press, 1996) 63. [*Chicago*]

> Stoughton, M. 1996. Why edit? In L. B. Jorgensen (Ed.),
> *Stet Again! More Tricks of the Trade for Publications
> People* (p. 63). Alexandria, VA: EEI Press. [*APA*]

> Tuchman, Barbara. *The Guns of August,* rev. ed.
> (New York: Dell Publishing Co., 1962). [*Chicago*]

> Tuchman, B. 1962. *The guns of August* (Rev. ed.).
> New York: Dell. [*APA*]

Capitalization or abbreviation of information also varies from style to style (*2d ed., 2nd ed., rev. ed.*). If the work is a compilation of articles, the author's name is given first and the title and editor of the work follow. Numerous other variations (two locations for the publisher, translation of a foreign work, report number for technical documentation, treatment of unpublished material, and so on) must also be dealt with. It's easy to see why you need a standard style manual or a style sheet from your own organization.

Here are two formats for a reference to a journal article.

> Chomsky, Noam, and Morris Halle. "Some Controversial
> Questions in Phonological Theory." *Journal of Linguistics*
> 1(1965): 97–138. [*Chicago*]

> Chomsky, N., & Halle, M. 1965. Some controversial questions
> in phonological theory. Journal of Linguistics 1(2): 97–138.
> [*APA*]

Look at the differences again. In the first case, the date follows the volume number of the journal; in the second, it follows the authors' names. Some styles use ampersands to connect multiple authors; some put the title of the article in quotation marks; some cite the issue number as well as the volume (*[2] above*) some use initial caps for the article titles.

The order of unnumbered references at the end of a section or a manuscript is also governed by style. The general rule is that works are arranged alphabetically (but even the system of alphabetization is a style question); works by an individual author precede works by that author and others; and works by the same author or authors are arranged chronologically. Works by the same author or authors in the same year are alphabetized by title.

Notes

Footnotes or endnotes contain the same information as references, in a slightly different format. Usually the author's name is given in normal (not reverse) order, and the elements are separated by commas rather than periods. Also different is the practice of abbreviating information, using such terms as *ibid.* (in the same place), *op. cit.* (the work cited), *loc. cit.* (in the place cited), and *id.* (the same). *Ibid.* refers to the work mentioned in the preceding note. No author or title is used with *ibid.*, but a page number or volume can be cited if the information differs from the earlier mention. (All these common terms that were previously set in italics because they were Latin have now entered the dictionary as English words; hence, they are no longer italicized. They are italicized here only because they are examples.) Again, a style guide is indispensable for editing notes.

Many publishers require that *op. cit.* and *loc. cit.* be replaced with references giving the last name of the author, a shortened title, and a page number. In a heavily referenced book, you could search endlessly for that earlier citation (*Adams, op. cit., p. 12*), only to discover that Adams was deleted in an earlier revision. It's also easy to confuse two works by the same author and reference the wrong one.

TABLES AND GRAPHICS: 14
Making Data Easier to Grasp

The Basics of Editing Tables

Tables present information in a concise form that makes it easier to grasp. The reader must draw inferences from or interpret the tables, and the copyeditor should make that task easy. As a copyeditor, you won't normally set up tables or decide on the specifications for table makeup; the author or substantive editor has presumably already made those decisions. Rather, you'll examine the tables in relation to the text and in relation to one another, suggest a subhead here or a footnote there, check simple math, and make sure the tables are consistent in format. Your goal is to ensure that the tables present information clearly, concisely, and logically. Many academic style manuals devote whole chapters to handling tabular material. Journalistic style manuals such as that of the *Associated Press* pass over the subject, but newspapers and magazines may well cover it in in-house style guides.

Different copyeditors approach tables differently; as you work, you'll develop your own approach and decide which practices serve you best. As a general rule, however, if the manuscript contains more than two or three tables, deal with them in a separate pass. First look at each table in relation to its description in the text. Does the table match its description? Does it prove or illustrate what the author says it does? Next, if working on hard copy, mark the table callout in the margin (*T. 1,* in a circle, for the first table) or highlight it so that the keyboarder can insert the table in the proper place.

Then edit the table for format and style inconsistencies. Note that many styles permit more abbreviations in tables than in text; for example, it's usually acceptable to use the percent sign rather than spell out the word *percent*. On the other hand, too many abbreviations can make a table hard to read; it may be better to run a line caption down to another line than to abbreviate half the words in it. Some styles require that all abbreviations used in a table be defined in a table footnote, even if they have already been defined in the text or in earlier tables.

Always check simple math and query any discrepancies. If percentages don't total 100 percent, you'll need a disclaimer on rounding: "Note: numbers may not total exactly because of rounding." Without such disclaimers, readers will assume that math is exact; errors leave readers suspicious and less disposed to accept the author's premises and assertions. Check to be sure that all figures in a column are carried out to the same decimal place; 2.92%, 3%, and 2.9% shouldn't appear in the same column. Look for blank cells: should they include either a zero or the abbreviation NA? And if NA is used, be sure to include a definition: Does it mean "not available" or "not applicable"?

Finally, look at all the tables together; this step brings inconsistencies to light. For example, the absence of a column head will be more glaring when one table is seen alongside others that do have such heads. Other format errors will be easier to see as well.

Tables may be set off from text by rules above and below. A few years ago, vertical rules (down rules) had somewhat gone out of fashion, both because they tend to make a table look cluttered and because they often had to be drawn in by hand (and thus added to publication expense). Software now makes such rules easier and less expensive to include than in the past.

Each entry or item in a table has a name.

Table: The term used to designate the entire tabular presentation.

Body: The "tabular" part of the table; excludes the title, headnote, and footnotes.

Cell: Any entry in a table.

Field: The area within the body of the table in which the figures are entered (excludes the *stub* and *boxhead*—see the discussion on page 232).

Footnote callouts usually appear in the table as superscript letters, although (especially in a table with dense text) numbers or symbols may be used. At the bottom of the table, the footnote numbers may be either superscript or level with the text of the note and followed by a period (1.). The presence or absence of commas in groups of figures is a style question, as are the format and order of the notes at the end. You must always follow the style guide and ensure consistency among the tables themselves.

Editing a table for clarity

Tables are very useful in that they present more data than would be digestible in running text and provide visual interest as well. But tables are hard to create. There are so many ways to go wrong—from simple inconsistency of format to puzzling wording. We took the table presented here from the *Mini-Digest of Education Statistics 1994* (National Center for Education Statistics, U.S. Department of Education, Washington, DC) and introduced several errors. Try to identify errors and missing or confusing information. A discussion of the problems to be resolved follows.

Table 18—Proficiency of 17-yr.-olds in reading, by selected characteristics: 1971, 1981, and 1992

Selected characteristics of students	1971	1980	1992
Total	285.2	285.5	289.7
Sex:			
Male	278.9	281.86	284.2
Female	291.9	289.2	295.7
Race/ethnicity:	291.4	292.8	297.4
White	238.7	243.1	260.63
Black	—[1]	261.4	271.2
Hispanic			
Control of school			
public	—[1]	284.4	287.8
private	—[1]	298.4	309.6
Parents' Education Level:			
Not graduated high school	261.3	262.1	70.8
Graduated high school	283	277.5	280.5
Post-high school	302.2	298.9	298.6

* Data not available

Formatting oddities and errors. First we'll discuss the format from top to bottom, then we'll look at the information presented and comment on the effectiveness of the table as a whole.

- At the top is the table number followed by the title. There are as many ways to style the table number and title as there are editors and publications; this one is perfectly acceptable. A possible oddity is the line length: Usually the title is the same width as the whole table. And since yr. is the only abbreviation in the entire table, it would probably be better to spell it out.
- In the *stub* (far left) column are four main divisions that should be similar in punctuation, capitalization, and indention scheme. Note the inconsistencies: The second main stub should be flush left, the third needs a colon, and the third and fourth are inconsistent in cap style. (You'll have to decide between caps and lowercase and sentence-style capitalization. The other main stubs offer no help because they are single words or the equivalent.)
- The indented *substubs* must also be in consistent format; the third group (under Control of school) needs initial capital letters. The group under the last main

stub is consistent but hard to read; we'd prefer that the runover lines be indented further, and obviously we'd fix the typo, too.

- The *field* (the actual data) is in three columns nicely aligned on the decimal points, and the em dashes fill the cells for which no data are available—good! (The dashes could be aligned on the right of the column if you prefer, but be sure the superscripts extend past the right side of the column if you choose right alignment.) The individual cells are nearly all three-digit numbers with a single-place decimal; those that are not should be looked at carefully. Near the bottom of the 1971 column, you might be tempted to add a zero so 283 will look like the other numbers, but don't. Adding a zero would falsify the data by saying tabulation of the results (or the experiment) was carried out to that decimal place. Query the lack of the zero instead. Consider rounding off the two numbers that have two-place decimals, and query the 70.8 in the 1992 column—it's just too different from the rest of the data to go unverified.

- Alignment is important in all tables. Note that the 1992 column heading aligns on the right side of its column; the other two align on the left. In this table, it's a subtle difference, but if the numbers in the columns were longer, the inconsistency would be more noticeable. The cells in the "Race/ethnicity" group are misaligned; apparently all nine numbers should move down one line (note that no data follow the other main stubs). In the last group, placement of the data line for a two-line stub is inconsistent. For this table either style would be fine. If the stub or the information in one of the cells ran to several lines, we would insist on first-line alignment.

- The footnote that explains the dashes has an asterisk, but its callouts in the table field are superscript 1. This kind of inconsistency is typical in tables as is having footnotes without callouts and vice versa. We would also expect to find the footnote under the base rule, but its placement here could be the publication's preferred style.

What does it all mean? If you revise the table according to the preceding discussion you will have a table that looks nice and is consistent, but will its meaning be clear? Looking good isn't enough. Does the title reflect the actual information presented in the stubs and column heads? No, the years are not the same. Does the center column present data for 1980 or for 1981 per the title? The column head for the stubs does mirror the table title, although we'd delete "of students" because "Control of school" is not a characteristic of students.

We also wonder if the substubs in the last group could be worded more simply: maybe "Did not graduate from high school," "High school graduate," "Some post-high school," or maybe express these categories in years of education: "Fewer than 12 years," "12 years," "More than 12 years."

The "Total" line is also puzzling: total of what? The columns would obviously not add up to those numbers (although they might be averages). A larger issue is the nature of the numbers themselves. No unit of measure is given: Are they percentages? Scores on a test? According to the table title, they are indicators of proficiency, but it is not clear exactly how. Perhaps they are average scores on a test that has 400 possible points. All we can do is compare the numbers with each other and note the differences or similarities across the three years in the column heads; what the numbers mean outside the context of the table is never explained, and that's essential if the table is to communicate its data clearly. This table needed a thorough copyedit.

Editing a word table for readability

Tables can represent details that would require several paragraphs and hundreds of words of text to describe; skillfully handled, they increase the authority and usefulness of any document. Rather than repeating the text, tables are generally used to present full data in a format that invites readers to compare kinds of information. But poorly organized or inconsistent tables may prevent readers from pursuing the details that tabular format is meant to illustrate.

Table Before Copyediting

Table 1. Early Subacute Period (7 to 72 Hours).

Area	Study	Effects of ECT
General Intelligence	Calev et al., 1991*b*	No change*
	Taylor et al., 1985	No change*
	Calev et al., in preparation	No change*
	McKenna & Pratt 1983	Improvement (on Digit Symbol Subtest of the WAIS)
Language	Taylor et al. 1985	Results suggestive that verbal fluency** is adversely affected
	Lerer et al., in press	Verbal fluency** adversely affected
	Taylor & Abrams 1985	No change (on a variety of language tasks)*
	Jones et al., 1988	One of 20 tasks (word fluency, assessing retrieval from semantic memory) affected**
Perceptual and Visuo-Spatial Function	Taylor et al. 1985	No change*
	Taylor and Abrams 1985	No change*
	Calev et al. 1991*b*	No change*
Motor function: Manual dexterity	Taylor & Abrams 1985	No change
Higher cognitive and frontal function	Taylor et al. 1985	No change*
Lawson et al. 1990	No change*	

* No change can be attributed to ECT.
** Calav et al. 1993*b* suggest this may be a memory rather than a language problem.

The table was adapted—greatly adapted—from an article in a National Institute of Mental Health journal.

A case in point is the "Before" table on this page, an editor's challenge if ever there was one because it's all words, no numbers. Specs require it to be a single column, and because space is at a premium, the table must be as short as possible while remaining readable. Try the techniques discussed here next time you're editing a word table this difficult to follow.

Table After Copyediting

Table 1. Effects of Electroconvulsive Therapy (ECT) in the Early Subacute Period (7 to 72 Hours After Administration).

Area and Study	Effects[1]
General Intelligence	
Calev et al. 1991*b*	No change
Calev et al. in preparation	No change
McKenna & Pratt 1983	Improvement (on WAIS[2] Digit Symbol subtest)
Taylor et al. 1985	No change
Language	
Jones et al. 1988	One of 20 tasks (word fluency in retrieval from semantic memory) affected[3]
Lerer et al. in press	Verbal fluency adversely affected[3]
Taylor & Abrams 1985	No change (on a variety of language tasks)
Taylor et al. 1985	Results suggest that verbal fluency is adversely affected[3]
Perceptual and Visuo-Spatial Function	
Calev et al. 1991*b*	No change
Taylor & Abrams 1985	No change
Taylor et al. 1985	No change
Motor Function: Manual Dexterity	
Taylor & Abrams 1985	No change
Higher Cognitive and Frontal Function	
Lawson et al. 1990	No change
Taylor et al. 1985	No change

[1] No change = no change that can be attributed to ECT.
[2] WAIS = Wechsler Adult Intelligence Scale.
[3] Calev et al. (1993*b*) suggest this may be a memory rather than a language problem.

Plan your editorial attack. An editor sizing things up might first note the obvious readability problem in the *column* on the right, but worse problems come to light quickly: Studies are arranged inconsistently, acronyms aren't explained, and the title and footnotes don't give enough information for the table to stand alone without reference to the accompanying text. There are also the usual editorial inconsistencies like *and* vs. ampersands and comma vs. no comma before the year in the study items.

If you're confronted with these kinds of problems, relax and take on one at a time. Do them in whatever order works best for you. Start with your personal strong suit. If you're primarily a consistency person, tackle the copyediting issues first. If you have an eye for organization, reorder the elements first and then clean them up. However you do them, here are the tasks necessary to salvage this particular table.

- **Make the citation style for studies consistent.** If the references in the text use author/year format, use the same punctuation in the table—this will take care of the comma/no comma and *and*/ampersand inconsistencies. Of course, you'll delete the period after *et*—a common error.
- **Decide on a consistent order for the studies.** Right now they appear to be in no order at all. The two possibilities are chronological and alphabetical:
  - If *when* a study was done is important for the data, or if the data show a *progression* of results (say, from little to considerable benefit after undergoing a procedure), choose chronological order.
  - In other cases, choose alphabetical order. Check the reference list for the document; if it's in alphabetical order, arrange the studies having the same first author in the same way in the table. This probably means you'll have the two-author studies before the *et al.* entries.

- **Check the main stubs (*Area*) for consistent capitalization.** Choose caps for all important words or only for the initial word (sentence-style caps), but be consistent.
- **Make sure the footnote style is optimum.** Use the footnote style that best matches the content. Numbers are generally used for footnote callouts in tables that are largely composed of words, letters are used in tables with number data, and asterisks are reserved for the various standard levels of statistical probability. Check the rest of the tables in the document and make this one consistent with them.
- **Make sure the title is descriptive.** "Early Subacute Period (7 to 72 Hours)" leaves the reader asking, "Early subacute period of what? 7 to 72 hours before or after what?" Although the main text will probably answer these questions, tables should be complete in themselves; the reader shouldn't have to study the accompanying text to figure out what a table means.
- **Verify that each acronym is explained.** The acronyms ECT and WAIS aren't explained. If the text doesn't provide the spelled-out terms, check whatever reference sources you have (an acronym dictionary is a wonderful thing!) or query the author. Even though this table is supposed to be short, it can't take substantive shortcuts. Find a logical place in the table to spell out the acronyms or add a note at the bottom. The revised table shows both solutions.
- **Try to simplify the wording.** Read through all the data for sense. Clarify or query any entry that isn't immediately clear to you. Look for ways to simplify some of the language in the "Effects of ECT" column without changing the meaning. Fewer, well-chosen words would help shorten the table and speed reader comprehension. And while you're cleaning things up, be suspicious of the single "No change" in this column without an asterisk. It's probably a simple typo, but you can't be sure; query the author.

Look for ways to improve readability. Now that the largely editorial matters are taken care of, you're ready to deal with the overall look of the table. Narrow columns are no problem with numbers, but this table is all words, and the information is hard to read. In fact, the narrow width of the table is the biggest graphic problem.

- **Column width.** If you spread this material over two columns, the table would be readable. Since the specs require that the table fit into a single column, you have two possible solutions:
  — Try a smaller type size, or
  — Combine the left and center columns

  Since the type is already pretty small, combining the columns is a better solution. Look at the revised table. We simply changed the column heads to read

"Area and Study" and "Effects" and subordinated the items in the column of studies under their appropriate topics. The resulting table has two columns instead of three, and the "Effects" column no longer looks like a column of words but instead offers readable blocks of type.

- **Runover lines in stubs.** Some of the main stubs, the Area items, contain a lot of words; the required runover lines will add to the length of the table. Try running these main stubs across the table instead of confining them to their column. Setting in bold or italics will make the divisions of the table data stand out and enhance readability.

- **Runover lines in columns.** What about the runover lines in the "Study" and the "Effects" columns? Your choices are to

  — Indent all runovers, or
  — Align all lines on the left.

  Indented runovers make it clear where one block of type ends and another begins. In this table, space between entries shows the reader where one group of data ends and another begins, so the indented runover lines aren't needed.

  We changed the runovers in the studies to align left. If all our efforts at shortening resulted in a table that was still too long, we could go back and close up the spaces between entries and indent the runover lines in both the studies and the effects column. The table would be on the dense side, but the indented runover lines would preserve its readability.

- **Alignment across columns.** Another format inconsistency that affects the readability of this particular table is the alignment of studies with the effects. The recurring effect "No change" is aligned with the end of its study citation, but the first line of each longer effect aligns with the first line of its study citation. This inconsistency is another common error in table formatting— with blocks of type like these, it's better to align first lines across the columns.

Look at the "After" table on page 235. For our trouble we have a table that's well ordered, understandable as a separate entity, and (maybe most important from a layout perspective) about an inch shorter!

The Basics of Editing Graphics

The term *graphics* embraces all kinds of illustrative material, including figures, exhibits, charts and graphs, photographs, and schematics. Some publishers also consider tables a form of graphics. Because graphics are often prepared and stored separately from the text, the margin for error increases. Check graphics in the same way as tables. First look at each graphic in relation to its description in the text. Does the graphic match its description? Does it prove or illustrate what the author says it does? Next, if working on hard copy, mark the graphic callout in the margin (F. 1, in a circle, for the first figure) or highlight it so that the keyboarder can insert the graphic in the proper place. Then edit the title and caption for format and style inconsistencies. Most style sheets specify the format for captions; if your particular style sheet doesn't, ask your supervisor or client.

Both graphics and tables should amplify, not duplicate, information in the text. The text may say, for example, that far more young men than young women are convicted of violent crimes; a pie chart can show the actual percentages of each. But if the text says that 88 percent of crimes are committed by young men and 22 percent by young women, a pie chart showing the identical statistics is redundant.

You will seldom edit the graphics themselves, but you may need to query the author about apparent discrepancies or errors. Graphics inserted into electronic files may appear easy to edit, but they can be minefields. Unless you know what program was used to create the graphics and are skilled in using it, you are well advised not to try to edit them online. Instead, print out the graphics and mark your edits on the hard copy.

Note that some options may make the graphics harder to understand. For example, a bar chart with three-dimensional columns is harder to interpret than a two-dimensional version. The three-dimensional effect doesn't detract from a pie chart, but neither does it add anything. If a pie chart has more than seven segments, it's likely to be hard to read; you may need to propose a different format.

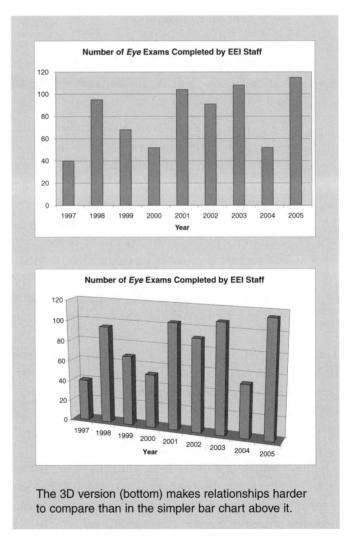

The 3D version (bottom) makes relationships harder to compare than in the simpler bar chart above it.

To edit graphics, you need some information about the publication in which they will appear. Is it a four-color journal? If so, color photographs are fine. But those great-looking photos will lose much of their impact if they're printed in black and white. A 2 × 2-inch illustration that works well in a three-fold brochure can get lost on an 8½ × 11-inch page.

Authors sometimes try to use graphics taken from the Internet. This practice raises two issues. The first is permission: Material that appears on the Internet is not automatically in the public domain. The author or publisher must obtain permission to reproduce it. The second issue is resolution: A photo can look fabulous on screen and dismal in print. Most photos on the Internet are small in size, so they look good at relatively low resolution. When blown up to printable dimensions, they look jagged or "pixellated." A low-resolution photo simply doesn't contain enough information to reproduce well on the printed page.

For a list of references to increase your familiarity with and understanding of concepts of graphic excellence, in printed and online publications, see www.eeicommunications .com/press.

ELECTRONIC EDITING BASICS: 15
Improving Workflow, Efficiency, and Quality

Since about 1990, the techniques of the editing profession have changed fast and, for some old dogs, painfully. Today, most copyeditors are expected to do the majority of their work at a computer, using electronic editing tools. Although some organizations and individuals have been slow to make this shift, paper-based editing is destined to play a small, specialized role in the future.

This chapter introduces you to the basic advantages of electronic editing—also called online editing and digital editing—for streamlining workflow:

- Edits don't have to be rekeyed (and checked) from marked-up paper drafts.
- Hundreds of manuscript pages are easily navigated, updated, and stored.
- Documents can easily be shared by work groups and sent to authors and reviewers.

Electronic editing can also improve the efficiency and quality of a copyeditor's work. Once mastered, text-manipulation tools and task automation offer the following advantages—a list that will doubtless grow as technology advances:

- Text is easily browsed.
- Text is easily inserted, deleted, and moved.
- Words and phrases can be searched for and replaced at the stroke of a key.
- Spelling checkers, although not infallible, quickly find and correct many typos.
- Other programs, databases, and electronic resources, including the Internet, offer access to everything from maps of Uzbekistan to lists of all known bird species. Fact-checking is faster and easier than ever.
- Software tools, macros, and add-ins can speed routine mechanical work by automating tasks such as building a table of contents, formatting headings, styling reference lists, and correcting repetitive errors.
- Everybody's favorite little button—Undo—instantly reverses mistakes, recovers original text, and can help you test and decide between alternatives.

This chapter also outlines some common problems that can befall the unwary editor working online. New editors, as well as experienced editors who are making the transition to working online, beware: The computer can be your ultimate editorial tool and best friend or your worst enemy, depending on how you approach it. It's not magic.

The genuine advantages of electronic editing are balanced by some serious liabilities:

- Text is a moving target and can be difficult to read onscreen.
- Automatic software features can modify a document "behind your back."
- Special characters, coding, and formatting are often lost when files are converted from one software or application to another.
- Without good file management, document versions are easily confused.
- Work can be quickly and completely lost.

Electronic editing as a skill set is evolving; although widely practiced, it is neither widely mastered nor universally standardized. Best practices are still being developed and pitfalls discovered. But today, technical proficiency (if not wizardry) in computer use is an essential requirement for professional editors. They're often described as "word people," but they are really word mechanics. Any editor who doesn't feel at ease with at least a few of the most widely used publishing softwares is at a distinct disadvantage. Of course, facility with electronic tools is no substitute for using good editorial judgment, but both are acquired the same way: with formal training, practice, and on-the-job alertness.

Computing Essentials for Editors

Because this chapter is not a software tutorial, we assume that you can already create and open word processing files; can use a mouse; are familiar with pull-down, toolbar, and keyboard commands; and can compose and edit text onscreen. These skills are fundamental to the work of most editorial professionals.

The greater efficiency realized by working electronically comes with acceptable trade-offs: software mishaps, version confusion, and formatting errors. Every editor experiences these mishaps occasionally.

Perfect computer literacy is not a reasonable goal. But editors are an easily anguished animal; they tend to have zero tolerance for the little digital surprises that might elicit a mere groan or rueful chuckle from others. Problem-solvers at heart, editors need and want to learn how to anticipate glitches, spot signs of trouble, and head off or reverse technical errors. That is what this chapter is intended to help you do.

Obviously, you would never intentionally introduce or overlook editorial problems into a text you're working on. But the quality and completeness of any online edit are compromised if you are on automatic pilot where technical considerations are concerned. If you've overlooked enough of the pitfalls listed here, you might even have to redo your editing of an entire document to correct the ensuing errors and omissions:

- **No file assessment.** When you receive a file from a writer or project manager, take the time to check for hidden tracked changes—that is, text that was at one point marked for deletion but that has not in fact been deleted. Like invisible ink, "undead" text can reappear when your copyedited file is converted (by production staff or a printer) to a new file format (say, in a desktop publishing software). If the new file format does not recognize the earlier instruction to delete that text, it will be "read" as live and be retained.

- **Obstructed view.** If you edit a document in Normal instead of Page Layout view, you will not see the text in a page footer or footnotes, so you will miss any grammatical errors or typos there.

- **Uncontrolled automatic changes.** If you edit a file with all the autocorrect, autocomplete, and autoformatting guns blazing, you are quite likely to be unpleasantly surprised by the results. When you key in a term, say, *special* on one line, the computer may "helpfully" change it to SPECIAL DELIVERY for you. When you key in an Internet address, your computer may try to underline and hyperlink it. The underline, which should not show in a printed copy the way it does onscreen, could easily be carried undetected through the production process and show up in the finished piece, to everyone's great embarrassment. Many people know how such glitches happen; but instead of saying "too bad," we tend to think, "Hmmm, the editors were not awake at the helm."

- **Reckless global changes.** Let's say that you've made a global change to upper-case the word *Exercise* throughout a book like this one. At some point, it is more than likely the authors have encouraged copyeditors to "exercise good judgment." Guess what will happen to the verb *exercise*? Right. The global change command does not discriminate or ask questions—it follows through with relentless, mindless consistency. Anticipate problems like that before making any global changes.

- **Blind grammar- and spell-checking.** As a final step, all copyeditors should grammar- and spell-check the document they have just completed work on. But the checking tool is going to mindlessly follow the instructions programmed into it, unless you override bad suggestions and correct errors in the program's dictionary and grammar advice. Again, you must use automatic tools with full awareness of how wrong they can steer you. For example, in a final spell-check of a document to be presented to highly critical managers, the abbreviation for the term National Association of Realtors (NAR) was "corrected" to *Nap* throughout.

- **Improper file-sharing protocols.** Your author or you might have spent a lot of time creating three head levels in a word-processing program by applying unique formatting rather than by marking head levels A, B, C, and so forth. But all your formatting keystrokes will be lost when the edited file is imported to a new application for page layout. Without clear formatting instructions from the copyeditor to follow a printout, and in the absence of embedded markup for head levels, a production specialist will treat the three head levels as one level, without distinction.

These types of problems and many others will come to light and can be corrected if copyeditors read through a document after all automatic changes have been made. Some editors call this a "read-behind step," and, ideally, it is done by a copyeditor who has not worked on a particular document. At the very least, spot-check all the "fixes" (from capitalizing a name that is also a common noun to adding or deleting a hyphen to a compound word) you have told the computer to make for you before sending it forward to production.

Know your software applications

First and foremost—and this cannot be over-emphasized—editors must know their software. Know it cold, inside and out. Know how to use every command on every menu. (And, while you're at it, you might as well learn everything you can about the software others are using, if you plan to share files with them.)

It is the nature of the business that, if there is one command you don't know how to use, you will accidentally execute it on a document five minutes before deadline, then be unable to undo it. Text assigned to an editor is precious to somebody, or else no one would aspire to print it. Imagine an automobile mechanic's workshop, cluttered with parts and tools. On one wall hangs a bizarre but scientific-looking item and a sign:

WARNING! DO NOT USE!
NO IDEA WHAT THIS IS FOR!

Would you take your Ferrari to this mechanic for a tune-up?

WYSIWYG

Once upon a time, onscreen text was green type on a black background. Today, word-processing applications such as Word and WordPerfect are WYSIWYG (pronounced "wis-ee-wig"), meaning "what you see" (on the screen) "is what you get" (in a printout). More accurately, they're almost WYSIWYG. For editors, that "almost" can make a difference, as when you attempt to query an author about a sentence that falls on the last line of your page 37, but the first line of the author's page 38. (For solutions to this common problem, see "Embedding queries in the text," page 280.)

And remember that the operative word in WYSIWYG is *you*. Page layout, fonts, and other formatting in Word and WordPerfect documents are notorious for changing when they're viewed or printed on another person's computer system that has different user and printer settings. Even with the same fonts loaded, two printers will break pages at different points. A page that breaks perfectly on the author's printer may produce a widow on the editor's printer.

Word and WordPerfect may behave differently depending on the devices on which they are running and the printers to which they are connected. Professional layout programs such as QuarkXPress and Adobe InDesign use PostScript—a page description language that controls the way a page will look. If you open a QuarkXPress or InDesign document and you don't have the correct fonts and images, you will receive a warning and an opportunity to repair the problem.

But in Word or WordPerfect, no such warning will be given, and missing fonts will simply be replaced by default fonts. There are options and utilities in Word and WordPerfect to help with this situation, but they are not immediately obvious or intuitive.

For these reasons alone—and there are many others—word-processing programs are tricky to use for layout. But in the real world, they're used to create many low-cost newsletters and other publications, so editors need to be aware of the pitfalls.

At the time of this writing, no software application is preferred industrywide for copyediting, and no application has been developed specifically for the copyeditor. Most editors use a general-purpose word-processing application such as Microsoft Word or Corel WordPerfect, because they offer a good mix of what editors need:

- Sophisticated text editing tools
- User-friendly text browsing and viewing options
- Ability to customize menus, keystrokes, and automatic functions
- Ability to open and read a variety of file types
- Operability on both Mac and PC platforms
- Nearly every formatting option available to printers
- Tools to create and edit tables, equations, and other graphics
- Tools to track and show revisions

Sounds great, right? But there are risks to using Word and WordPerfect. Formatting, especially, can become complex and unstable. Hidden coding can lurk under the surface. And those slick tools require knowledge and experience to use properly—or not to use (as anyone can attest who has managed, finally, to turn off Word's AutoFormat option).

You can also do electronic editing in other software applications, including page layout programs such as QuarkXPress and Adobe InDesign, Web page builders such as Microsoft FrontPage and Dreamweaver, and presentation programs such as Microsoft PowerPoint. The files you create in these applications may be larger, more complex in terms of available formatting options, less compatible with other applications, and more stable than Word or WordPerfect files.

This chapter will focus on the most widely used programs: Word and WordPerfect. But most of the principles and techniques are true for all applications.

File assessment before editing

In a happy world, electronic files arrive in your inbox or network drive like little presents, warming your heart and tempting you to meet yet another deadline with time to spare for a snack. All too often, in reality, one of those nicely wrapped presents disguises a bomb. Just as Coyote shakes packages from ACME before he opens them, the experienced editor—who has been burned, beaten, and blown off cliffs before—assesses new files before working on them. The following are important to determine before you set to work:

- **What is the file type?** Can you open it and read it? File type is indicated by a three-letter extension to the file name. The table on page 245 shows document file types commonly encountered by editors.

Along with the file type, it is important to consider which software version was used to create the file. Generally, later versions of word-processing programs can read earlier versions, but the reverse may not be true. Earlier versions may not be able to take advantage of the bells and whistles included in later versions. If you and the author are working with different versions of a program, be aware of that. Otherwise, the two of you may not understand why you see different things when you're looking at the same file.

If a your computer doesn't support a particular file type, often you can save it down to a compatible type, but you risk losing formatting or other information. Watch out: Always determine file type first, then save it down before editing. An easy mistake is to open an

Common Document File Types

File Type	Extension	Notes
Text	.txt	Text files contain only ASCII characters, or ASCII characters with line breaks. They can be created with almost any word-processing program, by cutting text from any source and pasting it into a plain text file or by "saving down" another file type to text.
Rich Text Format	.rtf	RTF is a step above plain text. It allows many of the formatting options available in Word and WordPerfect but not complex formatting or coding such as embedded comments, tracked changes, formulas and codes, or paragraph styles. This lack precludes the use of many advanced tools and software features.
Word document	.doc	Conveniently, Word and WordPerfect can read each other's files, with important limitations (see File Sharing). The conversion from Word to WordPerfect or vice versa may be quite rough; software utilities are available to make the transition easier.
WordPerfect document	.wpd	
Hypertext Markup Language	.html or .htm	HTML is the coding language used to create hypertext documents for use on the World Wide Web. These plain text files include formatting codes that tell browsers such as Internet Explorer and Netscape Navigator how to display text, position graphics, and display links to other pages.
Extensible Markup Language	.xml	XML is a markup language for documents that contain structured information.
Portable Document Format	.pdf	PDF is a type of formatting that enables files to be viewed on a variety of computers, regardless of their operating system or the source application originally used to create the files.
PowerPoint presentation	.ppt	PowerPoint is a presentation and graphics software application; it's part of the Microsoft Office package.

unknown file type, begin working on it, then attempt to save it—only to discover that you must save it to a different file type or version and will lose all the formatting.

- **What is the file size?** Files are measured in bytes, usually kilobytes (KB), megabytes (MB), or gigabytes (GB). Like a tailor with an eye for arms and legs, a good editor can guess a lot about a file just by its size. In assessing new files, make it a habit to reality-check the size against the content. If you're expecting a 20-page document and you receive a 100 KB file, chances are it includes embedded graphics. Such a file may be slow to save, and the graphics may obscure your edits when you track your changes. One option is to cut and copy the graphics to a separate file, edit the text, then put the graphics back in when the editing is completed.

- **Does the file contain special or hidden formatting and coding, or graphics or other embedded files?** If a file contains special formatting, coding, tables, or graphics that make it huge, you must consider whether your computer system can handle the file without slowing down or crashing. Greater file complexity will also make the edit trickier. Consider the destination of the file. Does the client need or want the original formatting to be retained, or is the file destined for a production process that will essentially strip out the formatting? If the latter, you may be able to get the file down to a manageable size by splitting it up or stripping out unnecessary coding and formatting.

If the file contains hidden formatting and coding, you must know how to view it lest your edits garble the file. Here are common examples of formatting and coding that hide in a document and can tripwire the editing process:

- **Indexes and tables** can be generated with automatic functions. They may look like ordinary text in some views, but you'll run into trouble if you try to edit this text.
- **Formulas** are another example of text that is generated by source coding. To edit this text, you must edit the source formula or strip out the coding.
- **Special coding introduced by an extension or plug-in** can cause trouble; this includes applications such as one that helps track references and permissions via a database.
- **Graphics** may have been created with the relatively crude graphics tools of a word-processing program, or they may be embedded or referenced/linked files, which are best edited in the source program. If you are expected to edit graphics as well as text, it's best to edit the graphics in the source program that created them. Some graphics, such as pie charts or tables created in Excel, can be edited

by simply double-clicking on them, because they are **linked** to the Word file. On the other hand, an **embedded** chart originally created in Adobe Illustrator and saved as a .tif (tagged image file format) file would have to be edited in Illustrator, resaved as a .tif, then reinserted into the Word file.

- **Text boxes** are a type of graphic that may not be visible except in page layout mode, or they may hide in the margins of a document, making the file unprintable. They are difficult to edit because as the text changes, the text box may or may not resize itself to accommodate. If a Word document with text boxes is saved as a plain text file, the text file may not preserve the boxed text.

- **Tracked changes and comments** are useful editing tools, but they can create problems. Since the tracking can be hidden both onscreen and in the printout, it's easy to forget that it's there. If tracked changes are not accepted or rejected, they can haunt a document later. If you use these tools, you may need to educate the author on how to deal with them.

- **Bulleted and numbered lists** do not always survive the transition from word processing to layout. Special coding may have been used to preserve these elements; this coding can make deleting, adding, and moving copy a nightmare. It may need to be removed; then the text can be properly restyled after editing.

Subsequent sections will tell you how to address these problems. At minimum, you must know how to discover them during file assessment; then you can deal with them or consult with someone who can help you.

Revealing Codes in WordPerfect

WordPerfect is a WYSIWYG program, but it includes a useful option to view, as symbols, the formatting codes applied to document text. When text misbehaves, this tool can help you determine why and correct the problem.

Here are some pointers to make life easier when working with Word, WordPerfect, or any word-processing application that allows more than just plain-vanilla text editing:

- We can't say it enough: Know your software!
- Keep file sizes small or, if the layout is complex, keep them even smaller. Break long documents into separate files.
- Keep formatting simple. Use as few styles as possible, but do use formatting and paragraph styles, and use them consistently.

- Use standard fonts (the ones that come with most computers).
- Turn off automatic functions.

File management for the whirlwind

While a lone writer might spend months or years working on a single document, copyeditors often work as part of a team on multiple projects with multiple documents from multiple sources. Moreover, the publication process often requires iterative phases of editing, querying, and proofing. As a result, the copyeditor is often responsible for managing a whirlwind of electronic files.

Each day, new files are created or copied from e-mails, disk, download, or network drives. Maintaining and organizing them is a necessary chore to avoid frantic searches for the "right" electronic file.

In some organizations, file management is the job of a project manager or a "traffic manager," such as a production editor. But the copyeditor must know how to preserve revisions and make backups of all edited versions of a publication. A history of the editorial phase can come in handy down the road.

File location for work and storage

Electronic files can be stored on—or saved to—personal drives, network drives, or a floppy disk, Zip disk, CD-ROM, or other portable media. For mechanical reasons, reading and writing files to a portable device can be relatively slow. In contrast, reading and writing files to a personal or network drive is as fast as the speed of thought; generally, this is the best place to locate files for editing.

A personal drive (hard drive or local drive) is the device inside the personal computer or laptop. It may or may not be networked and available to persons on other computers. While dependable, personal drives are vulnerable to such ordinary tragedies as theft, power surges, and coffee spills. Partly for this reason, large organizations usually network individual computers via cable or wireless technology to a common drive, which is mechanically similar to a personal drive except that it is larger, faster, and usually sequestered in its own VIP room with security, climate, and power controls. Most important, data on networks are usually backed up at the end of every day, so files can be recovered if something happens to them.

With good technology and administration, electronic file storage on a common network drive can be at least as reliable as paper storage. Errors, when they occur, are more often human than mechanical. For example:

- Depending on settings, deleting a file from a network drive may send it to oblivion, rather than to an electronic "trash can" from which it can be rescued if you have second thoughts.

The Copyeditor's Guide to **Substance**&*Style*

- The complexity of directories—or electronic "folders"—on a network drive can make it difficult to find a file accidentally saved (or dragged and dropped) to the wrong place. A possible solution: Operating systems and software applications track "recently used files." Once the file has been reopened, its properties (usually under the file menu) may disclose the file path. Or you can simply resave the file to the right location.
- Even if the file is saved where it should be, human memory may fail, especially when people are working with many folders and subfolders. If you often find yourself with printout in hand, file at large, one solution might be to add the file name and path to the footer of every document you work on. A simple macro can do this in one click (see Macros sidebar, page 281).
- Network drives may be available to many people in an organization, making files saved there vulnerable to the good intentions but perhaps poor editing of others. A "don't touch my stuff" culture helps. Another solution is to

Save, AutoSave, or Save As?

Save is your life insurance command. It overwrites old data with new data, and if you do it compulsively as you edit electronic files, it can protect against lost work in case of application or system death.

Control+S is the keystroke command for saving files in any application. On most personal computers, the F2 key will also save. Some applications, such as Word, offer an autosave option. Operating systems may also automatically save files as "temp" files. While useful for emergencies, temp files can clutter up directories and hog memory, particularly if you are working on big files.

AutoSave or **AutoRecover** will save your file while you're working. If you're editing a large, graphics-heavy document, your machine/file may suddenly seem sluggish while you're working because an autosave is under way.

You may prefer to make your own choices about when to save, rather than allowing the computer to save at preset intervals.

It is possible and sometimes useful to control the results of an edit by deciding when and what changes to save. For example, a good trick before attempting a risky change (such as a global search and replace) is to save the document, then execute the change. If you don't like the change, close the document without saving, then reopen it to recover the original text.

Save As is your witness-protection command. It gives you the opportunity to rename and relocate an active file. The original is closed and returned to wherever it was last saved in whatever condition it was last saved. The Save As command (via menu option or F12 key) is often used to copy a file to a new location, save a new version of a file, or save a file backup. Examples:

- After opening a document attached to an e-mail or located on an FTP (File Transfer Protocol) site, use Save As to rename and relocate it to your personal drive for editing.

- After opening a document on a network, use Save As to create a new file in a different directory, with a new name, for editing.

- After editing a document, save a backup to a disk or other external medium. Be sure to do a final save before you Save As, so the backup will include all changes.

The Save As command also can be used to "save down" a file, by designating a different file extension, to make the file readable by an older version of software or to strip out undesired coding and formatting.

password-protect important files. However, depending on settings, even protected files can be opened, saved as new files, and modified.

File organization and naming

Operating systems provide different ways to view and organize files. Generally, files are contained in virtual directories or folders. Windows Explorer, for example, uses an exploding tree system to show directory hierarchy and contents as well as individual file properties such as size, type, and date modified. Even though it is not "editing," the exploding tree system is something you should learn to use.

A sensible approach is to group files into a directory because they "belong together" for reasons of logical, chronological, categorical, or some other functional relationship. Of course, files may also "belong" with other files in other directories. This rather important limitation of a hierarchical filing system encourages file duplication, especially across office departments or work groups. As technology advances, methods of organizing files may change; but for the moment, folders rule.

The unique needs and styles of individuals and organizations make it impossible to advocate one file folder system over another. If you've ever cleaned your house and then been unable to find something important, such as your car keys, you can appreciate the fact that good organization depends on habit as well as logic. But unless you are working totally independently, some logic is helpful to improve communication on a work team. A logical system may also help your own performance; for example, if you must return to a project after a long vacation in Aruba. (Some of us have trouble finding files after a long lunch!)

For example, you might organize all old files into a folder called "Dead" and put current files in a folder called "Live." This simple method works well for simple projects. In most offices, multiple nested folders provide more detailed information about their contents. For example, the top-level folders of the editorial department of a book publisher might contain all files relating to particular book projects. Subfolders might contain administrative files such as contracts and invoices; original files from authors; copyedited files; and final files, with queries resolved, ready for layout and production.

One liability of relying on folders to describe the content of a file is that files often are separated from their folders; for example, when they are e-mailed to authors, other editors, or reviewers. For this reason, it is useful to provide as much information as possible in the actual file name, including

- Project name
- Document name

- Step in the process: substantive edit (SED), copyedit (CED), final version (FIN)
- Name or initials of person who last worked on the document
- Date finished

Older operating systems limit the number of characters allowed in file names, and some e-mail programs cut off long names when files are sent or received as attachments. This is less of a problem with current software and systems, but one still runs into it occasionally. Abbreviations may help.

Compressed Files

Compressing files may be an option when file size hampers the ability to distribute them electronically or when combining several files into one compressed file is advantageous. WinZip and StuffIt are popular software applications for compressing digital files. These applications can combine several files into one compressed archive. The amount of compression or reduction in file size depends on the file formats and the configuration of the compression program. Many compression utilities are available, and they are continually being upgraded with more advanced features.

If there are multiple reviewers, they might add their names or initials to the file name to indicate that their review is complete. If a file goes back and forth more than once between author and editor, your file names might look like this:

- chapter1.doc (original file)
- chapter1_Ced.doc (copyedited file)
- chapter1_AuRev.doc (author's responses to the editing)
- chapter1_RevEd.doc (author's responses reviewed by the editor)
- chapter1_RevEdAu.doc (editor's final changes reviewed by the author)
- chapter1_Final.doc (file that goes into production)

Underscores or hyphens can be used to delimit information items. For example, the file "MFD_5 Sting Fruit_CED_LM_112504.doc" describes a chapter 5, "Sting Loves Steamed Fruit," for a book called *Music for Dining*, copyedited by Lee Mickle on Thanksgiving Day in 2004. (Fortunately for Lee—and possibly for Sting—this is a hypothetical example.)

It can be argued that the date is unnecessary because file properties, which can be displayed in exploding tree systems, track the date when a file was last modified. However, the date last modified can easily be accidentally changed. For example, if you (or someone else in the office) opens an old Word document and prints it to a new printer, the pagination may change—so, when the file is closed, Word will ask, "Do you want to save changes?" If the user says "Yes," the date last modified will be updated and cannot be changed back.

Which information to put first depends on how you like to order your files to view them in an exploding tree system. For example, if you put the date first, the files in your directories will be ordered by default from oldest to most recent. If you put the step first, all copyedited files, all reviewed files, and all final files will be grouped together, which may reduce the number of folders you need.

Version tracking for integrity—and sanity

There are many good reasons for saving multiple versions of a file, particularly at important milestones in the publication process:

- Previous versions back up new versions in case of loss, corruption, or failure.
- Versions help track when changes are introduced to a document and by whom. In publications, responsibility for an error usually determines who pays to correct it.
- Versions provide proof of work accomplished.
- With the Compare Documents command in Word or the Redlining command in WordPerfect, the original version of a file can be electronically compared with the final version to show edits (e.g., for an author proof).
- Authors and reviewers may use older versions of a document as the basis for answering editorial queries or suggesting additional edits. An editor who has to incorporate into a new version changes located by their page numbers and paragraphs in a previous ("dead") version often must slog painstakingly back and forth between the two versions, trying to transfer changes without introducing errors. That should be avoided, if possible, but sometimes it must be done.

There are also pitfalls in saving multiple versions. A common problem is version confusion. When a document has multiple authors, editors, or reviewers, electronic versions can proliferate quickly. You may be the person responsible for controlling the live, or master, version. Managing your own electronic filing system is one thing; getting others to follow your procedures is a job for a general, not a copyeditor. One solution is to make everyone use a printout or PDF (an "electronic printout"), not the electronic version, to review the document.

Alas, deadlines sometimes make it necessary to compromise. If an electronic file must be shared, especially if it has already been copyedited, it is advisable to allow only one person to work on it at one time or, if the file is split up, one person to work on one piece at one time. It's important to note that after a file has been shared, you can no longer stand behind the document unless you read it through again line by line. For this reason, it is best to share the smallest part—by cutting and pasting—that you must share.

Flow sheets and cover memos help track a paper document as it travels around an office or back to an author for proof. A good flow sheet usually describes where in the process the document is, who has the original, where it will go next, and what the deadline is. Today, proofs are often shared electronically in PDF format. Information about the PDF proof can be provided in a separate e-mail or in a cover memo pasted into the PDF as the first page.

Ensuring compatibility for smooth workflow

In a perfect world, everybody in the publications lineup, from writer to editor to layout specialist, would use one kind of computer and one software program to do everything. In reality, however, computer hardware and software choices are myriad and specialized. Even within an organization, Mac and PC people may have issues. When freelancers, long-distance subject matter experts, and field staff are added to the mix, the workflow can seem like a free-for-all—or can grind to a halt.

Of the many challenges having so many "cooks" creates, perhaps the greatest is compatibility, a technical term meaning the capability of one kind or version of software to read files created by another. Compatibility is not always an on-off proposition; like a dimmer switch, it can range from floodlight bright to art gallery dim. In terms of publications work, dim lighting means that errors proliferate.

Who is the best cop for the compatibility beat? Often, it is the editor (who else can spot that milligram posing as a microgram?), regardless of when the errors happen (e.g., in the transition from the writer's WordPerfect to the editor's Word, or from the editor's Word to production's InDesign).

True, as an editor you cannot take responsibility for everything that happens on the production line. But you can be aware of potential problems and take steps to avoid them. You can ensure that edited files you pass along to production are squeaky clean. This means assessing and cleaning up the files you receive from writers or clients. Further, it means virus-checking all files you receive or download—even when they come from someone you know well, including your colleague in the next cubicle.

If you work in a company that has a production department, it should be easy to ascertain that department's needs. If you're a freelancer and don't know who will be dealing with the files later on, you can win friends and keep clients by sending along a memo describing the file type; software version used in editing; types of coding and formatting in the file; and your name and phone number or e-mail address so you can answer any questions that arise.

Traditionally, desktop publishers and graphic designers prefer Mac because of better graphics functionality; authors and editors prefer PC because of low cost and greater mutual compatibility. Many of the platform differences between Mac and PC have become cosmetic rather than functional—but not all. File naming conventions, fonts, and image formats still create problems between the two. For example, the same name may indicate a different font on PC than on Mac. Any nonkeyboard character—from the simple em dash to foreign-language characters—may run into compatibility problems. And the more elaborately a document is formatted, the more difficult it is to move from one platform to another. When you run into seemingly inexplicable errors of this kind, you can assume that the file was created on a different platform. Knowing that, you can watch out for formatting glitches and correct them as you edit.

Viewing, Browsing, and Editing Text Onscreen

On paper, the position of words, sentences, and paragraphs never changes. The editor's eye easily tracks from line to line, guided, if necessary, by the point of a pencil. Editors with good visual memory can often recall accurately the north-south-east-west page coordinates of a word or phrase, such as a table callout, from many pages ago. But on a computer screen, lines of text are continuously scrolling inside the frame of the application window and rewrapping as you insert or delete text. If there's a common complaint about electronic editing, it's probably this: Text is a moving target.

Viewing text onscreen

Your eye, tracking from moving line to moving line, must chase down mistakes. If you glance away from the screen, it may be difficult to find your place again, and it is usually impossible to locate recently viewed words or phrases by remembering where they were on the page. What to do? These tips may help:

- **Zoom.** The perfect level of zoom depends on the level of detail you are reading for in a particular pass through a document. When checking head levels, for example, zoom out to view one or more entire pages at once. When finessing sentences, zoom close. Some editors assign keystroke commands to two zoom settings, so they can switch quickly between big and detailed views.
- **Change the contrast and brightness settings.** Make sure the settings are optimal for your preference.
- **Get a bigger, better monitor.** A large, high-definition screen will also extend the useful life of your most important tool—your eyesight.
- **Hide toolbars you are not using.** To eke out every pixel of screen, you might also try shortening and combining toolbars by customizing them (an option in both Word and WordPerfect).
- **Go full screen** (an option for some applications, such as Word).

- **Split the screen.** This option in Word aids cross-checking by providing two views of the same document on a split screen, like picture-in-picture television. Mouse over the top of the scroll bar until the pointer changes shape, then pull down, splitting the screen. Edits can be made to text in either screen, according to where you click the cursor. Splitting also helps hold your place in one section of the text while you check something in another section.
- **Tile program windows.** When working on documents in two or more applications, it is often useful to tile the application windows vertically or horizontally to view multiple documents on one screen. In Windows, right-click on the taskbar and choose Tile Windows (choose Horizontally or Vertically). Mac windows must be tiled manually.
- **"Trace" with the cursor.** Some editors use arrow keys on the keyboard to trace the cursor through the text as they read. The cursor's repeat rate and blink speed can be customized. Some systems also allow you to make the cursor bigger or bolder or put it in color. There is one remote danger to tracing with the cursor: If autoformatting or autocorrecting tools are turned on, you might style a word by accidentally spacing after it. Instead of tracing with the cursor, you can use the mouse to trace with the pointer, but switching between keyboard and mouse is a slow way to work.
- **Use the cursor as a placeholder.** This is a good trick if you need to check something somewhere else in the document. Click the cursor where you are working and want to return, then use the mouse to go where you need to in the document. When you're ready to return, just hit the spacebar. The screen will jump back to your cursor location. Hit backspace to delete the space you added.
- **Use bookmarks.** In both Word and WordPerfect, an electronic bookmark can hold your place in the text, even if you close the document while you check e-mail or go out for a donut. Just remember to delete the invisible bookmark later, because it adds unnecessary coding to your document. A low-tech option: Key in a note to yourself with special characters or formatting that will be easy to find later. Remember to delete the note. Keying "[start]" where you left off is easy to do and easy to search for.
- **Show/hide paragraphs.** In Word or WordPerfect, this viewing option displays otherwise invisible spaces, tabs, and paragraph returns. This is especially useful to editors for cleaning up messy text pasted in from an e-mail or "typed" with spaces instead of tabs. This view is also helpful when you are tracking changes to help you maintain correct spacing between words.
- **Print out the document.** Its many advantages notwithstanding, onscreen editing isn't perfect. Many editors make a first pass onscreen, then print out the document for a second pass. It's often easier to flip through pages than to scroll up and down through a document, trying to find the right place to insert text,

for example. Reverting to paper from time to time can also reduce eyestrain, especially if there are lots of head levels.

Browsing text onscreen

The advantages of being able to browse text electronically compensate for the disadvantages of viewing text onscreen. Electronic browsing is fundamentally different from skimming or casually reading printed magazines or newspapers. Browsing is "linking"—moving forward and backward from reference point to reference point (e.g., from heading to heading, comment to comment, URL to URL, or search term to next instance of the term). For editors, browsing offers new ways to work systematically through a document to find errors, especially inconsistencies. Here are some methods:

- **Find or search on text.** Options—such as using wildcards, finding formatting, or matching case—can make searches more or less restrictive to return fewer or more results. Even in long documents, a savvy editor can quickly find a unique text (e.g., the first instance of an abbreviation) or variants of text (e.g., variant spellings of an abbreviation). In word-processing applications, search results are generally "returned" one at a time as in-text selections. The table on page 261 describes basic search strategies.
- **Go To commands.** In electronic documents, there is more to browse than text. You can also browse by any "marker," such as page, section, table, or graphic. For example, to quickly check the sequential numbering of all tables in a document, choose Go To…Table, and browse with the Next and Previous commands. After you get to the first one, it's faster to close the Go To box and use the little double arrows on the side scrollbar. Then the Go To box isn't in your way. This works for any kind of search.
- **Document maps.** In many applications, "maps" of the document can be viewed either in the primary window or in a split window. The map may be an index of headings and subheadings linked to the text, or a chart of thumbnails, also linked. Such views are especially useful to editors when checking head levels, confirming document flow, or moving large chunks of text to improve a document's organization.
- **Hyperlinks.** Anyone who has browsed the Web understands the utility of hyperlinks, which permit a "choose your own adventure" path through text. In online text, hyperlinks are both callouts and shortcuts to cross-referenced information, including references, tables and figures, and other pages. Even texts intended for print publication may include hyperlinks, as in automatically generated tables of contents. Hyperlinks may be identified by formatting or icons and may change color or shape on mouseover.

The Copyeditor's Guide to **Substance**&*Style*

Editing text onscreen

The keyboard and the mouse wire the editor to the onscreen text. Here are some keyboarding and mousing tips:

- **Learn to type well.** With practice, most people type faster and more accurately than they write. Because text is already keyed, editors who work online do not require blistering typing speed, but they do need sufficient skill to key in changes with eyes locked on the screen, not glancing down at fingers.

- **Use the keyboard more than the mouse.** The mouse evolved from the menu, and the combination has made working on the computer intuitive even if an application is unfamiliar. But when the application is familiar (as it should be—know your software!), it is significantly faster to execute a command with a keystroke than to interrupt keying, reach for the mouse, and hunt through menus. Somebody should rename the mouse the turtle. In races against deadline, the electronic editor who rides the turtle always finishes last.

- **When you do use the mouse, use mouse shortcuts.** Double-click or triple-click to select words or paragraphs. In Windows, right-click to pop up a menu of options to apply to your selection. Because of these shortcuts, the mouse is useful for many operations, but it requires the precision of a surgeon. A classic challenge is to select text beyond the screen view: One false twitch and you've selected half the document instead of just the paragraph you wanted. One more false twitch and you've dragged and dropped your selection up one line—an error that's easy to miss. A mouse wheel helps with these operations. In Word, setting the mouse to select whole words (see Tools…Options…Edit) makes selecting both easier and more complicated. When this option is turned on, one must select left to right, not right to left, to include punctuation that follows a word.

- **Use keyboard shortcuts.** Your word-processing software's Help menu offers lists of shortcuts. You may want to type up a list of the ones you find most useful; after you've used them a few times, you'll seldom have to consult the list.

- **Customize your own shortcuts.** Both mouse and keyboard can be customized to execute frequently used commands. For example, if you often highlight text, you may already have discovered that the command for selecting the highlighting tool does not have a keystroke shortcut in Word. Using Tools…Customize… Keyboard, you might assign a shortcut (such as Control+~) for highlighting or reassign a default shortcut you rarely use (such as Control+Shift+H, for hidden text).

Using Automatic Editing Functions

Many copyeditors consider what they do an art or a craft, but none would deny that their work is sometimes as mechanical as housekeeping. A trained monkey probably couldn't put away your CD collection in alpha order, but a computer might be able to. For editors today, the lucky fact is that computers do a fantastic job on tasks that are repetitive and laborious, provided they are also logical.

Here's a short list of editorial groaners a computer can do instantly, no complaints, provided you know the right button to click:

- In a numbered list, swap item 999 for item 3 and renumber the list.
- Find and capitalize instances of the word "federal," except those that occur in the reference list, in a 200-page government report.
- Build a table of contents for a 100-page document with five head levels, then update it after a text insertion shifts the page position of every heading.
- In a 500-page novel, change all straight quote marks to curly quote marks and all double hyphens to em dashes.
- With one click, style a heading with multiple formatting decisions and index it for browsing.
- Combine 10 separate reference lists, each containing 100 references, into one list sorted alphabetically by first word.
- Suggest corrections for the nine misspellings in this sentence: "A septuagenarian with a kaliedoscope suffered irreversable hemorraging in a periphreal dual with a mischievious aensthesiologist weilding a squeegee."
- Format footnotes in a document. Renumber them as they are added or deleted.

As those examples illustrate, automatic functions can accomplish work independently of the editor: sorting, renumbering, finding and replacing, building, updating, formatting, checking. They simplify and expedite busywork—granted, it's getting important details right, but it's busywork nonetheless. If you edit on a computer but do not use automatic functions, you are essentially working on an expensive typewriter.

But—and this is an important but—use caution. Just as instantly as they fix problems, automatic functions can foul things up beyond belief. The key to their proper use is understanding how they work. This, in turn, requires a basic appreciation for how computers "think": by rigid formula; by processing algorithms (aka "programs"); by asking x and doing z when the answer is a, then asking c, and so on.

A computer cannot do what all good editors can do: finesse, waffle, blur, make exceptions, tweak, adapt on the fly. At best, the computer can spit out a conclusion that is a shade of gray by working—with lightning speed—through a script of black or white,

The Copyeditor's Guide to **Substance**&*Style*

Exercise 30: Keyboard Commands Cheatsheet

Fill in this blank table with 10 new keystroke commands you want to learn. Copy the table and keep it by your computer. As you become familiar with the commands, fold the table on the dotted line to hide the keystrokes.

Command Name	My Mnemonic	Modifiers	Keys

yes or no, on or off questions. An editor can reason out the same conclusion in the same steps but is more likely to "just know"—that is, guess correctly based on previous similar experiences.

The limitations of computer "thinking" (verbatim execution of instructions, lack of creativity, literal-mindedness) lead to the following cardinal rule when using automatic functions: Check what the computer does! Be especially careful to check changes that are executed beyond your viewable window of document text, such as changes that result from Select All, Replace All, AutoFormat, and Update commands. "Globals" are changes applied to an entire document. Almost every editor experienced with electronic texts has been tempted to "do a global" to correct a problem discovered minutes before a deadline, and almost every editor has suffered the consequences when unexpected changes result.

The bottom line of good electronic editing is this: Either check automatic changes, or don't use them. Here are some specific automatic functions, with advice for avoiding hidden dangers.

Find and replace

Find and Replace is a basic yet powerful tool. Using it requires knowledge of search strategies described in "Viewing, Browsing, and Editing Text Onscreen," page 254, and adhering to these general principles:

- **Restrict your search.** You can catch a fish with a net or with a line. Browsing text with the search command is like fishing with a net: Use broad search parameters to catch a range of similar results. Finding and replacing, on the other hand, is like using a wooly bugger fly to catch a Saskatchewan lake trout: Restrict the search parameters to find text that is as specific as possible.
- **Include formatting in your search.** If text is not already distinguished by formatting, consider applying temporary formatting (e.g., highlight or font color) that can be undone later. For example, to change "behaviour" to "behavior" in the text of a psychology chapter intended for an American audience but *not* in the titles of the British articles in the reference list, first highlight the reference list, then search and replace <behaviour> (no highlight) with <behavior>. Then unhighlight the reference list.
- **Include special identifying characters,** both visible and invisible, in your search. Sometimes text occurs in the context of specific punctuation, symbols, spacing, or paragraph returns, any of which may be included to help identify the text itself. Just remember to add back the identifier with your replaced text. For example, in a document that consistently styles *p* (the symbol for

Search Strategies

If you want to...	Remember that...
Find whole words or phrases	Searching on "example" will not find "exam." Searching on "exam," will not find "exam."
Include formatting	You may want to find only underscored terms so you can change them to italics.
Match case	Searching on "Chapter" will not find "chapter."
Find part of a word or phrase	Searching on "exam" will find "exam," "example," "examination," etc.
Find all word forms	Searching on "ask" will find "asked," "asking," etc., but not "askew."
Choose "sounds like" or variant spellings	Searching on "bean" will find "been," "bin," and "bone," but not "blown."
Use wildcards	Use your word processor's Help menu to find wildcard search options. Using wildcards lets you tailor your search in a number of ways; for example, you can search for characters at the beginning or end of words or for words that include or do not include a specific character.

probability) as an uppercase roman P followed by a space, you might search for <P><space> (match case) and replace with <p><space> (italic).

- **Match case exactly in your search,** as in the example above.
- **Avoid using wildcards in your search.** Most find and replace functions do not allow you to selectively replace some characters and stet others found with wildcards; you must replace everything with something. For example, to change hyphens between number ranges to en dashes, one might be tempted to find <any digit><hyphen><any digit>. But what to replace with? In most applications, there is no option to stet <any digit>.
- **Think in multiple steps as you search.** To solve the above example, you might take these three steps: First, find <any digit><hyphen><any digit> and apply highlight. Second, find <hyphen> (with highlight) and replace with <en dash>. Third, find <any digit> (with highlight) and apply no highlight.
- **Find and replace one thing at a time.** Review and okay each change.
- **Use globals carefully—and do them first.** Use a global command (Replace All) as a "precleanup" step, so you'll be reading behind the computer's changes. If the global has created major problems, it's a simple matter to close the file without saving the changes. If it creates small problems here and there, you can fix them as you go along.

- **Use Find and Replace to correct ahead.** Writers tend to make mistakes consistently. If a mistake occurs twice, it is likely to occur throughout the document, so you might as well stop and make a global correction. You can use the Find Next command to get back to your starting point, then continue editing.

Find and Replace is your best friend for fixing these errors:

- **Punctuation.** For example, find <e.g. > and replace with <e.g.,>. Note that including the space makes the search more restrictive. Finding <e.g.> and replacing with <e.g.,> would change <e.g.,> to <e.g.,,>.
- **Capitalization.** For example, find <PHD> and replace with <PhD>, with whole words and match case selected.
- **Extra spaces, tabs, and paragraph returns.** In a document that uses double spaces after periods and colons, search for two spaces and replace with one space. (If you are tracking your edits, do this before you start tracking. Marking a space change after every sentence clutters up the document.)
- **Incorrect words.** Searching for whole words only will prevent introducing new errors. For example, finding <table> and replacing with <figure> will change every "stable" in the text to "sfigure," unless you select *Find whole words only*.
- **Grammar.** If you notice that a writer consistently makes a grammatical error, use find and replace to work ahead in the text and correct it, then return to your place and continue editing. For example, to correct "which/that" confusion, find <which> and replace with <that> on a case-by-case basis. To undo use of the serial comma, find <, and> and replace with < and> on a case-by-case basis; then do the same thing with <, or>. Adding serial commas is also possible but more tedious, because you cannot exclude nonserial *ands*: find < and> and replace with <, and> on a case-by-case basis.
- **Formatting.** For example, to italicize lowercase letters that follow the years in author-date citations, find <any digit><a> and apply highlight, then find <a> (highlight) and replace with <a> (italic), then undo or reverse highlighting. Do the same for b, c, d, and so on.
- **Style.** For example, find a spelled-out phrase and replace with its abbreviation, or replace % with percent (in this case, be sure to add a space before *percent*, to avoid changing 90% to 90percent: find <%> and replace with < percent>).

The Copyeditor's Guide to **Substance**&*Style*

Spelling and Grammar Checkers

Of the many automatic functions that can be integrated with today's word-processing applications, spelling and grammar checkers are probably the most widely known and used. Both tools are essentially glamorous cousins of find and replace; the authority popularly ascribed to them is undeserved, a point editors sometimes find themselves explaining (or arguing) to noneditors. Some writers and businesspeople rely exclusively on spelling and grammar checkers. The mixed results they achieve—some errors corrected, others missed, and still others introduced—arise from the limitations inherent in the way computers "read." For professional editors, understanding these limitations and the errors that can result is key to using or not using, or at least not relying blindly on, checkers. Generally, checker errors can be described as false positives (incorrect usages not identified as errors) and false negatives (correct usages identified as errors). The following examines both kinds of errors for each checker.

Remember: Checkers are a tool, not an authority—and they can steer you wrong if you accept their guidance without thought.

Spelling checkers

Give a spelling checker a list of common words, and it can tell you with 100 percent accuracy whether every word on the list is spelled correctly. But put those words in a sentence, and the checker is likely to make mistakes. This is because spelling checkers compare words in the text with words in their own dictionary, but they do not "know" how to spell, a distinction frequently lost on noneditors. If a word is in the checker dictionary, it is "right" to the checker; if not, it is "wrong."

But context affects whether words are spelled correctly. For example, spelling checkers may okay incorrectly used homonyms (bear/bare, do/dew); parts of speech (their/there, its/it's); or spellings that depend on usage (effect/affect, disc/disk). Likewise, checkers may flag as wrong perfectly correct spellings, including words with a closed prefix or suffix (posttraumatic, thirtysomething, computerwise); words with unusual capitalization, including proper nouns (eBay, L!BRARY, HarperSanFrancisco) and abbreviations (DoD, aka, SOHO, PHAs); and new coinages not in the checker dictionary. Spelling checkers flag duplicate words (*I saw the the cat running across the road*). But sometimes English allows them (*He said that that was precisely the problem*).

Most editors are aware—from painful experience—of these limitations. A problem more likely to be overlooked is that the checker dictionary is just a "word list," not a dictionary, as it contains no definitions. A checker is only as good as its list, which is most likely derived from a variety of good but unique dictionaries, including *American Heritage*, *Webster's New World*, and *Webster's Collegiate*.

Copyeditors are sometimes required to use a specific dictionary for a particular job. If the job calls for *Webster's Collegiate* but the checker is based on *American Heritage*, it's up to you to know which checker spellings to accept and which to reject.

Most checkers allow you to modify the dictionary or create a custom list to supplement it. Both options, especially the second, are useful if you frequently use the same dictionary. But this leads to another caveat: Be careful about making modifications. If you or someone else who's using your computer accidentally adds a misspelling to the checker dictionary, instances of false negatives and false positives on that word will thereafter be doubled until the problem is discovered and fixed.

Despite the liabilities, editors agree that spelling checkers improve their productivity, just as calculators improve an accountant's. Here, then, are rules to check by:

- Let's say it again: The spelling checker is a tool, not an all-knowing authority. Be suspicious!
- Use custom dictionaries if you edit similar documents that share a unique vocabulary.
- Restrict who can use your system and modify the dictionary.
- Be careful not to introduce misspellings into your primary or custom dictionaries. Once a misspelling is introduced, you may never see it again—until the computer suggests changing a correct spelling to the misspelling.
- Spell-check word by word. Do not let the checker make decisions for you. If you're unsure, look up words that the checker flags the old-fashioned way, in the dictionary specified for your job.
- Spell-check as a final step to catch new misspellings and typographical errors you may have introduced during your edit. If you return a document to an author or client with spelling errors that you have introduced, you will lose a tremendous amount of credibility.
- If you accidentally "ignore" a misspelling or "change" a word spelled correctly, you have three choices: (1) Start over. (2) Interrupt your check to find the word and fix it. (3) Write down the word and find it after your check is finished. If you fly through a check and cannot remember the word you ignored or changed, option 1 may be your punishment for rushing!

The Copyeditor's Guide to Substance&Style

Grammar checkers

Given the limitations of spelling checkers and the reasons why they are prone to false negatives and false positives, just imagine the fun a computer has trying to process the nuanced, bend- and breakable, context-dependent rules of grammar. Next time you want to blow your computer's little thinking chip, feed it this conundrum:

> For many sentences, the grammar, which determines the meaning
>
> of the sentence, is determined by the meaning of the sentence.

Is the grammar of this sentence correct? Yes, but a computer could probably never say so, because verifying the grammar that determines the meaning requires understanding the meaning. To illustrate, let's pretend we give this sentence to a grammar checker—and let's even be generous and assume that the checker correctly identifies the parts of speech and stifles its usual knee-jerk squeals about the passive voice. Now let's ask if the nonrestrictive clause "which determines the meaning of the sentence" should be restrictive, like this:

> For many sentences, the grammar that determines the meaning
>
> of the sentence is determined by the meaning of the sentence.

The answer is no. Written this way, the clause implies that sentences have multiple grammars, which is...um...*not what we mean*. But how would a grammar checker know? Unless it had a special line of code in its megabytes of script that somehow made it aware of the concept that "a sentence has only one grammar," the checker would be incapable of answering this question, which any good editor could do by thinking a moment about the writer's intent.

Even in very simple writing, sentences less puzzling than this example frequently occur, in which the grammar determines the meaning and the meaning determines the grammar. This is the fatal flaw of grammar checkers: If you cannot understand what a sentence is supposed to mean, you cannot correct the grammar. At best, grammar checkers identify possible problems. Often, they make writing worse by suggesting corrections that misunderstand the meaning. Here are typical checker "catches":

- Subject-verb agreement. Checkers may not recognize subject and verb when a modifier falls between them, or when their order is swapped, as in a question.
- Run-on sentences and fragments. Checkers generally don't like long sentences or fragments.

- Simplicity of language. Checkers may not like expressions that might be jargony, clichéd, wordy, or overstated. The suggested changes may result in a dumbing down or flattening of the writing.

Grammar checkers may be useful for people with a very poor grasp of English grammar, but a professional editor's understanding of the topic far outstrips the capabilities of today's programs. Most editors simply turn off the grammar checker.

Mind-Reading Functions and Automatic Paragraph Styles

A caveat: Automatic functions can be quite useful to editors, but they can also be a nuisance to undo (with Control+Z) when the computer's mind-reading is off the mark. Editors should know how and when to disable automatic formatting, correcting, and completing functions that are not useful and that might introduce new errors during an edit.

Autoformat, autocorrect, autocomplete

To speed word processing and document formatting, "mind-reading" functions in word-processing applications check text as it is keyed into a document and correct it automatically:

- Common spelling errors may be corrected.
- Common typos may be corrected, such as *teh* to *the* or two initial capitals (THe) to one (The). But the acronym CNA may also be incorrectly changed to *can*.
- Non-ASCII symbols may be substituted for ASCII equivalents:
- Double hyphens (--) may be changed to an em dash (—).
  - A hyphen with spaces (-) may be changed to an en dash (–).
  - Straight quote marks (" ") may be changed to curly quote marks (" ").
  - The letter c in parentheses (c) may be changed to the copyright symbol (©).
  - A colon and a closing parenthesis (ASCII for "smile") may be changed to a smiley face (☺).
  - A lowercase i may be changed to uppercase, even when you need to represent a Roman numeral.
- Formatting may be applied in cases like these:
  - Heading styles
  - Numbered and bulleted lists
  - Bold or italic
- Hyperlinks may be applied to Internet, network, and e-mail addresses.

The Copyeditor's Guide to **Substance**&*Style*

An option for handling headings

On paper, editors typically mark head levels A, B, C, and so on. Any text not marked is assumed to be body text. Onscreen, paragraphs may be typecoded, formatted, or "styled." The decision depends on the document's destination after editing.

If no production step follows (in other words, if you are working in the application that will print or publish the document), you may use whatever formatting you, the publisher, the writer, or the client prefers to make the document readable. However, most edited documents go through a production step to lay out their text in a brochure, report, book, Web, or other format. This process requires that the editor identify heads and body text for the layout specialist.

The choice among the following options will depend on available technology and the publisher's house rules:

- **Hard-copy markup.** Editors (and publishing teams) who are unable to use typecoding, formatting, or styles must resort to an old-fashioned paper markup. As a final step, many editors print out documents they have edited online and proof them. It is sensible and effective to mark head levels on this printout, then submit it with the electronic file for production. Alternatively, a clearly formatted table of contents may be acceptable.
- **Typecoding.** There is no single standard for typecoding. The preferred type-codes depend on how they will be read (by a human being or by a program). If by a human being, the typecoding—or, more simply, numbering—may appear in brackets.
- **Formatting.** Instead of typecoding, the editor can apply formatting to headings and body text to make their levels recognizable to production staff. This is a sensible option for documents with few head levels, but for more complicated documents, the distinction among head levels may become murky.
- **Styles.** Editors who are comfortable with the advanced features of their word-processing applications can use automatic paragraph styles to format heading and body text and code outline levels.

This last option—using automatic paragraph styles—is gradually becoming the standard for many publishing teams. A paragraph style is the sum of formatting decisions applied to a single paragraph, including font attributes, line spacing, tabs, and page break controls. To the word-processing program, a "paragraph" is anything followed by a hard return. For paragraphs that are headings, the style includes the heading's outline level. Paragraphs that are not headings (i.e., body text) do not have an outline level.

Automatic paragraph styles offer a number of advantages over manual formatting:

- **Efficiency.** With a single mouse click or keystroke, a number of formatting commands can be applied at once.

- **Consistency.** When a style is applied, it is applied the same way every time. A common error in manually formatting documents is to apply new formatting on top of old formatting, which often gives an inconsistent result. Style commands strip out old formatting first, then apply new formatting.

- **Flexibility.** If a style must be changed, all paragraphs coded with that style can be automatically updated throughout the document in one step. Updating all headings into a new font size can be a tedious manual task. Automatic styles make it easy.

- **Improved document organization.** Because styles code for outline level, they allow new ways to view the document (e.g., in outline mode) and browse it (e.g., with a document map). Finally, they allow automatic generation of the table of contents (see sidebar).

- **Improved file compatibility.** Outline levels can be retained when documents are imported into production applications.

The disadvantage of automatic styles is greater document complexity. Some editors complain that styles are just one more invisible factor to manage in electronic documents. For example, if one heading in a large document is not styled, it will not appear in the document map or an automatically generated table of contents. It can be extra work for the editor to make sure that all headings are correctly styled.

Other complexities are software-specific. Word, for example, likes to read your mind. If you apply extra formatting to a styled paragraph, Word may automatically add a new option to your style menu. Soon the menu has so many style options, it can be difficult to find your originals. However, creating new styles that are not based on the normal.dot template may be a better approach to ensure document stability. Default styles usually are included in the normal.dot Word template stored on the user's machine. If that template has been modified on a machine, the documents coming to that machine may be modified without any warning!

Automatically Generated Table of Contents

If all headings in a document are styled consistently, you can create and update an automatic table of contents. Table format and the number of outline levels can be customized. The automatically generated text is coded; the coding must be unlinked from the text in order to edit the table of contents. Usually, it's easier to edit the headings in the text, then regenerate the table of contents.

Software-specific complexities like these may be overcome by software-specific training and experience. Here are general tips for avoiding pitfalls:

- **Apply styles in a separate pass through the document.** Then check the automatic changes. View options such as the Document Map can help you browse for and apply styles quickly and consistently.

- **Guard against accidentally updating styles.** In Word, when new formatting is applied to a previously styled paragraph, Word will query whether you want to update or reapply the style. You want to reapply it, not update it.

- **Watch out for "formatting reversals."** Although rare, such reversals may occur when a style is applied to a paragraph with variously formatted text, such as a heading that includes a word in italic. If the heading style itself is italic, the italicized text may reverse to non-italic when the style is applied. This happens because computers use the same command, like a light switch, to toggle formatting on and off.

- **Beware of incorrect corrections.** AutoCorrect is a feature in Word that corrects spelling errors as you type. Occasionally, you may have to go back and correct the correction. If this proves too much of a struggle, turn off the AutoCorrect option.

Editing Tables and Lists Online

A table is a grid of cells that contain text or graphics. The dimensions of the cells are determined by gridlines, which may be visible or hidden. Cells, rows, and columns are changed, deleted, added, split, and merged by using commands on the Table menu.

A list is essentially a single-column table. "Delimiters" are the visible or invisible characters (e.g., bullets, commas, tabs, paragraph marks) or formatting (e.g., table cells) that separate list items. For editors, the content makes it a list; for computers, delimiters make it a list. The basic list is delimited by paragraph returns; for example, an alphabetically ordered reference list. A less obvious example of a list is a narrative comprising 10 paragraphs. An editor would not regard the narrative as a list; but to a computer, the narrative is 10 "items" of text delimited by paragraph marks.

Editing tables

Here are some pointers for editing tables in electronic files:

- Each cell, row, or column may have its own formatting, including font and paragraph properties, margins, and text wrapping or no-wrapping.
- There is a difference between selecting text inside a cell and selecting the cell itself. When a cell is selected, the entire cell—not just the text—changes color.

- New formatting can be applied to selected cells, rows, columns, or the entire table. Be careful to select the cell, not just the text, as described above.
- With the tab key, you can move from cell to cell and select their text contents. It is possible—and often essential—to use tabs inside cells. In Word, key Control+Tab.
- Table borders (gridlines) may be visible or hidden, both onscreen and in print-outs. If you open a document and notice that the text "acts funny" (e.g., the tab key jumps to and selects text, or text disappears into margins, or text wraps where it shouldn't), you are probably working in a table with hidden borders.
- The row of headings may be set to automatically repeat when the table runs over onto a new page. To edit a heading, you may have to edit it in the top heading row, not an automatically repeating row. Again, editing methods will vary slightly according to the word-processing software and will change to accommodate new versions.
- Page breaks may divide rows, causing text to wrap from the end of a cell on one page to the beginning of a cell on the next page. When you're editing long tables, it may be easiest to switch out of page layout view, so you can view the text uninterrupted by page breaks.
- Tables can do some spreadsheet tricks. For example, you can sort cells in alphabetical, numeric, or date order. You can also insert formulas to sum or perform other calculations to numbers in a row or column. You cannot edit text that is generated by a formula. To change the text, you must change the formula itself, or unlink and remove the text from the formula.
- Because tables are a kind of formatting, they increase file size and file complexity, which can affect other formatting and automatic functions, including redlining or tracking changes.
- You can convert tables to text. This option maintains cell contents but strips out table formatting. You can choose how to delimit the contents (e.g., with commas, tabs, paragraph returns, or custom characters). By the same token, you can convert text to a table. See "Editing lists" below.

Editing lists

Here are pointers for working with lists in electronic files:

- Numbered and bulleted lists are frequently used in business communications. Word-processing applications automatically number or bullet items and format them with a hanging indent. Delimiter options include a variety of number styles, outline number styles, bullets, checkboxes, and other dingbats.
- Editors frequently encounter problems changing the numbering of document headings that have been formatted as automatic lists. The solution is to use a list command or strip out the automatic coding and edit the numbers as plain text.

The Copyeditor's Guide to **Substance**&*Style*

- The advantage of maintaining automatic formatting is that the computer will automatically renumber list items if they are reordered.
- Lists, like tables, can be sorted in multiple ways, including alphabetically. (In Word, select the list and use the Sort command on the Table menu. The Sort command will work even if the list is not formatted as a table.)
- When sorting lists, be careful that your list is properly delimited, or the Sort command may split apart a list item that should be one unit. The best way

Editing in Plain Text

On yesterday's computers—less sophisticated than today's coffeemakers—editors who worked online generally used a word-processing application that could understand only the 128 characters of ASCII text, also know as "plain text." All non-ASCII characters and special formatting had to be hand-coded, that is, identified by the editor for the person or program next on the production line.

ASCII (pronounced "askey" and short for American Standard Code for Information Exchange) is a numerical code, not unlike Morse code, for 128 of the most commonly used western letters, numbers, and symbols. A nonprinting space, for example, is represented in ASCII as "0,32." ASCII can be read by just about any machine, platform, and program, from PC to Mac to Atari; from Windows to DOS to UNIX; and from Word to Quark.

Here's how the first paragraph of this chapter might look in ASCII text with manually keyed codes for formatting:

@ChapTitleA:Electronic<\n>Editing Basics:<\t>

@ChapTitleB:Improving Workflow, Efficiency, and Quality<\p>

@Body:Since about 1990, the techniques of the editing profession have changed fast and, for some old dogs, painfully. Today, most copyeditors are expected to do the majority of their work at a computer, using electronic editing tools. Although some organizations and individuals have been slow to make this shift, paper-based editing is destined to play a small, specialized role in the future.

@Body:This chapter introduces you to the basic advantages of electronic editing<\m>also called online editing and digital editing<\m>for streamlining workflow:

@Bullet:• Edits don't have to be rekeyed (and checked) from marked-up paper drafts.

@Bullet:• Hundreds of manuscript pages are easily navigated, updated, and stored.

@BulletLast:• Documents can easily be shared by work groups and sent to authors and reviewers.

The codes above indicate headings, paragraph returns, em dashes, and bullets. When the text is imported into a page layout application, in this case, QuarkXPress, these codes are interpreted and the appropriate formatting is applied.

The editor strips down (or "saves down") all incoming files to bare-bones ASCII, edits and codes the text, then passes the file—an idiot-proof and practically indestructible text file—to production for conversion to layout.

Because of the codes, the text is hard to read and slow to edit. Coding a bulleted list, for example, can be a tedious ordeal. But the simplicity of working in ASCII means that practically nothing can go wrong, and for some teams, that makes this method a very sensible choice.

to delimit complex lists (e.g., a list of names and addresses, in which every item has multiple paragraph returns) may be to use table formatting with invisible gridlines.

- Once you start a list, word-processing programs like to read your mind: If you return to a new line, the application will assume you want to continue the list. You may need to undo the continuation.
- Because they are a kind of formatting, automatically generated numbered or bulleted lists may not convert well to other applications. Bullets, checkboxes, and other non-ASCII characters may translate in surprising ways.

Coded Text: Notes, Citations, and Callouts

Electronic text can be coded to number it automatically and link it to other text, such as a note, a comment, or a reference. The linked text may appear at the foot of the page, at the end of the document, or in a popup on mouseover. A special command is generally used to insert coded text. This command may be executed by the application itself or by an add-in program such as a reference management software application (see the sidebar on page 277).

In a printout, coded text usually looks just like plain text. Onscreen, it may or may not, depending on your view options (in Word, for example, coded text might be shaded). However it is viewed, coded text is different: Underlying the innocent "plain text" displayed in your printout or on your screen may be lines and lines of software-specific coding. This coding is essentially instructions to the application for outputting the plain-text result displayed in the text itself, the linked text, or both. For example, a coded footnote callout might contain (a) instructions to count previous callouts and number this callout sequentially, (b) the content of the note, and (c) instructions for how to display the note at the bottom of the page.

Editors often encounter coded text in electronic documents that have footnotes, endnotes, comments, and citations to reference lists. Advantages include the following:

- The computer does the formatting work for you, including renumbering and repositioning coded callouts and linked text as you add or delete text.
- The plain text output of the coding can be easily updated as conditions change. For example, text may include a date that changes as the document is opened, changed, or printed.
- Coded items can be browsed with Go To and other commands.
- The ability to view linked text on mouseover or in a split window can make cross-referencing and editing easier.

Hypertexts Need Special Consideration

Hypertext is nonlinear, nonsequential writing organized by associative links. Unlike a traditional narrative, hypertext can be navigated by multiple paths determined by readers, not the author, in a "choose your own adventure" fashion. Hypertext published in virtual environments such as the Internet challenge other traditional assumptions about reading and authorship. Links, for example, may blur the boundaries of a text from one source with texts from other sources. Online text may also be generated or updated spontaneously, making it impossible to fix in time, quote, or reference with certainty.

The most common kind of hypertext is written in HTML, or hypertext markup language, a simple programming language that formats text and images so they can be displayed almost universally by many applications, known as browsers, on many computer systems. Most World Wide Web content is coded in HTML. XML (extensible markup language) is a markup language for documents that contain structured information. Most XML is transformed into HTML before it is put on the Web.

Example of HTML Source Code

This is coded text:

```
<html>
<body>
<p>
<a
href="http://www.eeicommunications.com">
This text</a> is a link to a page on
the World Wide Web.
</p>
</body>
</html>
```

It should appear as this:

This text is a link to a page on
the World Wide Web.

Editors who work with hypertext, especially Web content, may be expected to code text with HTML tags. More commonly, the editor works in a WYSIWIG program that does the HTML coding behind the scenes. Word can be used to write HTML pages, but other programs specifically designed to write HTML (such as FrontPage or Dreamweaver) write cleaner code, which results in Web pages that load faster. A document viewed with source HTML code may contain more than just text tags. Information about Java scripting, style sheets, and other automated processes may fill two pages of coding when only a paragraph of text is visible in the browser.

Because of the different kind of reading they enable, hypertext documents must be edited with special considerations in mind:

- Continuity of the text is unpredictable. Hypertexts do not have traditional beginnings and endings. Readers may join text in the middle, then jump out without finishing. To enable this, editors may add linkouts to relevant texts both within and outside the source text (while minding copyright restrictions). Conversely, to keep readers from leaving a text, editors may limit linkouts.

- Navigational links are different than indexing links. They help readers visualize the organization of hypertexts and work back or drill down to desired information. A tree-like outline or map of the content may be included on every page to help readers work back to the top of a text (e.g., the home page) for an overview or drill down to a new level of detail.

- Abbreviations and special terms may need to be defined everywhere, not just the first time they're used. This decision depends on the intended or expected audience.

- The editor must check not only grammar, spelling, and style, but often the functionality of the hypertext as well. The editor is often expected to follow links and confirm that they go where they're supposed to.

Like any automatic function, coded text also has disadvantages. Here are things to watch out for:

- If a coded callout is deleted, the linked text also will be deleted. A footnote callout, for example, may be easy to miss: a tiny superscript number closed up against a word. During editing, you might accidentally backspace over it and delete it. This deletes the note, too, and the Undo command may not get it back.
- Coded text can be converted to plain text, but once the coding is gone, so are the automatic functions, such as formatting, renumbering, repositioning, and updating.
- Linked text may be visible only in a printout or onscreen in page layout views. This makes it easy for editors and reviewers who view the document electronically to overlook the linked text.
- Because code is software-specific, file compatibility is compromised. Coded text, especially linked text, is frequently lost when documents are imported to production applications. It is important for the editor to revert coded text to plain text before files are shared. Because coded footnotes are notoriously lost in file conversion, house rules often specify formatting them as plain text in brackets immediately following the referenced paragraph. Plug-ins and extensions for programs such as QuarkXPress and Adobe InDesign are available and can be helpful, but sometimes there are trade-offs. Automated tools in your word processor can also be used to convert footnotes to plain text. The key is to have a consistent system that is used by both editors and desktop publishers.

Editing Graphics

Graphics can be created and edited in many word-processing applications. Word, for example, has a drawing toolbar with commands for creating lines and shapes that can be filled with text. Graphics created in one application can be embedded in another application file type. For example, an Excel chart can be embedded in a Word document. Copyeditors generally do not create graphics but may edit them, particularly if they contain text. It is usually inadvisable to edit the graphic electronically unless you can work in the source application that created it. Graphics may be embedded in text or linked from text to an unseen database or image.

Some subtleties are involved with the terminology for placement of graphics in Word. For example, an *embedded* graphic is different from one that is *linked*, which is different from an OLE (Object Linking and Embedding) graphic. Options for inserting images or graphics in Word include copy and paste, as well as these:

<insert, <picture

<insert, <object ("objects" can include files, such as PowerPoint slides and databases)

<insert, <file

Imagine a picture of your favorite production manager in JPEG (Joint Photographic Experts Group) format inserted into your document. If you were to open that JPEG in an image editing program and draw a mustache on it and save it, the change will not appear in Word if the picture is only embedded in the document and not linked. If it is linked, then the new facial hair will appear in the document picture.

Tracking and Showing Online Edits

Copyeditors are not oracles whose decisions are never questioned. Nor are they independent from oversight and collaboration. Often they rely on writers, other editors, and proofreaders to sign off on, read behind, and check what they do. Thus, it is important to record changes to a manuscript. Recording changes keeps the editor accountable and promotes communication and agreement.

In the days of pencil on paper, a common obstacle to review was getting a hard copy to the writer by fax, messenger, or overnight delivery. Now, files can be shared electronically in the blink of an eye. But this creates a new problem: How should the editor track and show changes in an electronic manuscript?

Blazing a trail to track changes

The crudest method is to apply formatting to indicate insertions and deletions. For insertions, it has become conventional to apply a color to the new text; for deletions, both color and strikethrough (a font option). The advantage of using color and strikethrough is that these options are intuitive, readable, and generally not used for any other purpose in a manuscript during the editing phase. These manual options imitate the tracking or redlining features offered in word-processing programs. Because they are manual, however, they cannot be automatically accepted or rejected. Italics, underlining, or boldface used to show edits may confuse anyone who is later charged with accepting and integrating the changes. All caps are sometimes used to show insertions when working in plain text (e.g., in an e-mail message), but only because more sensible options are not available. Because they seem to be SHOUTING, they may offend authors, and all-cap letters are difficult to read.

Showing changes to formatting can be a head-scratcher. Examples of formatting changes are setting the name of a ship in italics, setting AM and PM in small caps, or styling a heading in boldface Indigo Tahoma 14-point font. There is no good way to call attention to these kinds of formatting changes. Fortunately, it's usually not important for the editor to track them; when it is, the best solution is to note the change in a query or memo.

These low-tech methods to show changes are easy to understand and can be used in any software program that allows text editing. Changes are always viewable no matter what software options are turned on or off, and the document is not loaded down with special coding, which can cause file-sharing and -translation nightmares. Most important, marking edits with formatting allows edited documents to be shared electronically rather than in hard copy.

However, formatting each change can be extremely tedious and time-consuming. Also, after the changes are approved, somebody must manually update the document, which must then be proofread. Thus, this method is not much of an improvement over pencil-on-paper markups.

Change-tracking tools

Adobe Acrobat has many features and tools for editors to use. The main strength of Acrobat is portability. An Acrobat file created on a Mac using obscure fonts can be viewed with its design integrity intact on a PC on the other side of the planet. The file is portable because all the document information, including fonts and graphics, is embedded in the document, and because Acrobat file size can be kept small, allowing for easy electronic transfer.

Adobe Acrobat allows two documents to be compared to each other as in some word-processing programs. Acrobat also allows annotation or comment in PDF documents. Users may insert comments using graphical markup tools associated with notes, which can be easily compiled, summarized, and responded to. In the past, you needed the "full" version of Acrobat, as opposed to just the free Adobe Reader, to respond to Acrobat comments. Beginning with Version 7, however, Adobe has increased the ability to comment in Reader.

The two most widely used word-processing programs, Microsoft Word and Corel Word-Perfect, offer sophisticated tools for tracking and showing changes, tools that can result in great efficiencies when they're used correctly. Word calls it Track Changes; WordPer-fect calls it Redlining. When they are turned on, both tools automatically apply formatting to insertions and deletions and "remember" who (i.e., which user, identified by the software) made the edit. In both Word and WordPerfect, the default formatting is color and underline for insertions, and color and strikethrough for deletions. (In newer versions of Word, changes can be shown in "balloons" in the margin instead of strikethrough and underlining.) Also, marks or ticks in the margin identify lines with changes, and edits by different reviewers may appear in different colors. All these defaults can be customized, but the customizations may not travel with the document when it is shared. Thus, changes may appear in red on the editor's computer but in blue on the reviewer's computer.

Changes to formatting can also be tracked and shown in a different color. The best option is to show formatting changes with margin marks or ticks only. Some formatting changes "track funny"—they can be as unpredictable and unstable as an ink squirt. Paragraph returns, for example, will not close up until the change is accepted. In frustration, trying to make it look right, the hapless editor may redo, undo, redo, and undo the change until the result becomes anybody's guess. Automatically generated bulleted and numbered lists can also be difficult to modify when tracking changes. Renumbering of the list, as well as the hanging indent, may be thrown off until changes are accepted. Finally, some formatting changes, such as changes to margins, tabs, paragraph spacing, and table cells, cannot be tracked.

Reference Management Software

A number of software programs—including EndNote, Reference Manager, ProCite, Biblioscape, GetARef, and Papyrus—can be used with word-processing applications to insert, format, and manage citations and bibliographies. These add-in programs typically load into a word-processing application via a new toolbar or menu, which provides a command option to insert citations as coded text. Each citation is linked to a separate database that contains complete bibliographic information, including author names, publication data, and abstract. With other commands, all citations in a document can be formatted according to a selected publication style, and a reference list can be generated, also in a selected output style.

Writers, especially scientific writers, are increasingly using reference management software. Since about 1960, the number of scientific articles and books published each year has expanded exponentially. Because there are more sources to cite, and because electronic databases such as the National Library of Medicine's PubMed make these sources easier to find, documentation in scientific writing has likewise increased—to the point that reference lists for articles often exceed the page length of the articles themselves. Many scientific writers today generate bibliographies with thousands of entries. To manage these huge bibliographies, reference management software has become a practical necessity; thus, scientific editors frequently encounter documents that have coded citations and reference lists.

The same principles for editing any coded text apply. Most important is this: To use automatic reference management features such as formatting or renumbering citations, you must have installed the same brand and version of the software that the writer used. You may also need access to the writer's bibliographic database, either as a copy or via a network. If software and database are unavailable, the writer or editor should convert the coded text to plain text before the document is edited. The software itself may provide a command to do this, or coded text can be selected and unlinked. In Word, the command to do this is Control+Shift+F9.

Examples of Text Formatted to Show Edits

Original	Edited	Corrected	Notes
Always use spell-chaker.	Always use spell-checker. ~~spell-chaker.~~	Always use spell-checker.	Optionally, deleted text can also be set in color, but this requires an extra mouse click or keystroke.
Always use spell-chaker.	Always use spell-che~~a~~cker.	Always use spell-checker.	This edit is difficult to read and requires multiple clicks or key strokes to make. It is preferable to strike out and replace the entire word.
Read behind any global computer charges.	Read behind any global ~~computer~~ changes~~charges~~.	Read behind any global changes.	When striking out a whole word, be sure to delete a space accordingly. Conversely, when adding a word, add a space too.
Set chapter titles, such as The Copyeditor's Guide to Substance & Style, in italics.	Set **book**~~chapter~~ titles, such as ***The Copyeditor's Guide to Substance & Style***, in italics.	Set book titles, such as *The Copyeditor's Guide to Substance & Style*, in italics.	Boldface is readable, but it may confuse a noneditor who must later accept the change. In this example, would a noneditor know the book title should be italic only, not bold and italic?
Special tools, explained next, can make tracking changes easier.	Special SOFTWARE tools [DELETE , explained next,] can make tracking AND SHOWING changes easier.	Special software tools can make tracking and showing changes easier.	When using a program that edits only in plain (vs. "rich") text, such as Notepad or Web-based e-mail, you may have to resort to all caps.

A friendly—but dangerous!—option is to hide changes onscreen while you're working, so the changes are tracked but not shown. You can display them at any time. Think of this option as a kind of crystal ball that provides a view of how the document will appear when it's finalized. Just remember, you are viewing a possible future yet unrealized; all changes remain tracked and present in the document until they are accepted or rejected.

Furthermore, hidden changes, especially hidden deletions, can haunt a document if they are forgotten. Sensitive omissions or revisions can embarrass the author or editor if they're discovered by the wrong person, and text marked for insertion or deletion may not be recognized as such if it's imported to other programs. Another liability: From the computer's viewpoint, deleted text is still "there" and may interfere with search and replace commands. One final drawback is worth noting: Editors may turn Track Changes on and off as they work, tracking some edits and not others. When tracking is not shown onscreen, it's easy to forget whether the tracking tool is on or off.

Despite these risks, many editors prefer to hide changes while they're working, especially in a document that requires heavy swings of the editorial machete, because a mess of insertions and deletions distracts the eye, interrupts text flow, and confuses the sense of the writing. (This also happens when editing on paper.) A prudent solution is to edit, review, and hide changes in stages. Editors also like to hide changes because it makes spacing errors easier to spot and correct. Other editors hide changes at the end of the editing process, just before they spell-check the document.

The most efficient feature of Track Changes and Redlining comes into play when it's time to integrate changes and finalize the document. With the reviewing toolbar, the editor or author can browse, review, and accept or reject the changes one by one. It is also possible (although not always prudent) to accept or reject all tracked changes at once. This carries the same risks as any global change. Be sure all tracked changes have been accepted or rejected so the document is "clean" before turning it over for layout.

It is important to build in a final check step. After changes are accepted, review the text to correct missed or closed-up spaces and other typos that are difficult to see when the changes are showing. With electronic editing, particularly when change-tracking tools are used, many steps that used to involve multiple eyes and skills are collapsed into one person's work. It's a good idea to print copy out after editing and read it through before it goes back to the author or client for review, or moves on to production.

Queries and Incorporating Changes

Editors query authors (or clients or other reviewers) to provide missing information, clarify meaning, or approve a questionable edit. A number of methods can be used to add queries to electronically edited documents. Deciding which method to use may depend on the following:

- Will the author review the document and queries onscreen or in a printout? If a printout, whose? Different software settings and printer hardware may yield printouts with different pagination, and text that is revealed or hidden depending on the options selected. In general, if a printout is used, you should provide it—or send the document as a PDF. (See "Final Notes: Printouts, PostScript, and PDF" on page 283.)

- If the author will review the document onscreen, is the author working in the same software program and version as you are? If so, how proficient is the author with the software? Can the author use advanced tools, such as Comments, without calling you or tech support for help?
- Will the document be reviewed by multiple authors or reviewers? If so, do the queries need to be identified or sorted for the different reviewers?
- Can queries be embedded in the text, or will doing so significantly interrupt text flow and document formatting, hindering readability? If embedding will cause problems, you can use callouts to reference a separate query list.
- Will the author read the text word for word to find embedded queries? If not, how can you make the queries (or callouts) easy to find and browse?
- Who is responsible for incorporating changes to the electronic file after queries are answered? If you are, how should the author answer the query: by updating the file, or by submitting a separate answer list? If the latter, how should the author reference the query?

Because of the variety of possible answers to these questions, editors who work with electronic documents may resort to a number of query methods, depending on the situation. The following are three basic ones.

Embedding queries in the text

This low-tech method is often the most practical. Embedding means you key all your queries directly into the text in brackets, which are easy to search on because they are otherwise infrequently used. This method has two disadvantages. First, authors who do not read the text word for word may overlook the queries. Second, embedded queries—especially if they are detailed or numerous—may interrupt text flow and document formatting (e.g., in a table). Here are some tips for embedding queries:

- When multiple authors will review the document, preface each query with the appropriate author name to clarify who should answer it.
- When a single author is queried, preface the queries with QQQ (for "query") or CHK (for "check"). These standard callouts help make queries easy to find and browse with a search command. Writers and editors also sometimes use 0 (for "to come") to tag something missing, such as a date.
- To further distinguish queries from text, highlight them or set them in bold or colored font. Because highlight is infrequently used, it improves query searchability.
- It may also be helpful to highlight the specific text referenced by the query.
- Whatever the format, use it consistently.

The Copyeditor's Guide to **Substance**&*Style*

Using Macros to Automate Complex Tasks

Editors may routinely perform a series of commands, especially find and replace commands, in a rote order. For example, before editing a new document line by line, good editors like to preclean: globally search for and correct common formatting, spacing, spelling, and punctuation errors. At some point in the development of word-processing applications, someone decided it would be convenient for a user to be able to gather à la carte commands in one place, line them up in order, and save them for next time, when she—an editor, let's imagine—might snap her fingers and say, "Give me the usual." Presto: The computer executes all her favorite find and replace commands, opens the footer and inserts the file path and name, highlights every citation in one color and every table and figure callout in another color, and takes a word count. A macro—short for macroinstruction—is just such a thing: It executes a list of commands in one step.

Macros can be written in a software language (e.g., Visual Basic for Windows, AppleScript for Mac OS) or "recorded" with an application tool. Because every text is unique, macros can also introduce errors. For this reason, it is always important for a human editor to read behind text "edited" by a macro.

This simple macro, written in Visual Basic, will replace two hyphens with an em dash in Microsoft Word.

```
Sub EmDash()
'
' EmDash Macro
' Macro recorded 10/19/2005 by jsmith
'
    Selection.Find.ClearFormatting
    Selection.Find.Replacement.ClearFormatting
    With Selection.Find
        .Text = "--"
        .Replacement.Text = "—"
        .Forward = True
        .Wrap = wdFindContinue
        .Format = False
        .MatchCase = False
        .MatchWholeWord = False
        .MatchWildcards = False
        .MatchSoundsLike = False
        .MatchAllWordForms = False
    End With
    Selection.Find.Execute
Replace:=wdReplaceAll
End Sub
```

- Mind where you embed the query: Whether before or after the queried text, be consistent.
- If the author will review a printout, consider numbering the queries so they can be easily referenced in a reply document. You might insert numbers as codes to allow automatic renumbering as queries are deleted or added. When editing is complete, change the codes to plain text so they are static for the author.

Using a separate query list

It is sometimes difficult to get busy authors to review the entire text. In such cases, you may create a separate query list referenced to the text. A printed query list can be incorporated into the cover memo, commanding immediate attention. If the document will be reviewed electronically, you can e-mail the memo and query list.

Another reason to separate queries from the text is to maintain text flow and document formatting. This is important mainly if you are working near the end of the production process in a page layout application such as Quark or InDesign. It also may be important if you are sending edited drafts to multiple reviewers. In such cases, embedded queries intended for one author may distract reviewers who are expected to attend to other aspects of the writing. In addition, the queries might bias the reviewers or embarrass the author.

Normally, queries in a list are referenced to the text by page (and sometimes line) number. But the pagination of electronic documents—particularly HTML, Word, and WordPerfect documents—changes depending on user settings, which makes referencing problematic. The following are possible solutions:

- Number the queries. For a short document, you can number all queries consecutively; for a book, you can number them by chapter.
- Reference the queries by section and paragraph.
- Send the document as a PDF (see "Final Notes: Printouts, PostScript, and PDF" on page 283).
- Format queries as comments (see the next method).

Using the Comments feature

An advanced feature of Word, WordPerfect, Acrobat, and other software applications, a comment is text that is coded with automatic properties to display in a bubble, in a split window, in a list at the end of the document, or in a popup on mouseover or double-click. Like automatic endnotes or footnotes, comments must be inserted, modified, deleted, and viewed using special commands. The major obstacle to using the Comments feature in an electronic review is that the author may not be familiar or comfortable with it. If the document will be reviewed in a printout or PDF that the editor provides, comments can be a useful and attractive way to format queries.

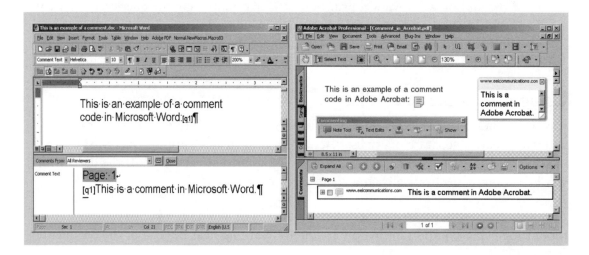

The Copyeditor's Guide to **Substance***&Style*

Whichever query method is used, editor and author must agree on how queries should be answered and how edits will be accepted or rejected. Usually this decision depends on the destination of the edited document.

If the author is responsible for its publication, you will return the edited electronic file. You may also provide instructions on how to respond to queries, accept or reject tracked edits, and otherwise prepare the file for layout.

Alternatively, you may be responsible for obtaining author responses to queries and approval of the edited document, and then passing along a final version for page layout and publication. In this case, you must ensure that authors and other reviewers do not introduce new errors after the edit. This is best accomplished by giving the author a printout or PDF to mark up or by carefully reviewing the electronic file that the author returns. The author must make any additional changes using an agreed-upon method (e.g., hard-copy markup, tracking and showing changes in the electronic review copy, or referencing changes to a printout or PDF by number). You will then transfer changes to the original file.

When authors return many changes, it may be tempting to use their copy of the electronic file, if they provide one. Best practice recommends against this: Even trustworthy authors may have introduced errors during review or corrupted the file (e.g., with templates or macros) in some way that is not immediately apparent. Unless the deadline is so tight that there is no alternative, the risk of errors and file corruption is almost never worth the time saved by using an author's file after the edit.

Final Notes: Printouts, PostScript, and PDF

WYSIWIG functionality makes it seem as if printouts of electronic documents are totally controlled by the software application. In fact, printouts are determined by behind-the-scenes negotiation between the software application and the printer. Printers come in many flavors, from the cheap desktop inkjet models many editors use to sophisticated prepress systems capable of producing high-quality, high-resolution images. Any printer is essentially an inking mechanism controlled by a little printer chip-brain, formally known as a raster image processor, or RIP. The RIP uses its own special language, called page description language, or PDL. When a document is sent to a printer from a software application, the RIP receives it as a bunch of code. The RIP translates this code into its own PDL. By this process, text is formatted and pages are laid out, and the right number and color of ink dots (the more dots, the higher the resolution) are squirted in the right places on a sheet of paper to produce the image.

In 1985, Adobe Systems introduced PostScript, a PDL that has become practically standard for desktop publishing and electronic prepress. Most RIPs now "speak" PostScript. PostScript is a reliable way to ensure that various printers accurately reproduce the appearance of the onscreen document.

Adobe also introduced PDF (Portable Document Format), a proprietary file format with a PostScript basis. Essentially, a PDF file is an "electronic printout," viewable onscreen, of any document created by any software application—such as Quark, InDesign, Word, or WordPerfect—that prints to a PostScript RIP. Because PostScript has become a standard page description language, the list of compatible software includes practically every application used in the publications industry. PDF files are created using a program called Adobe Acrobat. The Acrobat command to create a PDF is basically the same as the command to print, except that the document is "ripped" to a file rather than to paper. PDF files can be viewed, navigated, and printed using a free application called Acrobat Reader, which can be downloaded from Adobe at www.adobe.com. Acrobat Reader does not need a source program to view the PDF file, nor does it need any original fonts or graphics. And Acrobat Reader works on any computer platform and can print to any PostScript printer.

PDFs can be gently modified, using text touchup tools. They can be annotated with comments. And they can be programmed with interactive bells and whistles such as buttons, dropdown menus, and text fields. Editors generally do not use these advanced features. But they do frequently create PDFs of edited documents and share them with authors, for the following reasons:

- **To reduce file size.** Because PostScript is a relatively simple language, a PDF is usually smaller than the original file. This makes it easier to share via e-mail attachment.
- **To stay on the same page.** Formatting and page layout of PDFs is fixed no matter what platform or printer the author uses (except, in rare cases, when an author's printer does not have a PostScript RIP). This facilitates communication about the location of edits and queries.
- **To fix a view.** The editor can choose a particular view for the author, save that view as a PDF, and keep other information (e.g., coding) hidden. For example, if you have tracked changes in Word or WordPerfect, you can customize the display of the changes and save that display to PDF for an author who is unfamiliar with tracking or redlining commands.
- **To maintain control of the original.** When you are responsible for finalizing the electronic version of a document for publication, sending a PDF to the author or other reviewers helps prevent them from modifying the text.

The Copyeditor's Guide to **Substance**&*Style*

- **To help close the revision process.** Editors with deadlines may find themselves at odds with authors—particularly authors of the maniacal species—who seem always brimming with new ideas to improve their writing. At some point, the text must be surrendered and published. Psychologically, a PDF suggests to authors that "this is final," which may inhibit eleventh-hour tinkering.

Editing text in PDF documents usually is not desirable. While Acrobat does offer tools for editing text, they should be reserved for minor edits that do not involve line or page breaks. Each new version of Acrobat offers increased functionality with regard to editing text, but it is not yet appropriate for lengthy text edits. Plug-ins or extensions (software that adds functionality to another software application) are available for Adobe Acrobat, including some that make the job of editing text a bit less difficult in some cases and simply possible in others. One popular extension is Enfocus Pitstop, which allows text and images in PDF documents to be modified.

Another reason that editing in Acrobat may not be desirable is that PDFs are often made of documents from more than one source application; once the PDF is changed, the source files are superseded unless they are revised concurrently.

While a PDF review copy may not be appropriate in every situation, it is a useful option. The primary obstacle is usually the author's lack of familiarity with the format, but this is changing. Web publishers have helped to popularize PDF by using it to publish forms, reports, and other heavily formatted documents that would be difficult to convert to and publish in HTML. If you have surfed the Web, you have probably learned how to view and print PDF files. Still, it is important to verify that the author is familiar with the format and explain how he or she should return changes (i.e., as a marked-up printout or as a list of changes referenced to the PDF by page and line number).

Without explicit instruction, naive authors have been known to find creative, disastrous ways to edit a PDF. One such "solution" is to copy and paste PDF text into a new word-processing file, which is then edited and returned to the editor with a note to "please use this instead of the original." Text formatting and paragraph styles have been lost, non-ASCII characters have been mistranslated, and line numbers from the PDF have been captured and interpolated with the text. The editor must now comparison-proof the two texts to find the author's untracked changes and transfer them to the original. Advance communication is the best defense against these kinds of surprises.

Exercise 31:
Editing Checklist for Online
Practice—Let's Go Live!

To pull the lessons of the chapter together, use this checklist when you are doing the exercise on the EEI Press Web site. If you are ready to test yourself, go to the exercise and then compare your revisions with the work of an experienced online copyeditor. The test is on www.eeicommunications.com/press/onlinetest.html.

Electronic Editing Checklist

Assess the file.

❏ Identify the file type.

❏ Reality-check the file size.

❏ Assess amount of formatting in text and headings.

❏ Search for hidden coding: styles, footnotes, references, indexes and tables, formulas, special (non-ASCII) characters.

❏ Search for embedded content, e.g., files, graphics, and text boxes.

❏ Assess complexity of tables and consider editing them on paper.

Set up the file for editing.

❏ Save new version as desired file type. (Be careful about losing formatting when saving a file "down.")

❏ Choose the best view.

❏ Control or disable automatic functions.

❏ Remove unwanted coding, e.g., with Control-Shift-F9.

❏ Split content into separate files (e.g., separate text, tables, reference lists).

❏ Access online style sheets, dictionaries, and other resources.

Edit formatting before editing the text.

❏ Anticipate formatting that will be useful to build for or carry into the production step.

❏ Format text and headings using automatic paragraph styles OR do not format text and headings OR identify headings using typecoding or other system agreed upon for production.

❏ Use special (non-ASCII) characters OR identify special characters for the production step.

The Copyeditor's Guide to **Substance**&*Style*

Exercise 31, continued

Perform automatic functions first, then read behind the computer's changes.

❑ Spell-check first.

❑ Run custom macros.

❑ Rebuild and sort lists using automatic functions.

❑ While editing, search and replace forward to correct recurring errors.

Track changes and develop queries to the author.

❑ Agree with the author and others on the production team what changes to track electronically and how (e.g., with formatting or with Track Changes or Redlining): none OR only substantive change OR all changes.

❑ Agree with the author how to query: in text in brackets with bold or highlighting OR with comments or footnotes OR number queries in the text to correspond to a separate query list.

Finalize and QC the copyedited file.

❑ Reset spell-checker and check the file for errors introduced by the edit.

❑ Check page numbering.

❑ Add line numbering (for queries).

❑ Check content and links of headers and footers, first to last.

❑ Identify the document version on the first page.

❑ Put the file name and path on the first or every page.

❑ Build or update an automatic table of contents (if automatic paragraph styles have been used).

❑ Save as a new version.

❑ Create a printout or PDF for author review. Confirm that the review version matches the source file version.

❑ Explain to the author in a cover memo or flow sheet how edits have been tracked, how the PDF may be reviewed, and how answers to queries may be returned.

Incorporate answers to queries and finalize the file for production.

❑ Save as a new version.

❑ Remove queries and update the text.

❑ Accept or remove all tracked changes.

❑ Clean unnecessary coding and formatting from the file.

❑ Identify the file for production using a cover memo or flow sheet. Note special formatting or content.

GLOSSARY

absolute—descriptive word that can't be qualified with more or most (*unique, perfect, complete*)

active voice—*see* **voice, active**

actor—doer of the action inherent in a verb

agreement—grammatically, having the same number, case, gender, or person (subjects and verbs agree in person and number; pronouns and their antecedents agree in number, person, and gender)

alignment—position of a line of type, word, or individual type character in relation to another line, word, or character

　flush left—beginning at the left margin

　flush right—ending at the right margin

　justified—all lines even at the right margin (usually accomplished by varying the spacing between words in the lines and by hyphenating)

　ragged right—uneven right margin (spacing between words in the lines is the same throughout)

alphabetization—act of ordering a list according to the alphabet

　letter by letter—order by letters, ignoring word spaces and stopping only at punctuation or at the end of an entry

　word by word—order by letters in the word, stopping at word spaces

antecedent—word, phrase, or clause to which a pronoun or other substitute refers

　implied—antecedent is an idea rather than a single word

　unclear—antecedent can't be determined by context

appositive—second noun placed immediately following another noun to identify it more fully (George Washington, the first <u>president</u>, had wooden teeth)

　restrictive—appositive that provides essential information and therefore isn't set off by commas (My sister <u>Nancy</u>)

cadence—rhythm of the language

callout—first mention of a table, figure, footnote, or reference in the text of an article or chapter

case—form of nouns and pronouns determined by their usage in a sentence

> **nominative**—case used for subjects and predicate nominatives (*I, he, she, they*)
>
> **objective**—case used for direct and indirect objects and objects of prepositions (*me, him, her, them*)
>
> **possessive**—case used to denote ownership (*my, your, his, her, its, their*)

citation—mention, usually in abbreviated form, of the source for information just presented in the text of an article or chapter; the full information for the source is usually found in a list of references at the end

clause—group of words that has a subject and a verb and is used as part of a sentence—main or independent—clause that expresses a complete thought and could stand alone as a sentence

> **subordinate or dependent**—clause that requires a main clause to complete its meaning

collective noun—noun that is singular in form but can be plural in meaning (*staff, variety, herd, majority*)

comma splice or comma fault—incorrect use of a comma to separate two related main clauses in the absence of a coordinating conjunction; a run-on sentence is the result

compound sentence—sentence that has two or more main clauses

compound word—combination of two or more words that expresses a single idea; can be hyphenated (blue-green); closed, i.e., with no word space (*grandfather*); or open, i.e., retained as separate words (*follow up*)

conditional tense or mood—phrase or clause using the word would or could; conveys a feeling of uncertainty

conjunction—word used to join other words, phrases, or clauses

> **coordinating**—conjunction joining elements of equal rank (*and*)
>
> **correlative**—conjunction pairs joining elements of equal rank (*either...or, neither...nor*)
>
> **subordinating**—conjunction joining a subordinate clause to a main clause (*because, therefore*)

conjunctive adverb—adverb used to join main clauses by showing the relationship in meaning between them (*then, however*)

descriptive dictionary—dictionary that includes all words used in both written and spoken English, in contrast to one that prescribes correct usage

direct address—noun used to indicate the particular person to whom a sentence is directed (<u>Bill</u>, please go)

draft—version of a manuscript; also called an **iteration**

ellipsis—punctuation mark (three dots) that signals an omission from a direct quotation

endnotes—notes of explanation, emendation, or source placed at the end of a chapter or article

euphony—harmonious progression of words having a pleasing sound

extract—long quotation typeset in a block in which indention from the margins substitutes for quotation marks

format—appearance and arrangement of type elements on a page or in relation to each other; to check format is to ensure visual consistency

fragment—group of words presented as a sentence but not conveying a complete thought; fragments usually lack one element of a main clause, such as a subject or verb, or else are subordinate clauses

gender—feature of personal pronouns that differentiates between masculine, feminine, and neuter antecedents

gender-neutral—*see* sexist language

gerund—verb form that ends in *-ing* and is used as a noun (<u>Driving</u> is difficult)

heads/subheads—short titles at the beginning of sections in a piece of writing; also called **headings/subheadings**

infinitive—verb form preceded by *to* and used as a noun, adjective, or adverb

inverted sentence—sentence in other than the usual subject-verb order; e.g., most questions and all sentences beginning with *there*

iteration—*see* **draft**

jargon—terminology characteristic of a particular group, profession, or activity; also overuse of a discipline's vocabulary

layout—design or arrangement of elements on a printed page

modifier—word, phrase, or clause used as an adjective or adverb

    misplaced—modifier that can't grammatically or logically describe the word it appears to describe

    nonrestrictive—modifier that presents parenthetical information about the word it describes; also called **nonessential**

    restrictive—modifier that presents information needed to identify the word it describes; also called **essential**

           The Copyeditor's Guide to **Substance**&*Style*

modify—to describe or qualify the meaning of another word, phrase, or clause

mood—property of a verb that tells the manner in which the writer regards the action or state of being

    imperative—mood that gives a command (<u>Give</u> him the book)

    indicative—mood that makes a statement of fact (The trees <u>are</u> very old)

    subjunctive—mood that conveys a condition contrary to fact, improbable, or doubtful (If I <u>were</u> a rich man…)

nonrestrictive—*see* **modifier, nonrestrictive**

noun—word that names a person, place, or thing

noun string—several nouns being used together as if they were adjectives and having no intervening prepositions or articles

parallel construction—idea that sentence elements in a series should have the same grammatical structure (He likes <u>to run, to swim, and to ski</u>)

passive voice—*see* **voice, passive**

person—point of view conveyed by personal pronouns

    first person—the one writing or speaking (*I, we*)

    second person—the one reading or spoken to (*you*)

    third person—the one written or spoken about (*he, she, it, they*)

predicate—part of a sentence containing the verb and all its modifiers

predicate adjective—adjective used in the predicate to refer to the subject (She is <u>pretty</u>)

predicate nominative—noun or pronoun that follows a linking verb (one that shows state of being) and renames or modifies the subject of the sentence (Joe is the <u>manager</u>)

prescriptive dictionary—dictionary that prescribes correct usage rather than including all words in use by writers and speakers of English

proofreading—checking the most recent version of a manuscript against the original

query—question an editor asks an author

redundancy—use in a sentence of several words or phrases with the same meaning (*new innovation, past experience*)

references—sources for information contained in a piece of writing; each reference consists of author, title, and publication data (place of publication, publisher's name, year for a book; periodical name, volume, page number, and year for a journal article); usually listed alphabetically by author's last name at the end of an article or book chapter

relative pronoun—pronouns *who, whom, whose, which,* or *that*; used to introduce an adjectival subordinate clause

restrictive—*see* **modifier, restrictive**

serial comma—comma used after the next-to-last element in a series; also called a **series comma** and a **terminal comma** (*red, white, and blue*)

sexist language—wording that includes masculine but not feminine nouns and pronouns; can be alleviated by using gender-neutral words (*journalist,* not *newsman; salesperson,* not *salesman*) or by pluralizing (*the authors/they* rather than the *author/he*)

smothered verb—verb that has been turned into a phrase based on its noun form (*make reference to*)

style—choice among acceptable alternatives in spelling, abbreviation, capitalization, punctuation, numbers; usage conforming to a particular publications manual; literary expression of a particular author

    house style—style choices of a particular organization, usually set down in a style guide or style sheet

subject—part of a sentence that names the person, place, or thing that the sentence is about

    compound—subject consisting of two or more elements of equal weight

tense—form of a verb that shows its time of action—past, present, or future

unit modifier—two or more adjectives that function as a single entity to modify a noun; individual words in the unit don't, by themselves, modify the noun (*well-fed cat,* but not a *well cat* or a *fed cat*)

verb—word conveying action or state of being

    compound—two or more such words having equal weight and serving as the action or state of being in the sentence (The doll <u>walks</u> and <u>talks</u>)

voice—property of a verb that shows whether the subject is the doer or receiver of the action of the verb

    active—verb form used when the doer of the action is the subject of the verb (The dog <u>catches</u> the ball)

    passive—verb form used when the subject of the verb is the receiver of the action (The ball <u>is caught</u> by the dog)